Practical Guide to Salesforce Communities

Building, Enhancing, and Managing an Online Community with Salesforce Community Cloud

Philip Weinmeister
Foreword by Paul Stillmank

Apress®

Practical Guide to Salesforce Communities: Building, Enhancing, and Managing an Online Community with Salesforce Community Cloud

Philip Weinmeister
Powder Springs, Georgia, USA

ISBN-13 (pbk): 978-1-4842-3608-6   ISBN-13 (electronic): 978-1-4842-3609-3
https://doi.org/10.1007/978-1-4842-3609-3

Library of Congress Control Number: 2018948157

Managing Director, Apress Media LLC: Welmoed Spahr
Acquisitions Editor: Susan McDermott
Development Editor: Laura Berendson
Coordinating Editor: Rita Fernando

Cover designed by eStudioCalamar

Cover image designed by Freepik (www.freepik.com)

Distributed to the book trade worldwide by Springer Science+Business Media New York, 233 Spring Street, 6th Floor, New York, NY 10013. Phone 1-800-SPRINGER, fax (201) 348-4505, e-mail orders-ny@springer-sbm.com, or visit www.springeronline.com. Apress Media, LLC is a California LLC and the sole member (owner) is Springer Science + Business Media Finance Inc (SSBM Finance Inc). SSBM Finance Inc is a **Delaware** corporation.

For information on translations, please e-mail rights@apress.com, or visit www.apress.com/rights-permissions.

Apress titles may be purchased in bulk for academic, corporate, or promotional use. eBook versions and licenses are also available for most titles. For more information, reference our Print and eBook Bulk Sales web page at www.apress.com/bulk-sales.

Any source code or other supplementary material referenced by the author in this book is available to readers on GitHub via the book's product page, located at www.apress.com/978-1-4842-3608-6. For more detailed information, please visit www.apress.com/source-code.

Printed on acid-free paper

To Amy Weinmeister, who, through her support, encouragement, and love, made this journey a joy.

Table of Contents

About the Author xiii

About the Technical Reviewers xv

Foreword xvii

Acknowledgments xxiii

Introduction xxv

Chapter 1: Why Salesforce Communities? 1

Why Salesforce? 1

Why Communities? 2

    Member Personas and Interactions 3

    Business Data and Processes 4

    User Experience 5

Why Salesforce Communities? 6

    A Cross-Cloud Approach 6

    Transformation, Innovation, and Enterprise Readiness 7

Recap 9

Chapter 2: Planning and Preparing for Success 11

Establishing a Vision 11

Verifying the Approach/Frame of Mind 13

Other Areas to Consider 15

    Audiences 16

    Data Sources and Types 17

    Measuring Success with KPIs 19

Recap 20

Chapter 3: Licenses and Member Groups: Employees, Partners, and Customers..21

Licenses for Salesforce Community Users 21

Community License Types 22

Community License Functionality...24

Community License Application 27

Disabling Community Users 30

User vs. Login-centric Licensing 30

Communities License Management 33

The Concept of Member Groups 34

Blending Member Groups Within Communities 37

Multiple Member Groups Within a Single Community 37

One User in Multiple Communities 38

Recap 39

Chapter 4: Community Template Types: Tabs, Visualforce, and Lightning..............41

Template vs. Bolt..42

Introduction and High-Level Categorization.......................................43

Overview and Assessment 47

Tabs 47

Visualforce...48

Lightning..49

Impact of Template Selection..52

Relevant Functions and Features 52

Efficient Community Creation..55

Technological Foundation..56

Flexibility and Extensibility 57

Hybrid/Transitional Options..58

Recap 60

Chapter 5: Community Builder for Lightning Communities **61**

Overview 62

Getting to Know Community Builder 63

Left Sidebar/Tabs... 64

Top Navigation Bar 97

Recap 115

Chapter 6: Pages and Components in Lightning Communities............................ **117**

Lightning Pages 119

Navigation Menu Bar... 126

Lightning Components 128

Understanding Components within Communities 129

A Real-World Example 133

Recap 142

Chapter 7: Setup and Administration **143**

Setup.. 143

Initial Setup 144

Additional Communities Settings 146

Administration... 148

Preferences 150

Members 155

Tabs 157

Branding 158

Login & Registration 160

Emails.. 168

Pages... 170

Reputation Levels 172

Reputation Points 173

Rich Publisher Apps... 175

Recap 178

Chapter 8: Access, Sharing, and Visibility 179

Community Authentication and Access 180

    Authentication (Private vs. Public) 180

    Community Member Access 182

Object and Field Access 182

Record Sharing 184

    Organizationwide Sharing and External Users 185

    Customer Community vs. Other Community Licenses 187

    Sharing Sets 188

    Share Groups 196

Recap 199

Chapter 9: Topics in Communities 201

Overview/Purpose of Topics in Communities 202

    Topic Data Model 202

    Topic Presentation/UI 204

Topic Types 205

    Standard Topics 206

    Navigational Topics 208

    Featured Topics 211

Other Topic Areas 213

    Internal vs. Community Topics 213

    Unlisted Chatter Groups 213

    Topics and Articles 214

    Management within Community Builder 214

Recap 215

Chapter 10: Community Knowledge (Articles) 217

Prerequisites and General Setup 217

    Licensing/Permissions 217

    Lightning Knowledge 219

    Knowledge Administration 219

Articles in Communities 222

    Article Visibility 222

    Articles and Topics 223

    Articles in Global Search 228

Recap 229

Chapter 11: Process Automation in Communities 231

Workflow 232

    Community Case Creation Notification 233

    Community Group Membership Notification 236

Process Builder 237

    New Community Member Actions 239

    Community Member Reputation Point Notification 242

    Other Examples/General Approach 245

Flow 246

    Warranty Status Check 247

    Community Engagement Wizard 249

    Placement of Lightning Flows in Communities 253

    Paused Flows 256

Recap 257

Chapter 12: Audience Targeting and Personalization 259

Overview 260

Audiences 262

    Profile 263

    Location 264

    Domain 265

    User Object 265

    Record Type 267

    Audience Criteria Logic 269

    Bringing It Together 270

Audience Targeting Types 272

    Branding Sets 272

    Page Variations 278

    Component Audiences 284

Other Considerations 286

    Testing 286

    Suitability/Application 287

Recap 288

Chapter 13: Lightning Bolt for Communities 289

Building a Bolt 292

    Bolt Creation in Community Builder 295

    Bolt Installation 298

    End-to-End Overview 300

Lightning Bolt for Salesforce 301

Recap 304

Chapter 14: The Best of the Rest: Additional Communities Topics 305

Analytics 306

Moderation 307

Deployment 310

    Site.com Export 311

    Change Sets 313

    IDEs and the Metadata API 314

    Packaged Lightning Bolt 315

    Manual Replication 315

Salesforce App (Previously Salesforce1) 316

Search 319

Messages 320

Notifications 321

Chatter Streams 322

Other Capabilities 324

Guided Setup 325

Marketing Cloud 325

Quip 326

Einstein for Communities 326

CMS Connect 327

Recap 328

Chapter 15: Next Steps: Keep Learning **329**

Trailhead 329

WeinBlog 330

Release Notes 331

Twitter 332

Dreamforce, TrailheaDX, and World Tours 333

Salesforce Training and Certification 334

Pluralsight 335

Recap 335

Index **337**

About the Author

Philip Weinmeister, Salesforce MVP, is the VP of product management at 7Summits, where he is focused on building innovative components, apps, and bolts that enable impactful, transformative communities on the Salesforce platform. Phil is 18x Salesforce certified and has delivered numerous Sales Cloud, Service Cloud, and (primarily) Community Cloud solutions to a variety of organizations on Salesforce since 2010. Phil authored *Practical Salesforce.com Development Without Code* (Apress, 2015), which has earned an average rating of almost five stars on Amazon.com. Phil has been a Salesforce MVP since 2015 and, in 2017, was named the first-ever Community Cloud MVP at the Lightning Bolt Trailblazer awards at Dreamforce.

A graduate of Carnegie Mellon University with a double major in business administration/IT and Spanish, Phil now resides in Powder Springs, Georgia. He spends most of his "free" time with his gorgeous, sweet wife, Amy, and his children, Tariku, Sophie, Max, and Lyla. When he's not trying to make his kids laugh, cheering on the Arizona Cardinals, or rap battling his wife, Phil enjoys traveling, playing various sports, and growing in his walk with Jesus.

Stay updated on Phil's most recent insights and blog posts by following him on Twitter (@PhilWeinmeister).

About the Technical Reviewers

Jarrod Kingston is a Salesforce MVP and solution architect with Appirio. He has seven Salesforce certifications and eight-plus years of experience in the support, training, and advancement of Salesforce. Jarrod lives in Kansas City and is an avid Jayhawks, Chiefs, and Royals fan. You can follow him on Twitter (@jarrodmichael).

David Litton is a Salesforce MVP and the director of solutions architecture at Ad Victoriam Solutions. He has been working with Salesforce for more than six years and began working with Salesforce as a customer before transitioning to a partner. David has 18 Salesforce certifications including Application Architect, System Architect, and Community Cloud Consultant. He lives in Birmingham, Alabama, with his wife Missy and dog Ziggy. You can visit his Salesforce blog at salesforcesidekick.com to see what he is currently up to, and you can follow him on Twitter (@DavidLittonSFDC).

Foreword

Innovation. That's where the buck stops. No doubt about it. Innovation anticipates buyer needs, commands new markets, and completely disrupts business models. It is all about invention, modernization, and improving things. I have no doubt that's what makes a guy like Elon Musk tick. Looking past the potential to what's truly possible. Looking through the possibilities that myriad trends of our age are shaping and getting out in front of them. Anticipating. Leading. Visioning. Several years ago, I had a eureka moment of my own. I saw a world being shaped by *social*. I just knew that the world would change once the social constructs amplified by new media swept through popular culture. I was right. Let me explain.

Companies have been chasing after market share, increased revenues, and better productivity for as long as any of us can remember. And all of this time they have been asking the rudimentary questions "what?" and "how?" What can we do to improve? How can we expand? What is the market asking for? How do we improve getting our product into the market? What should we do? How can we do it better? The most essential question might seem obvious in retrospect; however, at the time, it was a revelation: "who?" That is the question that drives everything. And that "who" was at the center of my thinking back then. Customers, partners, and employees. That's who! Can we enable them to build a business for a company? Social constructs said yes. That's crowd-sourcing. That's what people have become accustomed to. That's what businesses now count on. A brand promise was born: "to enable your customers, partners, and employees to build your business for you." I liked it. I was no longer a pariah waiting in the wings for my moment. That moment had arrived. So, in 2009, I risked it all and launched a company dedicated to the notion that the creation of online community experiences would transform businesses and enhance people's lives. A friend of mine announced, "So, you're going to take a big risk; you're an entrepreneur." Years later, I realized that entrepreneurs aren't really big risk-takers; rather, they so deeply believe that their idea will change the world that they are willing to risk everything to see that world come to fruition. That was me back then. Fast-forward almost ten years, and my company, 7Summits, sits at the forefront of community experience design, creating digital solutions that drive measurable business value that is dramatically amplified by collaboration.

- *Customer supportals* afford self-service, raise conversion rates, affect product advocacy, and glean much-needed insights to fuel product roadmaps and go-to-market strategies.

- *Partner networks* streamline partner onboarding, serve up relevant content and tools, assist in matching leads, and provide important feedback to optimize channel performance.

- *Employee social intranets* provide a highly accessible and served knowledge base, drive open communications, crowd-source ideas, and turn every business process into an effective, efficient practice through collaboration.

- *Developer networks* open lines of communication between customers, driving tremendous value resulting in higher renewal rates.

- *Alumni networks* align mentors with mentees, match interests to opportunities, and share information at the opportune moment to serve both the alumnus and school in the most beneficial ways.

The list goes on and includes solutions for every industry from manufacturing to high tech to healthcare to financial services.

This, itself, is simply incredible. The world has gone from "being social" to collaborating in entirely new ways. Even the most discrete of business processes is made more transparent, more measurable, and more efficient. This is a critically important evolution because a lot more has been happening over the past ten years as well. At the writing of this book, we are, as a civilization, well past the front door of what we now call the fourth industrial revolution (4IR). This revolution revolves around new technologies fueling and stemming from areas such as artificial intelligence (AI), robotic process automation (RPA), the expansion of the Internet of Things (IoT), and innumerable other new sources of Big Data that continue to reshape the data management landscape as we know it—both producing and consuming this information in ways that will, no doubt, completely change the world that we live in.

So, what does this all have to do with *Practical Guide to Salesforce Communities*? Well, to begin with, communities *are* data. I'm not talking about content, files, and dashboards. I'm speaking to the tacit interactions between the actors consuming that information. How they work with them. How they consume them. How they collaborate with and through them. Those interactions between employees, partners, and customers revolve around a wide range of linkages: employee to employee, employee to partner, customer to customer, customer to enterprise, and customer to partner. And each of those audiences, each of those linkages, is interacting with processes, content, and data as well. That means more information, more data, and more insights. It is not a far leap, then, to understand that capturing these interactions is tantamount to applying automation thinking to your business. To boil it all down, companies cannot capitalize on the promise of AI and RPA if they do not have the substantial data sets that are needed by these neural networks to crunch and inform highly accurate outcomes.

I see many smart companies that moved on this notion almost a decade ago. The Big Data movement spurred them on. Now they are ahead of the game. Others are now catching up through substantial R&D investments, acquisitions, or both. For those companies that either were not ready to invest or were too skeptical, there is still an opportunity to capture the most important data of all: the data specific to your own business, processes, and audiences. That's *your* specific data and, properly harnessed, it can continue to propel your purpose, products, and services in a market that is about to become unsettlingly competitive.

Let me be clear here. There is no more superior way to do this than to put a community motion in front of the people performing that work to capture that data. Salesforce.com provides the platform engine needed to bring business processes, audience context, and data management together for this most important building block for every company's future. How important is it then to make it easy to get through this step, a key building block, to a much bigger purpose? That's where Salesforce, communities, and this book come in.

Phil Weinmeister is a master at helping others simplify their thinking so that they can find the best approach to solving a business process on the Salesforce platform. If I had to pick one thing that Phil is absolutely all about, it is "speed to solve." I'll come back to that shortly, but first let me tell you how I came to know Phil. My first encounter with Phil Weinmeister encompassed walking into the office of my head of technology, John Price, and noticing a stack of books on his desk that he had been supplying to his staff as they joined his team: *Practical Salesforce.com Development Without Code*. It was Phil's first book. Of course, I had heard of Phil from colleagues in our industry, but I had yet to meet him. I asked John, "Is this a good book?" John replied that it was *essential.* As the CEO of a rapidly growing Salesforce integrator, I quickly followed with, "Should we be going after this guy?" As it turns out, I had actually reached out to Phil over a year prior via LinkedIn to inquire if he might be interested in joining our firm. This time, I approached things with fervor—I read his book! It is an essential text for development on the platform. The reality of "the Salesforce economy" came into sharp focus for me after that read. Phil was making it easier and clearer for countless individuals to understand and make the transition toward developing on this platform. And he was focused on the notion that configuration trumped customization, paving the way for a leaner implementation that leveraged the richness of the platform to deliver value to the end customer. I liked it! So, I read Phil's book and then called him to invite him to join me at our headquarters in Milwaukee, Wisconsin. It was a great meeting of the minds for me. And I could tell that he was intrigued. Unfortunately, his schedule just would not permit it. The following week, I flew to meet him in person in his home town of Atlanta, Georgia. It turned out to be fortuitous. I had a vision for 7Summits and this market that well eclipsed the notion of simply building online communities. I wanted to see a different world in ten years: people unleashed to create, compete, and innovate in entirely new ways. Phil agreed. We have been working together at 7Summits now for almost 18 months, so I have firsthand experience with his own vision, insight, and influence. He wants to change the world by leveraging scalable technology to deliver truly remarkable results. "Speed to solve"—that is Phil Weinmeister.

So, let me expound on this speed-to-solve notion. What does that mean? It means being expert enough, niche enough, and select enough to be able to make things easy, clear, and consumable for others. For you, the reader, this is great news! It means providing an avenue to perform work effectively and get the utmost from the platform without over-customization. Phil is expert here, as well. And he backs up that knowledge with a very strong set of credentials. Phil is a three-time Salesforce MVP (starting in 2015) and 18x certified on the Salesforce platform. He is a Salesforce platform strategist bar none and one of the leading experts on the Salesforce Lightning Framework. He is the author of *Practical Salesforce.com Development Without Code*. He hosts his own Salesforce blog, the Weinblog. And he is the first-ever Community Cloud MVP and Trailblazer award winner (Dreamforce 2017). People leveraging Phil's approach to the Salesforce platform have gone on to start solid careers in the Salesforce ecosystem. Moving from a prior discipline to a Salesforce-related discipline. Moving from a purely business-side domain to a blend of business and technical acumen together, progressing their careers along the way. Phil has not just become a part of this ecosystem; rather, he is guiding others on their path to and through it. He is simply an amazing individual with an amazing perspective on business, technology, and the power of the Salesforce platform, making him the ideal author of this important text.

I thoroughly enjoyed Phil's approach to this book and learned a great deal myself as I walked through chapter after chapter. He starts things out at the exact right place by answering the essential question, "Why Salesforce communities?" He covers the core elements that are fundamental to a successful communities initiative. A great start! Next, he navigates a clear approach beginning with vision (not features!) and walks the reader through audiences, data, and success measures. These are the essential elements of a well-planned community. License models and management are next. Phil has reached a mastery level here for sure, and I have seen him, firsthand, create the architecture and strategy to maximize value for customers where license management is concerned. Phil then dives into community templates including the forward-thinking Lightning concepts. The Salesforce Lightning Design System is at the heart of innovation and speed when developing on the Salesforce platform. This is the true genius of Salesforce as a company. Lightning Bolts and Lightning components revolve around the notion that Salesforce partners (and customers) can create capabilities that more rapidly extend the platform than if Salesforce were to imagine and create things completely on its own. Talk about speed to solve! This opens up the door to a world of rapid development and platform proliferation that we can only imagine. My own company, 7Summits, imagined a world with prebuilt, purpose-driven communities way back in 2009. Salesforce has put that concept on steroids and delivered an environment through Community Builder, which will fast outstrip its competitors as both functional and industry-related Lightning Bolts and components become available on its software exchanges. In fact, I just spoke with a customer this year that wants a niche industry solution on Salesforce so that they can take advantage of that capability extended into the full richness of CRM and more. Someone will, no doubt, build that niche capability and make it available to the general market for that industry. Genius.

Moving further along, be sure to thoroughly review the part on visual workflow. This straightforward approach to themes and layouts and how they can be applied to community page designs truly demonstrates the flexibility *and* extendibility of Lightning-based communities. This thinking makes real the Lightning pages and Lightning components that Community Builder manages and supports.

Multiple layers of functionality are demystified so that Community Builder can be leveraged quickly to create, modify, extend, and maintain a community as it grows with and becomes shaped by its participants. Another best practice! So, at the heart of this book is the same elemental theme that Phil brings to everything he touches: speed to solve. From themes, components, and pages to groups, topics, and measurement to authentication, security, and community membership, this is the definitive text on Salesforce communities, how to configure them, and how to position them to take your business forward. That's why the notion of speed is so important. You've got a business to understand, to transform, and to take through the fourth industrial revolution. Salesforce communities are essential toward getting you there, and *Practical Guide to Salesforce Communities* is an indispensable reference for helping you to do so.

Paul Stillmank

CEO, 7Summits

Acknowledgments

David Green and **Adi Kuruganti (Salesforce)**: David has been instrumental over the past few years in providing guidance and clarifying various features and functionality for me. Adi was my go-to contact on the Community Cloud team when I first started down the communities path and led the way for future growth.

Mike Micucci (Salesforce): Mike set the recent direction for this amazing "cloud" and has enabled a vibrant ecosystem that has embraced innovation at every step.

David Litton (Ad Victoriam) and **Jarrod Kingston (Appirio)**: David and Jarrod both provided professional, meaningful reviews, making the final piece as solid as possible.

Paul Stillmank and **John Price (7Summits)**: Both Paul and John have wholeheartedly supported my ideas and thought leadership at 7Summits, paving the way for this book.

Rita Fernando Kim and **Susan McDermott (Apress)**: Rita, Susan, and the entire Apress team provided top-notch support every step of the way.

Amy Weinmeister: My wife fully supported this time-intensive endeavor from the beginning and actually reviewed each chapter. Simply put, she is amazing in every way.

And none of this would have been possible without **Jesus**. My career and abilities are ultimately gifts from Him, and I hope to reflect Him in all I do.

Introduction

In February 2014, I received an email from a gentleman at Apress. He had recently engaged in a conversation with an acquaintance who implored him to consider expanding the breadth of technologies in the Apress repertoire to include Salesforce. While Salesforce was hardly a small company by that point, the price of the CRM stock (Salesforce's ticker symbol) was less than half of the 2018 high. The email described how this publishing company editor had read my blog and wanted me to write a book for Apress—its first on Salesforce. I immediately shared the news with my wife to make sure I wasn't crazy; it was all a little unbelievable. Technology books are cranked out all the time...but this wasn't a self-publishing or mom-and-pop publisher situation (both can be great options by the way). This was a fairly large technology publisher. At that point, I did what any reasonable person would do: I called the editor to make sure I was not getting pranked! Until I heard a real person confirming what I had just read, I wouldn't believe it.

Fortunately, it wasn't a mirage. Apress formally accepted me as its first Salesforce author, and the rest is history; *Practical Salesforce.com Development Without Code* hit the shelves at the beginning of 2015. In that book, I explored the world of declarative development, which was what originally drew me to the platform when I first used it in 2010. The journey as an author has been a special one. Perhaps the most fulfilling and rewarding aspect of the overall experience is the real, material impact that the book has had on other people's careers. Here are a few reviews that particularly struck me follow:

- "Purchased this because I've been involved in migrating Salesforce orgs in last 8 months and felt like I needed a refresher in the declarative aspects of Salesforce. This was better than a refresher—I learned new things. The material is very well written in a logical, progressive & complete sequence. ... Unlike some books and many websites that throw things in an unorganized manner and hope the audience 'gets it' this book shows Mr Weinmeister has very firm grasp of the topics and can communicate it to others."

- "If you are planning on any Salesforce development or taking the DEV 401 exam, this book is for you. It effectively covers all the major topics in depth to gain a full understanding of the process and what's going on 'under the hood.' Although certain chapters such as the one covering formulas do cover more than what is on the exam, it allowed me to fully grasp the concepts. Rest assured if I do need to leverage custom formula functions or fields I feel full capable after reading this book. I've read multiple Salesforce practical guides and this is the first to not just skim over the top of major topics like automation, workflows, formula fields, and functions. Outside of Salesforce's official documentation, this book will likely be my go-to source."

- "Although I am not completely finished reading the book yet, I am very pleased with the content, layout, and approach that Mr. Weinmeister uses to explain the extensive list of functionality. I have found it an important and necessary accessory training tool to complement the Trailhead training modules in Salesforce. I actually think I can learn how to program again after so many years of being in a different occupation."

This feedback has continued to fuel my desire to share what I know and teach the community at large. After wrestling with the idea of writing another book over the past few years, I decided that it was the right time to embark on this journey once again. As tempting as producing another version of my original book was, I felt that I could have the biggest impact by entering new territory: the world of Salesforce Community Cloud.

In this book, I have thoughtfully reflected upon my years of experience working with Salesforce communities and identified those areas that would be most beneficial to potential readers. The final, chosen topics lend themselves to a balance of conceptual illumination and practical, real-world guidance; readers will discover that I have employed both approaches over the next few hundred pages.

It is important to me to lay a foundation before the book begins, specifically to ensure that expectations are aligned with my vision of the book's actual content. Readers should know the following:

- My overall goal is to share what I have learned and to empower others to become effective and successful "builders of communities" in various aspects.

- Although I know there tends to be a desire for nice, clean categorization in life, this book is really for individuals across all levels of current communities knowledge: beginning, intermediate, and advanced. Readers in each group will use the book differently, of course, but value will be found along the full spectrum of learners (whether in the form of discovery or affirmation).

- The book covers numerous features, functions, and capabilities of communities. I delve fairly deep into some of these but provide more of a high-level introduction to others. Correspondingly, a reader's specific needs may or may not line up with the deeper topics. For example, a reader looking for a textbook on CMS Connect won't find that here, but I will discuss it briefly. This is intentional; it's an area of significantly growing interest, but it's also evolving rapidly and will likely look very different six months after this book's release. I hope each reader finds significant value throughout the next 15 chapters (and also understands that supplemental material may be needed for an exhaustive dive into a particular area).

- This book continues my journey of providing solutions that do not require coding abilities. Without a doubt, technical individuals who know how to leverage Apex, Visualforce, and/or Lightning components can significantly extend community capabilities in a myriad of ways. While there are absolutely community-specific development tips and best practices, two considerations should be kept in mind.

  - Much of the underlying, community-specific aspect of custom development has to do with the platform and things such as sharing and user schema. Those are covered here.

- Much of the development, especially the front-end user experience, is channel-agnostic. In other words, many Lightning components can be made fully "community-enabled" by adding *forceCommunity:availableForAllPageTypes* to the *implements* attribute. Yes, some scenarios require handling of community scenarios, but not always. "Standard" Lightning component development instruction will be immensely helpful for building Lightning communities, so technical readers should not have to hold out for literature on Lightning component development for communities (although that would be great if/when a book is made available).

- While I do discuss Visualforce communities and considerations to be made when selecting a template, I approach the overall endeavor of community building from a Lightning-first perspective. While very niche use cases may warrant assessment of Visualforce versus Lightning, Lightning is the future of Salesforce communities. It has greatly matured over the past few years, and I would rather look ahead than hang on to remnants of the past.

- Salesforce will continue to expand communities, resulting in certain new enhancements that won't be found here as we move into the 20s (yes, it feels odd to type that...). I have a couple thoughts on this subject.

  - Everyone knows that the role of printed literature in the world of technology has changed over the years. When I first considered writing a book on Salesforce communities, one individual discouraged me from doing so and told me that "print is dead." I can say from first-hand experience that it is not. It has a specific role and can be extremely valuable and helpful to individuals. I see the book as a complement to online resources and a reference guide that is as much of a one-stop shop as is feasible.

  - In my final chapter, called "Next Steps," I discuss how the learning can continue. It's possible that I will produce subsequent versions of this book in the future; however, until then, look for expanded content in my blog.

- Readers should not consider the foreword as optional or extraneous! Paul Stillmank is a true pioneer and visionary in the world of online communities. Before community building gets underway, the adventure starts with Paul's thoughtful piece that sets a great basis for why Salesforce communities should have our attention.

And that's the story. Thank you for going on this journey with me. I cannot wait to see a wave of new "community builders" emerge to help drive positive, lasting digital transformation around the globe!

CHAPTER 1

Why Salesforce Communities?

There are two distinct parts of the question posed in this chapter's title—Salesforce and communities—and they cannot be sufficiently addressed in one response. To provide a holistic answer, we must look at three separate questions.

- Why Salesforce?

- Why communities?

- Why Salesforce communities?

Before we delve into the hands-on, practical aspects of building, moderating, and managing a community on the Salesforce platform (or, the "what" and "how"), I want to take a step back and truly communicate the "why." To put it simply, if I didn't believe there were strong, persuasive answers to the previous questions, I would not have written this book.

Why Salesforce?

My overall journey with Salesforce started in 2010. I had just taken the role of Business Systems Manager with an up-and-coming, SaaS-based email marketing automation company in the Atlanta, Georgia, area. This startup not only used Salesforce as its corporate CRM but served as a key partner for Salesforce in the days before the acquisitions of Pardot and ExactTarget (now Marketing Cloud). At the time, I was completely new to Salesforce. I still recall an interesting moment during the interview process. One of my soon-to-be-colleagues mentioned how the team was responsible for "managing Salesforce," and I nodded with a smile, not having the slightest idea what that would mean to the business world or to my own career in the years that would follow.

© Philip Weinmeister 2018
P. Weinmeister, *Practical Guide to Salesforce Communities*, https://doi.org/10.1007/978-1-4842-3609-3_1

Fast-forward to late 2017. Salesforce announced in August that it would eclipse a $10 billion run rate for the first time. Weeks earlier, Forbes announced that the cloud computing giant had reclaimed the top spot on the Forbes Most Innovative List after two years of "falling behind"...to the #2 spot. Keep in mind that Salesforce was designated as the #1 most innovative company in each of the *four consecutive years* prior to the dip to second place. The innovation alone is an amazing achievement, but it takes on a completely new meaning when we consider the size of the organization (more than 25,000 employees) and the tendency for innovation and creativity to dwindle as a company grows beyond a certain point.

As for me, I've fully embraced the platform. In 2014, I wrote my first book, *Practical Salesforce.com Development Without Code*, to explore the world of declarative development and provide guidance on building applications using "point-and-click" methods. In 2015, I was honored with the distinct title of Salesforce MVP, shared with a small group of experts and evangelists that includes administrators and CEOs. Along the way, I've learned enough to achieve nearly 20 certifications on the platform.

I bring up the progress and accolades for one reason: to help show unequivocally that this is an organization and a platform that warrants—no, *demands*—your attention. I can speak for thousands upon thousands of employees out there who have discovered a canvas for building business applications unlike any other. The platform has grown immensely, with "clouds" fully dedicated to sales, service, marketing, commerce, analytics, Internet of Things, artificial intelligence, and more. The breadth of the platform is undoubtedly impressive, but it's the quality in the array of products that sets the platform apart.

Why Communities?

Call them social websites, business portals, or online communities. The nomenclature may vary, but the goal generally remains the same: to engage, enable, and/or empower the customers, partners, and/or employees of one's organization. Communities are often misunderstood as nothing more than websites, which is absolutely not the case. Many of those who will read this book are likely to have deep understanding of online communities, but others may still be struggling to grasp them clearly and with confidence. As I see it, the following three elements are critical in a community:

- Member personas and interactions

- Business data and processes

- User experience

I'll walk through each of these key components and the value they bring to communities.

Member Personas and Interactions

Have anyone ever heard of a community without people? Unless it's a community of four-legged animals or something similar, the answer is no. Merriam-Webster defines types of community as follows:

- **1d** "a group of people with a common characteristic or interest living together within a larger society"

- **1e** "a group linked by a common policy

- **1f** "a body of persons or nations having a common history or common social, economic, and political interests"

- **1g** "a body of persons of common and especially professional interests scattered through a larger society"

- **3c** "social activity"

Sure, every website (in theory) involves people. However, it's not necessarily the case that a website considers the *personas* within the audience. A community needs to consider who is involved and in what capacity or role. It's one thing to have generic viewers and a very different thing to understand who is involved and in what capacity. Faceless "hits" become individuals with personalities, interests, and opinions. People generally desire to be known and heard...and community allows that to happen.

I can take this a bit further and discuss a second, related item, which is the enablement of interactions that these individuals may have within the context of a community. These no-longer-faceless people want to share, learn, influence, collaborate, buy, sell, discuss, and so on; an online community serves as the framework to support all of this. To be clear, however, the focus is not solely limited to system-focused transactions; a healthy, well-designed community always incorporates the individual into the activity.

Business Data and Processes

The concept of member activity within a community perfectly segues into the next area, which addresses the data with which these individuals are interacting and how those interactions are happening. This business data and the processes related to that data further differentiate standard websites from online communities. Intertwining members with meaningful, applicable data through community interaction and business processes is where the value of a community truly lies.

A traditional business portal minimizes the role and value of the individual members and their activity, while a typical website doesn't have CRM-rich data and business processes behind the scenes that would serve as the foundation for a Salesforce community. Let's take a look at a visual representation in Figure 1-1. This diagram captures the community members, their activity, and the business data and processes.

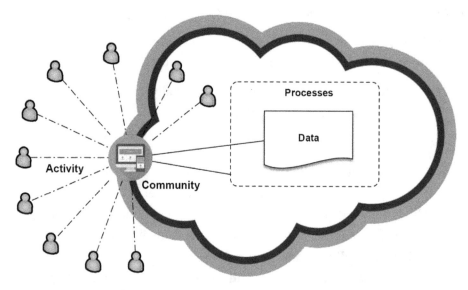

Figure 1-1. *Data and the individuals interacting with that data are essential to online communities*

It's important to understand the concept of how both people *and* data play such a key role, so I've provided another view in Figure 1-2. Notice the interconnectedness between community members and community data; data provides the context for the interactions, not only enriching the interactions between community members but providing much more valuable results for the organization as a whole.

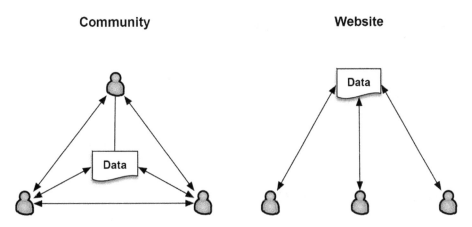

Figure 1-2. *A community changes how individuals interact with data and each other*

User Experience

A third critical element of a community is the user experience. For those of us who are not in the worlds of front-end development or graphic design, it's important to clarify that user interface and user experience are not equivalent. While a user interface (UI) focuses on page elements, layout, and interaction behaviors, effective user experience (UX) incorporates a holistic strategy to consider how to support meaningful user actions and activities while providing the desired aesthetic and enabling the relevant business processes.

Admittedly, the "business portals" of the past left us longing in this area. Creating an impressive, impactful experience for business users was just not seen as a requirement by the majority of organizations. While it could be argued that a general website still demands more in the area of UX than a CRM-driven online community, the gap is fairly negligible. In my current role with a Salesforce partner focused on community-led, multicloud implementations, I see the focus on UX firsthand. It is no longer an afterthought or a "nice-to-have"—an eye-catching UX is assumed to be present from the onset of the project. And, fortunately, communities are finally delivering this to customers. Instead of seeing a community as a trade-off between business data and user experience, it's fair to expect the ability to have cake and eat it, too—by combining a slick, modern user experience with critical business data and valuable member interactions.

Why Salesforce Communities?

Salesforce is a growing, innovative behemoth. Online communities are digital hubs that can connect people, enable business processes, and drive the bottom line in ways that traditional websites or old-school business portals cannot.

But what about communities *from* Salesforce? Let me take a moment to explain why Salesforce's communities offering, Community Cloud, warrants close attention.

A Cross-Cloud Approach

It is true that the Salesforce communities product, Community Cloud, has, to a degree, flown under the radar for much of its life, especially in the last few years. Followers of this "cloud" may have noticed a much more subdued communities message at Dreamforce, World Tours, and Trailhead Live events, giving way to bold, clear announcements about Service Cloud, Sales Cloud, and other areas of the platform. At a glance, this development might suggest a diminished role for communities in general.

However, with a closer look at the situation, those paying attention will see that it's quite the opposite, with online business communities playing an increasingly integral part in how organizations manage their business on the Salesforce platform. Instead of focusing on a community as a siloed solution, underlying business-enabling tools for specific areas of sales, service, and marketing are driving the need for communities. Businesses need to connect with customers, partners, and employees; Figure 1-3 illustrates the "cross-cloud" nature of Salesforce communities.

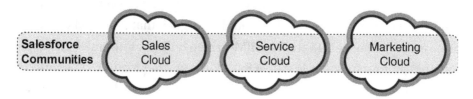

Figure 1-3. *Communities cut across the other "clouds"*

Companies are looking to engage and connect with community members *in the context of their business*. For example, an organization heavily focused on sales will likely incorporate some aspect of their sales processes into the community. Figure 1-4 shows how a community brings out this key business context through the means of a community.

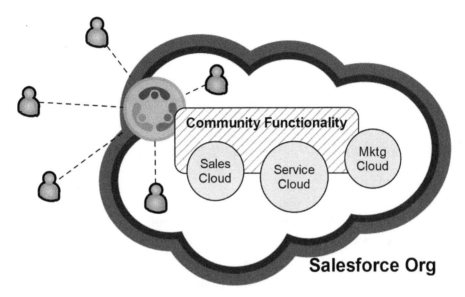

Figure 1-4. *A community provides the user experience and security model to deliver functionality (e.g., sales, service, marketing) to a specific audience*

Transformation, Innovation, and Enterprise Readiness

I am fortunate to have been close to Salesforce's communities product, Community Cloud, since its inception. My first solo implementation was in 2013. While working for a Chicago-based Salesforce services organization as a senior business analyst, I was tasked with delivering a support-centered community for a global leader in authenticated payments and secure transactions located in Mentor, Ohio. The reality at the time was that the product was so new and, frankly, so functionally limited that "expertise" loosely equated to knowing what was *not* possible with a Salesforce community. Figure 1-5 provides a glimpse back to those days and what we were working with.

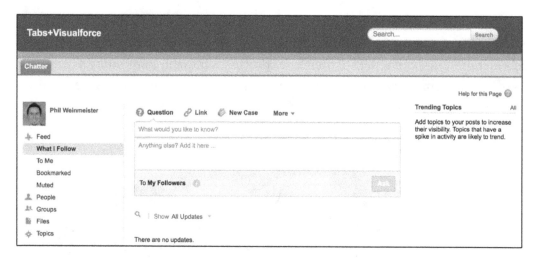

Figure 1-5. *A look at the only "point-and-click" option for building communities, circa 2013*

It's a nice anecdote, but why highlight the shortcomings of the platform about which you are about to read hundreds of pages on the topic? I bring this up because the Salesforce communities of yore—or yesteryear—are nothing like those of today. Technically, tab-based communities are still around, but they are absolutely not Salesforce's focus. Now, it's all about Lightning, and communities are no exception.

In 2015, Salesforce introduced the Lightning Community Builder and the Napili template to the world. This was a mammoth leap from both tabs-based and Visualforce-based communities. Alongside the benefits of reduced implementation time and increased UX flexibility, an immediately visible effect of this new direction was the extension of control from purely technical resources to include "technofunctional" resources looking to employ declarative methods first. Administrators and business analysts had always been a key part of communities implementations, but their post-design role had historically dwindled when requirements were complex. The reality was that when a significant amount of Apex and/or Visualforce came into the picture, a dependency on technical resources was also introduced.

Don't get me wrong; the picture I'm painting is typical of any customized or personalized software. Big changes mean bringing in the "big guns" in the form of traditional developers. And that is exactly what has fundamentally changed within Salesforce communities. Earlier, I carefully used the language "extension of control" as opposed to "shift of control" because as it becomes easier to make changes declaratively within communities, the ability to extend communities continues to increase. This is a not an "admin versus developer" discussion; it's a discussion on how to best utilize multiple roles and skill sets when building a Salesforce community.

Ultimately, this shift benefits communities customers. It means that a community that has been properly designed, developed, and implemented will result in a streamlined solution that requires minimal maintenance and can be further enhanced or extended without overhauling the existing solution. I'll dive more into the details in Chapter 3.

The huge strides in establishing an accessible platform that uses modern development and design standards are not to be ignored. Ultimately, however, the proof of success lies not with those building but with those buying communities. Are communities, especially Lightning communities, enterprise-ready? Take a look at these 2018 numbers and consider the story they tell:

- More than 18,000 active Salesforce communities

- More than 7,000 active Salesforce communities built on Lightning

- More than 200 active Salesforce communities with more than 100,000 members

- More than 225,000,000 Salesforce community members

Recap

This chapter provided the foundation for the rest of the book. I answered the question of "why?" before heading into the more tactical, hands-on sections that focused on the what and the how. Call me crazy, but I think it's important that anyone in this space understands the benefits of building communities on Salesforce and why this platform is one that will continue to grow to meet the demands of the future.

CHAPTER 2

Planning and Preparing for Success

As tempting as it may be to just dive in and start building a Salesforce community—especially considering the declarative capabilities of the platform I discussed in Chapter 1—proper planning and design of a community will firmly establish a much more likely path to success. Ironically, the presentation that I've delivered the most over the past few years has been my "Create a Lightning community (in 30 minutes)" session; audiences in Atlanta, Boston, and Chicago have seen me start from scratch and build a branded, functional community in minutes. However, that session was not about the process to address business needs and customer challenges through a community but rather to show the flexibility of the platform and its enablement of rapid development.

In this chapter, I'll explore a few key areas that need to be considered and explored before any "doing" happens. The more thoughtful the planning is, the smoother the implementation is bound to be.

Note Depending on the scope and complexity of a community, the planning phase could range from a few days to months; ultimately, successful planning will establish a clear picture of both *what* an organization will be building…and *why*.

Establishing a Vision

As obvious as it might seem to read in print, true "digital transformation" is not born out of a list of requirements. We've all seen it before: the meticulously crafted and organized spreadsheet with hundreds of rows describing in detail each of the functions, capabilities, and attributes of a new system. The organization may have even been able

© Philip Weinmeister 2018
P. Weinmeister, *Practical Guide to Salesforce Communities*, https://doi.org/10.1007/978-1-4842-3609-3_2

to deliver on it, meeting each and every requirement that came along. However, it's important to keep in mind that what a community technically does or allows should not be considered to be the vision or purpose for that community. For example, consider a service-related scenario from both sides. Implementing a specific feature such as Live Agent might serve as a key piece of a service-driven community that will very likely bring quantitative value. At the same time, it's critical to understand the long-term community goals for the service organization as a whole go far beyond a specific feature like Live Agent.

To help grasp this concept, one needs to visualize the difference between a vision-led community and a feature-driven community. Figure 2-1 conveys this idea. This visual shows the process of building a community as a supplemental exercise; start somewhere, add some new functionality, and arrive at the intersection of the current state and the added features. This is how many communities evolve.

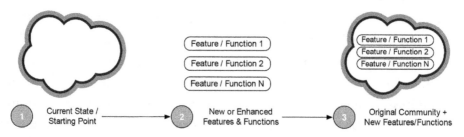

Figure 2-1. *A feature-led approach to building communities*

Now, consider a different path. What if individuals and organizations truly embraced the concept of digital transformation and envisioned the end state first? Instead of focusing on the figurative nuts and bolts that are required to build the machine, they would focus on the machine itself. By first thinking of the goals for the machine, the nuts and bolts needed to build it will naturally come into clear focus. Take a look at Figure 2-2. The "what" (the vision) is then *followed by* the "how" (the supporting elements to achieve that vision). In Figure 2-1, the "what" was simply features and functions without a strategy or vision.

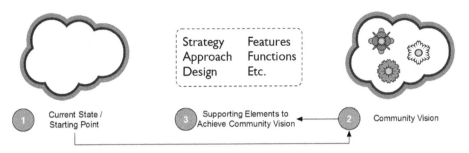

Figure 2-2. *The "how" can and should follow the vision for a community*

The depth and breadth of planning needs will vary among organizations. Let's say an individual works for a small firm with an even smaller budget looking to have some form of an online presence via a Salesforce community. It's unlikely that this person will have the resources to craft a grand vision for a community—and that's fine. One can still think ahead and come up with a long-term plan that will help to prevent a short-term, feature-focused community that ends up on the shelf after the novelty has worn off.

Verifying the Approach/Frame of Mind

How can community builders tell whether they are on the right track in community planning and preparation? An easy way to identify the common misstep of focusing solely on features or requirements is to do a quick role-play activity. Consider a hypothetical conversation with an executive sponsor of the community to explain what it's all about in a one-minute summary (i.e., an elevator speech). If the content coming out revolves around page layouts, specific components, or sharing rules, it might be appropriate to feel a bit concerned.

So, what would be compelling to a community's executive sponsor? Take a look at Figure 2-3. In this visual, I convey two very different sets of community drivers and identify which set shows long-term vision.

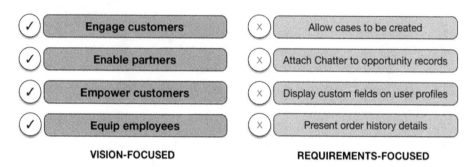

Figure 2-3. *Examples of vision versus requirements (and yes, aspects of the vision may start with a letter other than "E")*

Even if a builder has already ventured down the requirement-centric path, he or she can always take a step back to better understand and communicate the purpose of the community. This calls for a moment to focus on community vision-crafting. To establish the strategic direction for a community, one will need to identify the corresponding why, what, and who. Figure 2-4 provides a sample of questions that could help formulate this vision.

Know the:	By Clarifying:
Why	• Why is a community being considered? • Why would the expected audience use the community? • Why is the existing solution, if any, not satisfactory?
What	• What are the known business drivers? • What are key business challenges? • What is the expected outcome of the community?
Who	• Who will have interactions via the community? • Who will be impacted by communities activities? • Who could be considered a stakeholder?

Figure 2-4. *Asking the right questions early in the community planning phase*

The items in Figure 2-4 are just a sample of the types of questions that one will want to ask during your planning phase. With an understanding of information from questions like those shown here, community administrators, managers, and developers will find that the presentation of a compelling, succinct story of an envisioned community will flow with relative ease.

Note   I'll assume that if someone is involved in building a community in any way, he or she will understand the basics (and criticality) of gathering detailed requirements and establishing use cases. This chapter is not intended to provide an overview on business analysis; rather, it is to help provide to have the right mind-set when establishing an online community to ensure that builders think of key elements and ask the right questions.

Other Areas to Consider

As you individuals gather, analyze, and assess requirements and use cases and prepare to build a Salesforce community, there are a number of functional and technical topics to potentially address.

- Licensing

- Org strategy (multi-org, new versus existing org)

- Community type (templates)

- Reporting and analytics

- Security (access, visibility, sharing, permissions)

- Topics and knowledge articles

- Branding

- Process automation

- Deployment

- Management and moderation

- Activation, onboarding, and training

- Login/SSO

- Page variations and dynamic branding

I will jump into these topics in the coming chapters. However, in this chapter on planning and preparation, I want to call out a few specific areas that warrant particular attention early in the process.

- Audiences

- Data

- Metrics /KPIs

Audiences

Identifying all relevant audiences is a key step in preparing for a community build. Community administrators might not yet have all community users categorized, but they should have a sense for the individuals who play a direct or indirect role in the community. It may be fairly straightforward to determine the active "doers" in the community (although there are definitely exceptions to that statement); however, it's critical not to forget the "receivers" of community activity. For example, community activity may result in data that is routed to users who are not obvious, direct participants. These impacted users *are* still part of a community audience and need to be considered. Figure 2-5 gives a visual representation of audiences associated with both primary and secondary user groups within a community.

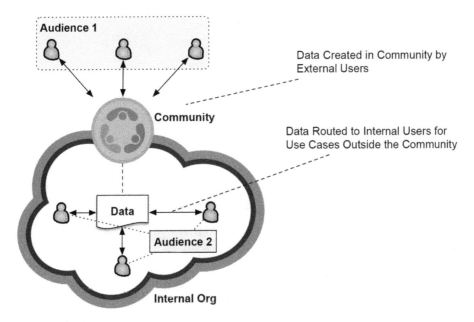

Figure 2-5. *Make sure to consider all potential audiences within the community*

Data Sources and Types

Admins must know their data. Along with its members, a community's data will serve
as the lifeblood of a community. Requirements and use cases should help to extract this
information, but a systematic approach is needed to ensure that all bases are covered.
Admins should step through the following and identify which of these components will
come into play in your community:

- Standard objects

    - Standard fields and corresponding field types

    - Custom fields and corresponding field types

- Custom objects

    - Standard fields and corresponding field types

    - Custom fields and corresponding field types

- External systems

    - Data types

    - Data fields

    - System of record

While an organization's setup may not require having to peer outside the Salesforce cloud, many communities will leverage data from outside sources. Figure 2-6 gives a picture of what this might look like.

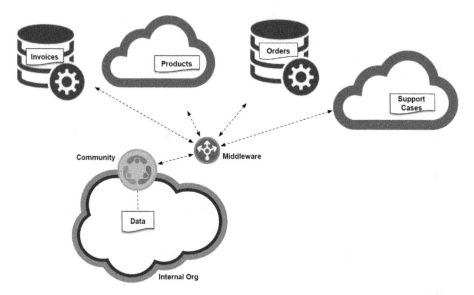

Figure 2-6. *Take an inventory of all potential sources of data when planning a community*

I stress having this familiarity with the community data because unaddressed issues at the data level—be it missing data, improperly mapped data, or data integrity issues—will plague a community from day 1. Inevitably, an initial negative perception will adversely impact the adoption of the community. Like a famous dandruff shampoo brand once stated, "You never get a second chance to make a first impression."

Measuring Success with KPIs

Even with a moving vision for a community and an extremely comprehensive set of detailed requirements and user stories, success is not guaranteed. While an organization may have positioned its community well to make a positive impact, there is one way to ensure that it has achieved your goals: by establishing key performance indicators (KPIs) and monitoring corresponding community activity over time. With quantitative, measurable goals, those building communities on the Salesforce platform can eliminate subjective conjectures and provide facts on how the community is operating, at least to a degree.

While the measuring comes post-implementation, one can start thinking about defining the KPIs as early as desired. Figure 2-7 shows examples of some metrics that warrant consideration, depending on the community's audience (or audiences) and use cases.

Community Metrics (Sample)	
Member registration	Call volume (measuring deflection)
Member logins	Case volume, response times
Page views	Opportunity volume, amount, closure
Likes, posts, comments	Lead volume, quality
File uploads, views, downloads	Customer satisfaction score (CSAT)
Reputation activities	Net promoter score (NPS)
Record/data activity	Order volume, amount

Figure 2-7. *Examples of community metrics to consider before the build starts*

Note   The high-level metrics in Figure 2-7 are a sample of potentially relevant community metrics. It's likely that some of these won't be applicable to a community, while other, unlisted metrics should be added to this list.

Recap

This chapter explored a critical, but oft-underestimated phase of the community lifecycle: planning. A general foundation was provided for achieving success upon deployment of a community, although one will need to go much deeper with your organization's specific needs, requirements, and use cases. The main takeaways from this chapter should be grasping the criticality of a vision for an online community and knowing where one is headed...and *why*.

CHAPTER 3

Licenses and Member Groups: Employees, Partners, and Customers

A critical element of any community-building journey will be the identification of corresponding member groups, as I generally discussed in Chapters 1 and 2. In particular, those building a community will need to identify which members make up a particular group (e.g., employees, partners, or customers), what capabilities are needed for each member to achieve success in his or her role, and how the members mesh with new or existing business processes in the context of system behavior. To a degree, this relates to the access and permissions that will be granted to each member group. However, the focus in this chapter will primarily reside at a more foundational level: community user licensing. While the constitution of a communities license mix can be changed over time, an unplanned shift in a set of licenses will come at a cost. Fortunately, such impacts can be avoided by establishing a proper understanding of license types and how they apply to a community early on in the project lifecycle.

Licenses for Salesforce Community Users

An essential aspect of building a successful Salesforce community is the understanding and application of appropriate licensing. To do this, I will explore a few areas.

- License types (which licenses exist for Salesforce communities)
- License functionality (the access/permissions that each license type provides for individual users)

© Philip Weinmeister 2018
P. Weinmeister, *Practical Guide to Salesforce Communities*, https://doi.org/10.1007/978-1-4842-3609-3_3

- License application (how licenses are applied to Salesforce users)

- User versus login-centric licensing

- License management

Community License Types

To clearly explain the various licenses that are available, it's helpful to first group them.

- Standard community licenses

- Legacy community licenses

- Employee licenses

- Standard licenses

Standard Community Licenses

I have been building communities for a number years; I have seen a wide variety of different use cases that need to be solved and different constituencies that make up the community audience. The vast majority of community-related licensing, as one would expect, comes from this bucket. There are three license types that fall into this group.

- Customer Community

- Customer Community Plus

- Partner Community

Note   Technically, each license type in the previous list is associated with two child license types: User (named member) and Login. I will address these subtypes later in this chapter.

Legacy Community Licenses

There are community licenses that are no longer available to new organizations looking to build a community but are grandfathered and still applicable to some existing communities. I won't dissect the access or functionality associated with these licenses since community admins won't need to know them outside of understanding how legacy communities are built.

- Customer Portal Manager Custom

- Customer Portal Manager Standard

- Gold Partner

- High Volume Customer Portal

- Overage High Volume Customer Portal

- Possibly others

Employee Licenses

For those wondering why employee licenses aren't grouped with the other community licenses, it's because employee licenses are a bit of a different beast. The biggest differentiator is that these licenses allow for direct access to the internal org, not just the corresponding community or communities. Salesforce refers to these as Salesforce "Platform" licenses.

- Lightning Platform Starter

- Lightning Platform Plus

Note   Prior to the Lightning Platform licenses, Employee Apps licenses were the closest active equivalent. Of course, these may change again; make sure to always discover the latest when researching licenses.

Standard Licenses

I'm grouping a number of licenses into this bucket. Most notably, the typical/most common license for internal users is found here. Users with these licenses can be granted access to an external community; an additional license is not needed. I won't go into all the types in the "other" bucket, but know that there are many "noncommunity" license types that provide users with the ability to log in to communities.

- Salesforce

- Other types

Community License Functionality

A key aspect of the licensing around communities is the set of capabilities and functionality that each license type provides.

Standard Communities Licenses

The most common question I get about licensing is about the difference between the various license types and what each type grants a user, in terms of access, permissions, and system capability, for the purpose of making a wise decision on the purchase of licensing. Ultimately, it comes down to a question of whether the base communities license, Customer Community, will suffice or whether specific requirements warrant an upgrade to a more flexible (and costlier) license.

Let's take a step back and look at the picture from a high level. It's important to understand which areas in Salesforce are made available through these license types. Take a look at Figure 3-1; it shows the access each type provides to "standard" Salesforce (internal) and to communities (external).

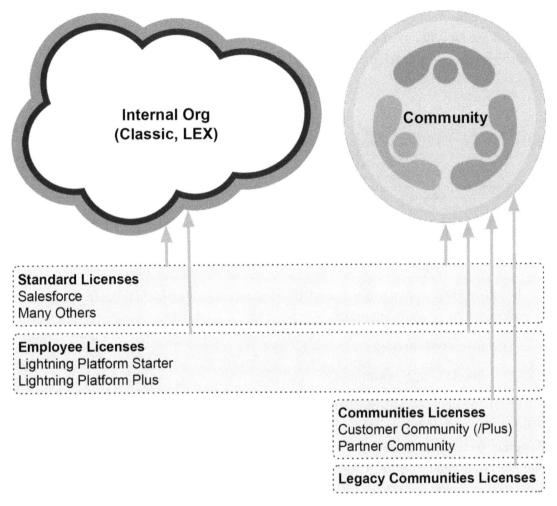

Figure 3-1. Community-specific licenses do not provide "internal org" access

The main takeaway of Figure 3-1 is that a number of licenses provide internal access (via the classic or Lightning Experience interface) and external access (via communities) access to Salesforce, while communities-specific licenses are intended only for external access.

Now, I'll zoom in and take a closer look at communities licenses to understand what makes sense for different use cases. Figure 3-2 shows a layered view of functionality available to users with each of the three communities licenses.

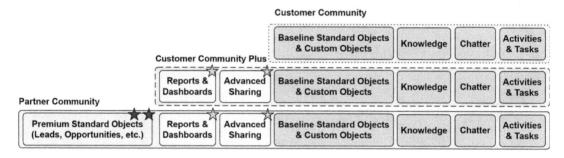

Figure 3-2. *A simplified view of key functionality in community license types*

Based on my personal experience delivering communities, most licensing decisions come down to two requirements.

- Advanced sharing

- Access to opportunities

I'll go into detail on access, sharing, and visibility in Chapter 7, but it's important to understand what "advanced sharing" means in the context of licensing here. With customer community licensing, the sharing model and sharing settings that we've all come to know and love within the classic or Lightning Experience interface is, for the most part, not available. That's correct—users based on standard customer licenses can't leverage any of the "advanced" elements of standard sharing. That means that while admins *can* grant general read-only or read-write access for a specific object to external users, they *can't* manually share records, set up sharing rules, or even set a community user as the owner of a record through the UI. User sharing is bound by Sharing Sets, which can be extended a bit with creativity but significantly limit what is possible. If an organization needs to be able to granularly control who can see what, it will need advanced sharing, requiring *at least* the Customer Community Plus license.

The opportunity object speaks for itself. It is Salesforce's bread and butter, and Salesforce isn't sharing this loaf for free anytime soon. It might seem odd that access to a few objects (leads and a few others, in addition to opportunities) would command a separate license in a model with only three license types. However, think of it this way:

the real money is made around these objects. They have everything to do with driving revenue, and companies will pay for a platform that will help them to do that effectively and efficiently.

> **Note**   Licensing is an ever-evolving practice at Salesforce. License types, names, functionality, and prices change fairly regularly. Make sure to directly contact Salesforce when making a purchasing decision to ensure that your licensing information is accurate and up-to-date.

Employee License Functionality

While employee licenses don't technically fall in the "communities" bucket, they are an ideal option for providing employees with low-cost access to both the internal org and one or more communities that are a part of the org. Figure 3-3 shows a high-level view of functionality in the two types of employee licenses.

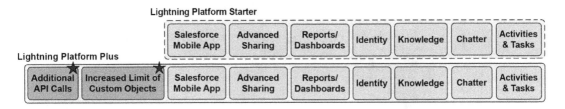

Figure 3-3.   *Additional custom objects are a major reason for "Plus" licenses*

Community License Application

The actual application of communities licenses is not intuitive, as it fundamentally varies from the process of applying a standard license to a user. Let's walk through the process for each scenario.

> **Note**   There are different tactical ways to carry out the application of licenses (e.g., via the UI, via Data Loader, etc.). The focus here is to provide more of a conceptual understanding of how community-related users come to be.

Standard Salesforce Users

To create a standard/employee user, an administrator can follow a simple, traditional approach, as shown in Figure 3-4.

1   Create user record; save.

Figure 3-4. *Creating a standard user is simple and straightforward: create the user record*

Customer Community Users

When we shift to the application of communities licenses, other steps come into the picture. A key understanding is that communities licenses are never applied by navigating to Setup ➤ Users and directly creating a user record. Figure 3-5 shows the process for setting up users with Customer Community and Customer Community Plus licenses.

1   Identify contact to be enabled as a customer user.

2   Enable contact as a customer user.

Manage External User > Enable Customer User

3   Create customer user record; save.

Figure 3-5. *Creating a customer community user involves the creation of a contact record*

Partner Community Users

For partner users, there is an additional step: establishing the account as a partner account. Figure 3-6 shows the steps to set up a partner user for communities.

1   Identify contact to be enabled as a partner user.

2   Enable contact's account as a partner account.
[Note: Required only one time per account]

Manage External Account ➤ Enable As Partner

3   Enable contact as a partner user.

Manage External User ➤ Enable Partner User

4   Create partner user record; save.

Figure 3-6. *Establishing partner community users impacts both contacts and accounts*

Associating Users with a Community

In all scenarios, the final step to creating a user for the purpose of enabling that user with community access is to associate the profile or permission set of that user with the community. I'll cover this in more detail later in the book.

Note   An organization does not have to use the classic or Lightning Experience (LEX) interfaces to set up communities users; a tool such as Data Loader can be used to create users in bulk.

Disabling Community Users

While it's not discussed or performed nearly as much as the activation of community users, the act of disabling community users is also an important activity to be familiar with. Four primary functions exist, two at the account level and two at the contact level.

- *Account ➤ Disable Partner Account*: This deactivates all partner community user records associated with contacts on the account.

- *Account ➤ Disable Customer Account*: This deactivates all customer community user records associated with contacts on the account.

- *Contact ➤ Disable Partner User*: This deactivates the partner community user record associated with the contact.

- *Contact ➤ Disable Customer User*: This deactivates the customer community user record associated with the contact.

User vs. Login-centric Licensing

Each of the three communities license types that we previously covered has a corresponding "login" license type. For example, both Customer Community Login and Customer Community licenses are available for providing users with customer-level access to a community.

The idea is simple. For users who do not log in frequently, providing them with a "named user" license is unnecessarily costly. On the other hand, providing an active user with a login license is not sensible, either, as they will also incur avoidable costs.

Salesforce suggests that the crossover point is 3:1, based on the list price of these two license types. This means that if a user logs in three or more times per month, they should be a named user. Figure 3-7 shows this decision point.

Note   The cost ratio of named-to-login community licenses is subject to change. Confirm with Salesforce where the recommended line exists before making a decision.

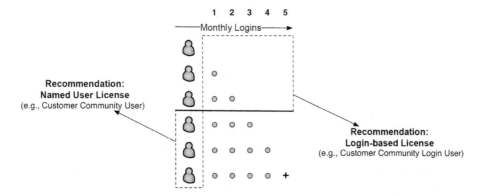

Figure 3-7.   *Users who log in three or more times a month should be named users*

Choosing wisely between named users and login-based users is critical and can significantly impact the bottom line. Let's walk through this with a fictitious company, Bunker & Jones. Assume Bunker & Jones has six community users with varying login activity. Figure 3-8 shows the login activity by users over a given month.

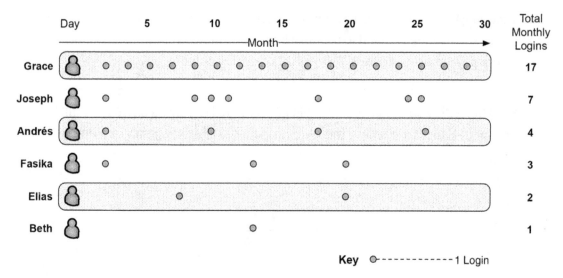

Figure 3-8. *Login activity for Bunker & Jones community users*

While the licensing decision may seem simple, success is dependent on an organization's ability to predict future activity and apply licenses accordingly. This is obviously a bit more variable than having a set of users with completely repetitive, predictable behavior. Take a look at Figure 3-9. In this example, I show four possible approaches for applying license types to Bunker & Jones and the ramifications of each. The high-cost option would cost the organization more than twice the optimal option!

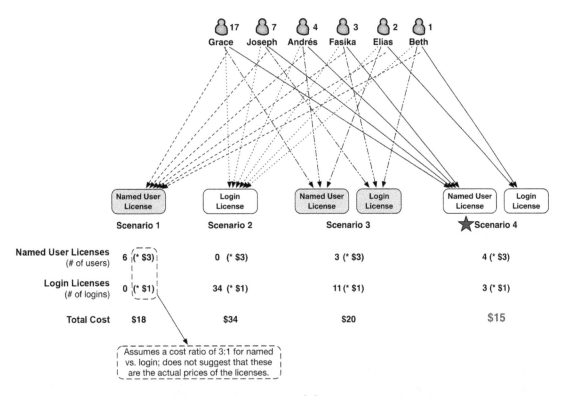

Figure 3-9. *The optimal licensing scenario (4) comes in at less than 50 percent the cost of the least optimal scenario (2)*

Communities License Management

A final key point specific to licenses is that there are specific capabilities regarding a change in licensing for a specific user. I will place these types of changes into two buckets: *named versus login* and *license type/level*. A user can be switched, with relative ease, between named and login user licenses, as shown in Figure 3-10. Of course, this assumes available licenses of each type, which would be necessary for the switch.

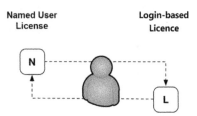

Figure 3-10. *Assuming license availability, an admin can move a user between named and login-based licenses*

Named versus login is a fairly straightforward concept. Changes of license *type* are a bit trickier. Figure 3-11 shows what is possible between standard communities license types.

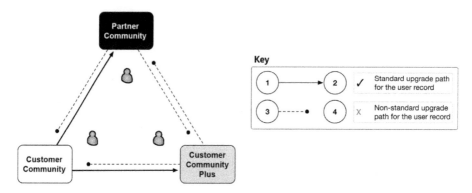

Figure 3-11. *The upgrade and downgrade paths between community licenses are not intuitive. Know these before making a license purchase*

Note   The nonstandard upgrade path does not mean that a community member that falls into that scenario cannot be migrated from one license type (e.g., Partner Community) to another (e.g., Customer Community). It does, however, mean that the process is much more involved, requires more time and analysis, and may result in data loss.

The Concept of Member Groups

Familiarizing oneself with the various communities licenses and what functionality those licenses encompass is necessary for community success. However, I can't simply leave the conversation there; the concept of "member groups" goes beyond a license label. It is critical to clearly understand what it means when hearing terms like Employee Community, Partner Community, and Customer Community.

Technically, organizations do not exactly "buy a [member group] community." I'll explain what I mean in the rest of the chapter. Consider our fictitious company, Bunker & Jones, for a moment. True, Bunker & Jones can subscribe to a community license bundle that has 100 percent employee licenses—with zero partner and customer licenses—for a community named Bunker & Jones Employee Community. In that sense, Bunker & Jones just purchased an employee community; however, it's important to understand that the community name is arbitrary and doesn't necessarily have anything to do with functionality or capabilities, and the mix of licenses can be changed at any time. If a partner license is added and leveraged for this community, is it still technically an "employee community?" This question is rhetorical; the point is that it's up to the organization to determine whether this community is still labeled as an "employee community" or not.

Some may be thinking, "Wait, I thought Salesforce had a Partner Community offering...so you *can* buy a community type!" That is a partner *template*, which technically can be leveraged with a variety of license types; it is not limited to partner licenses. Additionally, nonpartner functionality can easily be added to a community using this template. I'll discuss templates, or Lightning Bolts, more in Chapter 13.

The key takeaway in this section is that the labels of *employee, partner*, and *customer for a community* do not directly relate to off-the-shelf community SKUs from Salesforce; the supporting licenses do. In the context of the community itself, these labels are descriptors and serve two purposes by clarifying the following:

- The spirit/essence of the community

  - Functionality, capabilities

  - User experience/presentation

- General licensing structure

  - Distribution of available community licenses in the org

  - License distribution of users actively logging into the community (e.g., a community leveraging only customer licenses would be considered a "customer community")

As an organization's needs to connect with employees, partners, and customers expands, it becomes easier to see that Community Cloud is a true platform that allows for a spectrum of community manifestations that aren't limited to one specific audience type. I created Figure 3-12 to assist in that line of thinking. This figure shows potential overlap between function, vertical, and community member group; notice that each vertical and function includes more than one member group.

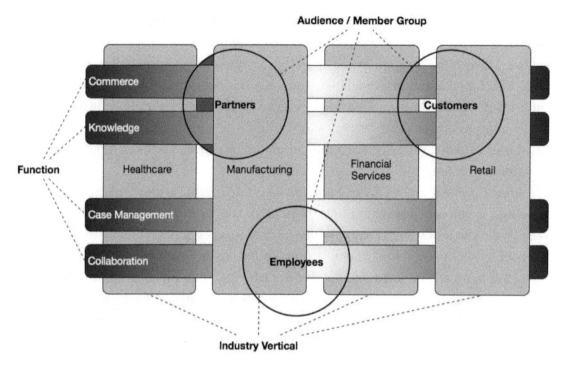

Figure 3-12. *Salesforce communities can support various combinations of audience, function, and industry*

With all this said, I need to be clear on one point. I said quite a bit about understanding the concept of member groups, specifically clarifying what exactly it means to label a community as a certain type (e.g., "employee community"). It is extremely common to label communities in this way, and I am not discouraging the application of these labels whatsoever. Ultimately, it is by far the simplest way to describe the purpose of a community, even if 100 percent of the members aren't from the same bucket. My main goal here is to provide you with a deep comprehension of what a community comprises that goes beyond a simple label.

Blending Member Groups Within Communities

We benefit from a couple major paradigm shifts that occurred when Salesforce introduced communities and started moving away from portals. First, multiple member groups can be enabled within a single community. Second, an individual user, regardless of member group, can be enabled in multiple communities and *at no additional cost* to the enabling organization. Let's dive into both and better understand how they impact the development of a community.

Multiple Member Groups Within a Single Community

Within a Salesforce community, multiple member groups can coexist. This is no small revelation, as pre-community "portals" did not allow for this. At that time, an organization would build a "partner portal," and it would be limited to a few license types associated with the partner portal. The concept of mixing multiple license types did not exist. Well, the game has changed, and we are all beneficiaries of that change.

If one does want to slap a label of Employee Community, Customer Community, or Partner Community on a community, let's at least open it up to the full gamut of possibilities. While both admins and users will definitely hear those three labels most commonly, there are four additional member combinations that need to be considered.

- Customer & Partner Community

- Customer & Employee Community

- Partner & Employee Community

- Customer, Partner, & Employee Community

Figure 3-13 shows how these member groups can come together to form blended communities.

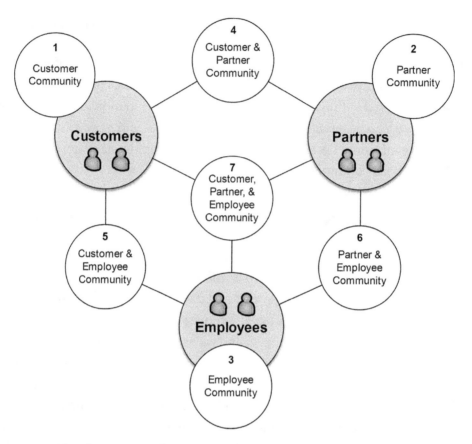

Figure 3-13. *The three most obvious community types are not the only ones available to you; 4, 5, 6, and 7 are hybrid communities*

One User in Multiple Communities

Another major revelation in communities is that a single user, regardless of member group, can be enabled in multiple communities. Additionally, this can be done *at no additional cost* to the enabling organization. Not only is this ideal from a financial perspective, it means you can manage a single identity for an external user who may need to be part of multiple communities. No one wants multiple user accounts anymore, especially on the same platform for similar use cases. Figure 3-14 depicts what this potentially means for an individual user.

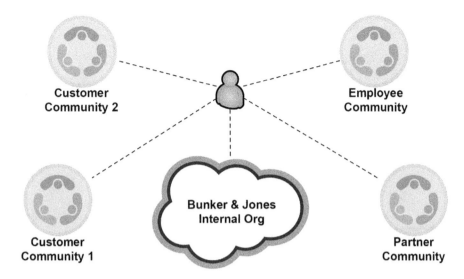

Figure 3-14. *One user can be granted access to an internal org and all the communities within that org*

Recap

In this chapter, I dove headfirst into the world of licensing and how licenses come together with the concept of member groups such as customers, partners, and employees within Salesforce communities. I reviewed various aspects of licenses, including types, functionality, application, and management. Additionally, I explained the idea of named users versus login-based users and how to approach your licensing purchases in light of these options. Finally, I opened up the concept of multicommunity users, as well as communities with multiple member groups.

CHAPTER 4

Community Template Types: Tabs, Visualforce, and Lightning

Technically, the first choice one is required to make when creating a new community is selecting an appropriate template. One could argue that this decision is even more critical than the selection of license types, as those can be changed without impacting the community (see Chapter 3 for some caveats to this statement). As I see it, a community template has four primary purposes.

- To provide an organization with relevant functions and features that will support the community requirements

- To enable an organization to build a community as efficiently as possible

- To establish the appropriate technological foundation to support declarative and/or programmatic development

- To support flexibility and extensibility for maintenance, management, and future changes

In this chapter, I will describe what top-level choices exist when selecting a template (tabs, Visualforce, and Lightning), break down specific templates and their corresponding pros and cons, and explain how template selection drives the four purposes mentioned previously.

© Philip Weinmeister 2018

P. Weinmeister, *Practical Guide to Salesforce Communities*, https://doi.org/10.1007/978-1-4842-3609-3_4

Note   This chapter will focus on general template types and give corresponding guidance on what to consider when selecting the most appropriate template for your community. Subsequent chapters that dive into template-specific functionality will focus almost solely on Lightning-based communities.

Template vs. Bolt

Before I dive in, I need to make sure to clear up confusion around Salesforce terminology, specifically *community template* and *Lightning Bolt*. I love the Salesforce platform, but I also want to be real and transparent; the coexistence and overlap of these two terms has been difficult to understand within the Salesforce ecosystem. Let me first state a few truths. First, every community is created from a (community) template. Second, an organization can take a community and create a "Lightning Bolt" from it, serving as the community's template. I once had a Community Cloud employee tell me that a "template" implies creation by Salesforce and a "Bolt" implies creation by a partner or customer (i.e., not Salesforce). That may be helpful, although it definitely doesn't clear up the whole issue. To be precise, a community template is an xml-based outline of a community that defines what elements should be included and how they should be configured at a community's point of inception. In other words, a community template is a "starting point" for a community, from where it can be further configured and customized. The term "Lightning Bolt" is, for the most part, a synonym for "community template." made available by Salesforce; this will be the focus in this chapter. A community template not created by Salesforce but by an individual (administrator, developer, etc.) or a partner organization, is considered a Lightning Bolt. Confusion can potentially occur because the template selection page (shown immediately after clicking New Community) is titled Lightning Bolt, as shown in Figure 4-1. My suggestion is to consider that every community starts with a community template; some templates are offered as customized solutions that are referred to as "Lightning Bolts." Make sure to read Chapter 13 for more detail.

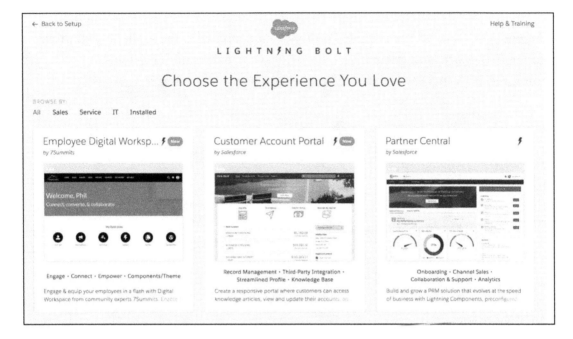

Figure 4-1. *Admins see this page immediately after clicking New Community*

Introduction and High-Level Categorization

Technically, the specific template choices available when creating a community are not split into the three categories mentioned in the chapter title. As of early 2018, the following are the available templates from Salesforce:

- Salesforce Tabs + Visualforce

- Lightning

    - Customer Service (Napili)

    - Build Your Own

    - Partner Central

    - Customer Account Portal

    - Aloha

    - Koa (no longer available in new communities)

    - Kokua (no longer available in new communities)

For now, I will discuss Lightning as a single, general template choice. Although differences do exist between Napili, Partner Central, and all of the available Lightning templates, they are fundamentally similar and leverage the same core tools for community building. See Figure 4-2 for an example of a Lightning community.

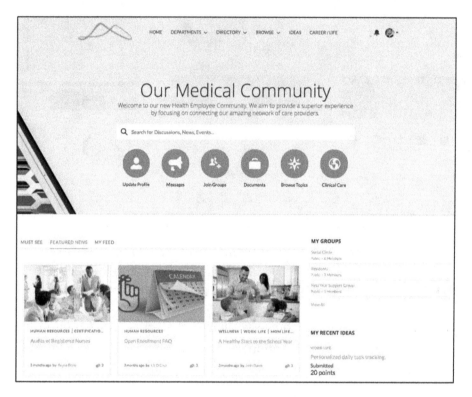

Figure 4-2. *An example of a Lightning community*

While tabs and Visualforce are actually part of one template, I will look at these as two distinct choices in this chapter.

When I mention a "tabs-based community," I am specifically referencing a community created with the Salesforce Tabs + Visualforce template that uses the standard, out-of-the-box navigation menu bar and sidebar. It's possible that the community leverages Visualforce pages and/or tabs, but the shell of the community is declarative, not custom. Figure 4-3 provides an example of a tabs-based community.

Figure 4-3. *A tabs-based community*

When I discuss a "Visualforce community," I am referring to a fully custom community that does not employ a standard, out-of-the-box navigation menu bar or sidebar. Everything in a community like this would be custom. See Figure 4-4 for an example of a Salesforce community built on Visualforce.

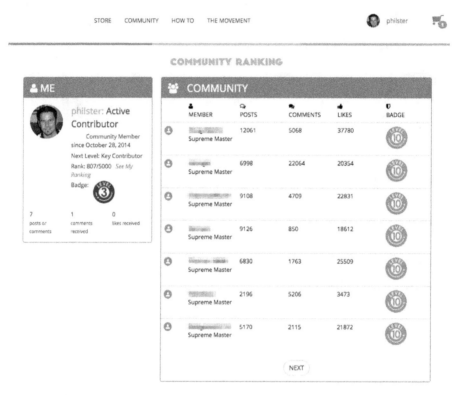

Figure 4-4. *A custom leaderboard page within a Visualforce-based community*

This leaves me with these three main template types to discuss in this chapter:

- Tabs
- Visualforce
- Lightning

Overview and Assessment

I am going to spoil the ending now: community builders should exhaust all reasonable scenarios when selecting a Lightning template when creating a community considering tabs or Visualforce. However, as of 2018, these are still available options, so I will walk through each one and outline the pros and cons of each.

Tabs

Tabs provide a declarative, no-code option with which one can build a community. However, I cannot with a good conscience suggest to anyone—for any reason—to build a tabs-based community in 2018 or beyond. Even in the situation where an organization wants to create an extremely basic community and does not plan on using technical resources, Lightning is going to be the best choice. The user experience within a Lightning community is significantly better than that of a tabs-based community; additionally, the ease with which one can drag and drop his or her way to a finished masterpiece with Lightning puts tabs in the rearview mirror once and for all. Figure 4-5 shows a view of a key administration page within a tabs-based community (I will cover administration in detail in Chapter 7).

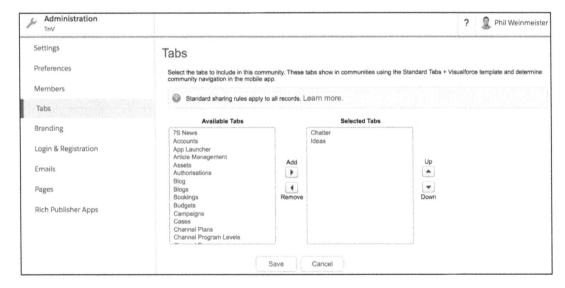

Figure 4-5. *Adding tabs to a tabs-based community*

Visualforce

By nature, Visualforce allows for an essentially limitless palette. Since a Visualforce community is built almost solely on code, those building the community can granularly control the user experience and functionality. However, it's important to understand that this comes at a cost. With Visualforce communities, one will find a solid correlation between the output and the investment required to get there. If an organization wants extremely complex business logic with a bespoke UI, they had better be ready to pay for it. In other words, "clicks" won't get those building a Visualforce community very far,; this template shrinks the pool of resources that can build this type of community. Figure 4-6 shows the administrative area that one would frequently use when building a Visualforce community.

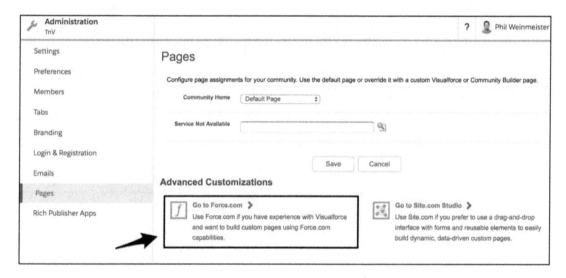

Figure 4-6. *Force.com admin section, used heavily in Visualforce communities*

Lightning

Lightning truly changes the game. While the technology is still relatively young as of 2018—when compared to Visualforce and tab options—it has matured significantly since its inception in late 2014. I have built communities using tabs, Visualforce, and Lightning, and I have no hesitation when pushing a recommendation of Lightning for new communities. Why? I'll provide a few reasons.

Extreme Productivity for Noncoders

To say that Lightning does not require code or technical resources in general is a bit misleading. Yes, technically, like with tabs, an individual can create a community with fairly useful functionality from scratch in short order without a line of code. However, to truly deliver a digital transformation, it is highly likely that custom Lightning components will come into the picture. As we all know, those custom components will require code. To be clear, though, this will be the case with any highly transformative solution, whether delivered with Visualforce, Lightning, or another front-end platform.

I think it's more appropriate to say that Lightning communities enable and empower those of us who are not programmatic developers (in other words, noncoders) in ways never before possible within the world of Salesforce communities. Not only can a functional resource efficiently configure a Lightning community, but he or she can assemble something much greater than the individual parts. I will share a few personal examples of this to illuminate the concept.

Since starting to work with Lightning communities, I have found myself in multiple situations where the availability of technical resources was extremely limited or nonexistent, but an inventory of existing assets (in the form of custom components) was at my disposal. I have been able to take these assets and, through reassembling and reconfiguring them, create a different application. Of course, the ability to do this depends on the flexibility of the original components, but this scenario is not a pipe dream.

I'll provide a few specific examples of taking disparate solutions and declaratively combining them. I have taken commerce and CPQ (configure/price/quote) elements from different providers and, by leveraging the related components and some additional platform tools, created an end-to-end CPQ plus checkout/purchase application in a Lightning community. Another example is with Lightning flow; I have taken custom components built for one specific purpose and, without any communication with the original developer, leveraged these components within a flow as part of a Lightning community. I simply learned what attributes were available and set them according to the need within the community. Figure 4-7 provides a visual of what I'm describing.

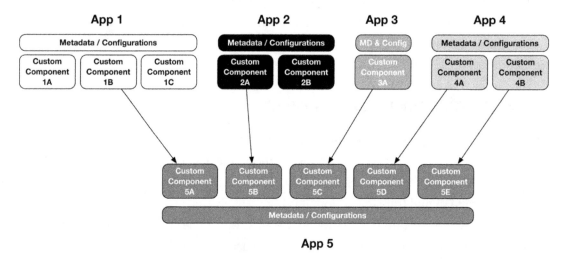

Figure 4-7. *Lightning allows the creation of new Lightning applications by consolidating and configuring components from disparate applications*

WYSIWYG Editor with Drag-and-Drop Control

Neither tabs nor Visualforce offers a what-you-see-is-what-you-get (WYSIWYG) community editor. That is a fairly significant limitation when you consider that you are building an online visual experience for your audience (or audiences). Sure, you can preview the community, but to have little or no visual context while you are building is not a desirable situation.

Lightning offers this with Community Builder, which I will dive into in the next chapter. Just understand for now that this is a major advantage over tabs and Visualforce. Seeing what you are building saves a significant amount of time in the long run.

Additionally, with Community Builder, you can drag and drop components onto and off of Lightning pages. Administration UX has made a major shift in this direction over the past decade, and it's fairly intuitive to most of us in an admin or developer role. This is also helpful for efficiency; what's faster than clicking, dragging, and unclicking to make a new element appear on a page?

Salesforce Lightning Design System

The Salesforce Lightning Design System (`https://www.lightningdesignsystem.com`) means that even a rudimentary Lightning community will provide a largely acceptable level of aesthetic pleasure for users. SLDS is used out of the box within all Lightning community templates, as you would expect. This means a much slicker, more modern look and feel than you'll find with tabs or most Visualforce communities. So, what's included in SLDS?

- *Components*: Building blocks of Salesforce applications

- *Utilities*: Utility classes that apply a single rule or simple pattern to components

- *Design tokens*: Elements that store visual design attributes and are used in place of hard-coded values

- *Icons*: Library of icons that support the Salesforce interface

True, SLDS is at least partially supported within Visualforce. It is not recommended by Salesforce for retrofitting into existing pages but is an option for new Visualforce pages.

Focal Point for New Functionality and Innovation

Since it's not an immediately impactful area, the future roadmap and potential innovation related to a template choice can be easily overlooked. However, it should be a key factor in any organization's decision when selecting a community template. Salesforce is investing heavily in Lightning; this includes major investments in Lightning within a community context. It should not come as a surprise that Salesforce is not spending much at all on Visualforce these days.

So, what does that mean for an organization looking to build a Salesforce community? It means that the decision to build with Lightning will reap benefits well beyond the launch date. No organization launches a community without hope of long-term success; it's fair to look a few years out when thinking about how a technology decision could impact the future. Sure, Visualforce might suffice today and even boast a few capabilities that haven't yet arrived in Lightning. But what about next year? Or the year after that? It's not a wise bet to overlook the future maturity and expansion of

Lightning and, likewise, not insightful to bet on an aging technology that is relatively stagnant. Figure 4-8 provides a conceptual view of how innovation has played out among these three template types over time.

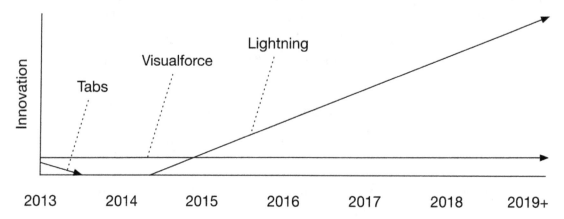

Figure 4-8. *Lightning is where the innovation is at on the Salesforce platform*

Impact of Template Selection

Why is template selection so critical when creating a new community? I will walk through a few areas that warrant serious consideration and explain why.

Relevant Functions and Features

Even with setting aside the almost limitless world of customization to extend a community, there exists a plethora of community-specific and community-enabled functionality that is provided out of the box on the Salesforce platform. While many organizations leverage some custom functionality and others may even want a completely tailored, pixel-perfect community, the vast majority want to maximize the platform and what is possible without reinventing the wheel or spending unnecessary funds.

To that end, templates come with or support specific functionality. As you may have deduced, that means some templates *don't come with or support* specific functionality, making your template choice that much more critical. Let's take a look at a few examples.

Ideas

Although it hasn't received much love in recent years in the form of enhancements, the Ideas module is still used by thousands of organizations with Salesforce. The Ideas module is available and supported out of the box as a tab (see Figure 4-9) but is not via Visualforce or Lightning (as of early 2018). Leveraging Visualforce or Lightning would require customization to create a user interface for the Ideas back-end application.

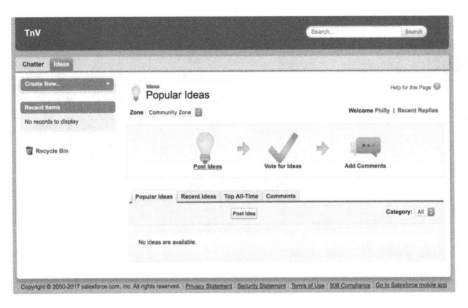

Figure 4-9. *Ideas within a tabs-based community*

Featured Topics

While topics in general are supported in tabs and Visualforce, only Lightning templates enable featured topics out of the box. Featured Topics is a standard component that can be dropped into a Lightning community; Figure 4-10 shows a configured instance of this component.

Figure 4-10. *The Featured Topics component within a Lightning community*

Flow

Flow, or *visual workflow*, is an extremely powerful business process automation tool on the Salesforce platform that does not require programmatic development. I will go into depth on how Flow can bring a Lightning community to life in Chapter 10. For now, I will frame it in the context of templates. Flows can be enabled and displayed on a Visualforce page and within the standard Flow component that was delivered in Salesforce's Winter '18 release version, but there is no out-of-the-box home for flows in a tabs-based community. Figure 4-11 shows the Flow component in a Lightning template.

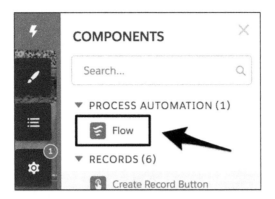

Figure 4-11. *The Flow component in a Lightning component*

Efficient Community Creation

The previous section addressed how to ensure that what you will need in your community is supported or enabled. Let's now shift to focusing on how your template selection can get you to the finish line as quickly as possible. While different templates may support various functions, notable work might be required to get them up and running.

I need to make sure that a key point is not missed here: only Lightning communities can come with site elements prepositioned and preconfigured. With tabs and Visualforce communities, you always start from scratch. Figure 4-12 gives an idea of the overall concept.

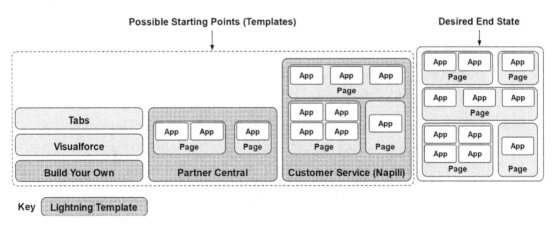

Figure 4-12. *Each community template brings with it a certain amount of out-of-the-box functionality*

Technological Foundation

Choosing the appropriate template is much more than a consideration of available or supported functions and features. With Lightning now on the scene, your choice has an immense impact on how your organization will develop and maintain your community. Figure 4-13 provides some of the corresponding factors that you'll want to consider.

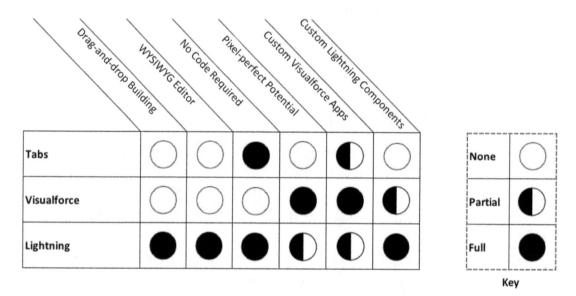

Figure 4-13. *Attributes of each community template type*

Here are some of my additional thoughts on each of these items:

- *Drag-and-drop building*: Visualforce requires code; tabs require clicks. Lightning enables you to drag and drop components onto your Lightning community pages.

- *WYSIWYG editor*: Only Lightning (via Community Builder) provides this. Plan for a lot of clicking/tabbing back and forth between screens when building your community with Visualforce or tabs.

- *No code required*: Tabs and Lightning hit the mark here, requiring zero code. Visualforce is completely the opposite, as it requires code.

- *Pixel-perfect potential*: I believe we have finally reached the point where I can legitimately say that Lightning allows for pixel-perfect site building. You'll have to build your own custom theme and custom Lighting components, but you can do it. On the other hand, Visualforce has always been known as the option that allows you to "do whatever you want."

- *Custom Visualforce apps*: Of course, there's no issue with leveraging these in a Visualforce community. You can leverage the Visualforce Page component to wrap Lightning-enabled Visualforce pages for use within Lightning communities. Also, you can create a Visualforce tab for a Visualforce page and use that tab in your tabs-based community.

- *Custom Lightning components*: There are no options for using components in a strictly tabs-based community, although you can leverage Lightning Out (https://developer.salesforce.com/docs/atlas. en-us.lightning.meta/lightning/lightning_out.htm) to potentially place components within a Visualforce page. Components, of course, can live in a Lightning community template.

Flexibility and Extensibility

Factors in choosing a template that are easily overlooked are flexibility and extensibility. Think of flexibility along the lines of configurability: how easily can you make changes without customization (aka code)? Extensibility stresses the ease with which you can add to, or extend, the solution.

Again, Lightning stands out here. Virtually every aspect of Lightning can be modified without code. Of course, to change the essence or nature of a specific Lightning component, you'll have to modify the code in that component, but you can easily configure the community and the components with clicks. As far as extensibility goes, you can add new Lightning components with extreme ease.

As for the other options, not so much. Yes, you can configure a tabs community and make changes without code. However, the ceiling of what you can change is much lower. Extending a tabs solution also doesn't leave you with tons of options without diving into code.

Visualforce communities are inherently inflexible, unless significant time was spent up front to inject configurability into the solution. They can definitely be extended (back to the "do whatever you want" mentality), but customization will be required for any extension that you consider.

Hybrid/Transitional Options

It is important to understand that, for those heavily invested in Visualforce, a transitional option does exist. Lightning communities support Visualforce pages within a Visualforce Page component available in Community Builder. To use a page in this component, the corresponding Visualforce page must be available for Lightning communities via the checkbox shown in Figure 4-14.

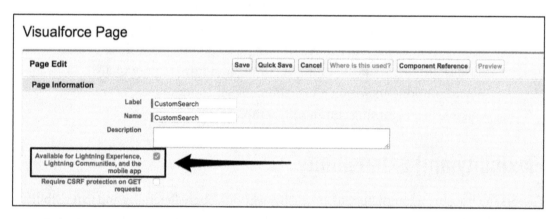

Figure 4-14. *Visualforce pages must be enabled for Lightning communities before they can be exposed in a Lightning community*

The Visualforce Page Lightning component can be dragged and dropped onto a Lightning page within Community Builder, as shown in Figure 4-15. Chapter 5 will explore Community Builder in depth for those without an understanding of that tool yet.

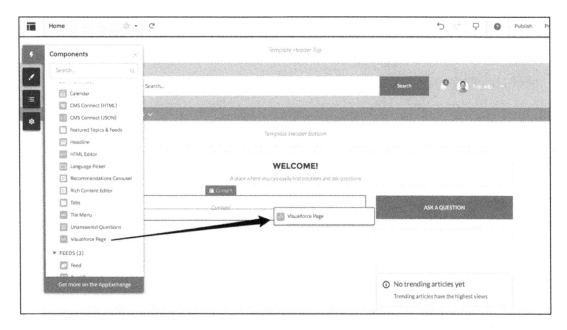

Figure 4-15. *The Visualforce Page Lightning component*

Once configured, a Lightning page that contains a Visualforce page is established.
See Figure 4-16.

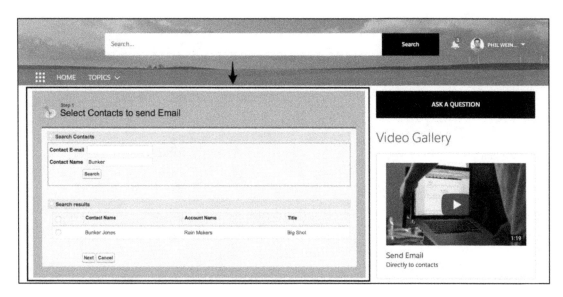

Figure 4-16. *Visualforce in Lightning*

Note   The reverse of this is also possible; Lightning components can be displayed on Visualforce pages via Lightning Out. However, this is not necessarily recommended, unless use cases warrant that approach.

Recap

In this chapter, I reviewed the three top-level options for building a community: tabs, Visualforce, and Lightning. Considering criteria such as efficiency, flexibility, and available capabilities, I looked at each template type and provided pros, cons, and recommendations. The clear takeaway? Heavily consider Lightning first; if Lightning doesn't satisfy a showstopping requirement, take a look at Visualforce. However, consider the long-term trajectory of the different template types and where things will be headed with upcoming Lightning innovation; a short wait to jump on Lightning might be worth it in the long run.

CHAPTER 5

Community Builder for Lightning Communities

For those who have decided to leverage a Lightning-based template as a starting point for a new community, a major bonus awaits. That bonus is (Lightning) Community Builder, the primary tool with which all Lightning communities are constructed. Community Builder, as shown in Figure 5-1, is found as a unique section within the community workspaces and provides the paintbrush, paint, and canvas for those creating a community from Napili or any other Lightning-based template. This tool has significantly changed the community creation process and has enabled and empowered many technical noncoders in the Salesforce ecosystem to develop functional, effective, and vibrant communities.

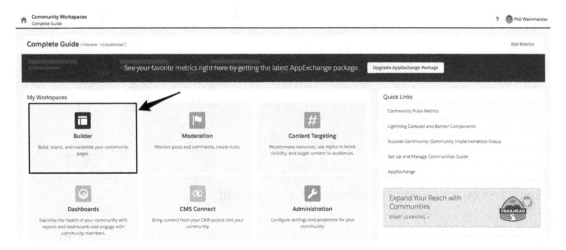

Figure 5-1. *The Builder workspace*

Note   Tabs and Visualforce-based communities do not use Community Builder.

P. Weinmeister, *Practical Guide to Salesforce Communities*, https://doi.org/10.1007/978-1-4842-3609-3_5

Overview

Community Builder is a visual tool that allows those responsible for building a community to see it come to life during the creation process. Community Builder is a what-you-see-is-what-you-get (WYSIWYG) editor that provides the ability to drag and drop the main building blocks of a Lightning community—Lightning components—to achieve the desired end state. The closest equivalent on the Salesforce platform as of 2018 is Lightning App Builder (another WYSIWYG tool), which allows administrators to construct Lightning apps for Lightning Experience. Lightning Experience is for users of "internal" Salesforce, not of communities. See Figure 5-2 for a view of Lighting App Builder.

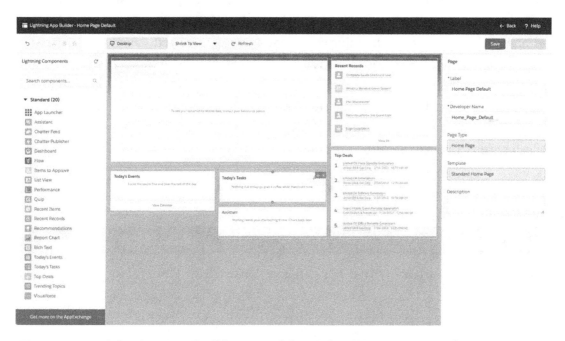

Figure 5-2. *Lightning App Builder, a tool for Lightning Experience that most closely resembles Community Builder for communities*

However, while Lighting App Builder does provide a palette of components for use and allows changes to the overall page layout, Community Builder (Figure 5-3) incorporates much more.

Figure 5-3. *A look at a new community from within Community Builder*

Within Community Builder, administrators can perform the following functions, among many others:

- Add, remove, position, and configure standard and custom Lightning components

- Configure community page attributes (e.g., layout)

- Manage sitewide branding colors, fonts, and images

- Create audiences for page variations and branding sets

- Preview and publish a community

In this chapter, I will walk through each of the sections, describe how to use them, and explain how they contribute to the overall creation of a community.

Getting to Know Community Builder

Community Builder is a broad, multifaceted application. To intimately understand the ins and outs of the tool, a systematic, comprehensive walk-through of each area is needed. I will divide it into two main sections, as shown in Figure 5-4: the left sidebar/tabs and the top menu bar.

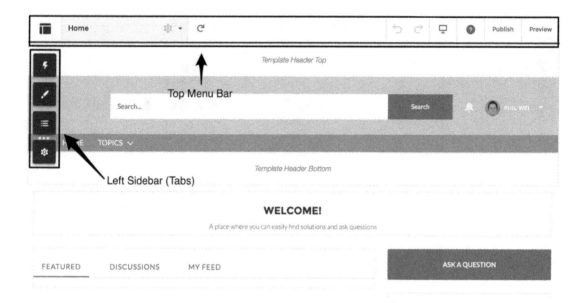

Figure 5-4. *Basic structure of Community Builder*

Left Sidebar/Tabs

A significant amount of time building communities is spent using the left sidebar. This sidebar within Community Builder houses four tabs.

- Components

- Theme (previously called Branding)

- Page Structure

- Settings

Note   As documented in this section with the Theme tab, Salesforce does somewhat regularly change terms and user interfaces related to communities functionality. While some of the labels and screens may change over time, the content and the essence of the actions won't necessarily change too much.

Figure 5-5 shows where each of these tabs is located.

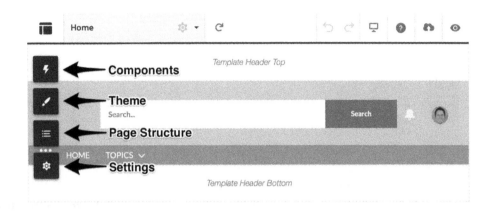

Figure 5-5. *The tabs in the left sidebar within Community Builder*

Components Tab

A community template, or Lightning Bolt (to be discussed in detail in Chapter 13), provides a basic assortment of prepositioned components already placed on pages to be configured. However, it is inevitable that community creators will eventually want to tap into the available pool of additional components to fill out their community and plug functional gaps. Insert the Components tab.

If I go with the analogy that a Lightning component is to a Lightning community as an individual Lego piece is to a finished Lego project, then the Components tab serves as a bag of various Lego pieces. The tab is essentially a list of available Lightning components. Each component is represented by three items: a text label, an icon, and a description that is shown upon hovering over a component. See Figure 5-6 for an example.

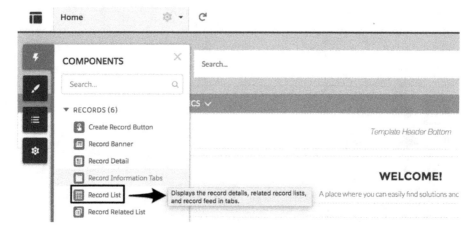

Figure 5-6. *Each component listed in the Components tab has a label, icon, and description*

The Components tab has two primary groupings: standard components, listed first, and custom components, listed last. However, admins will not see both of these exact section headers; Salesforce displays subgroupings within the standard component section. So, while community administrators will see a Custom Components section, they will see sections such as the following that comprise the standard component group:

- Analytics

- Cases

- Content

- Feeds

- Files

- Gamification

- Messages

- Process Automation

- Records

- Support

- Topics

Additionally, one can search by a text string to filter for any component that contains that string. As a bonus, the section headers persist in the search results. See Figure 5-7 for an example of a possible component search.

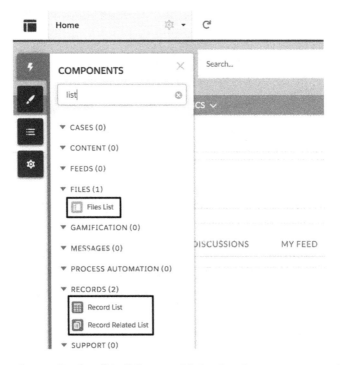

Figure 5-7. *Search results for "list" from within the Components tab*

To add a component from the Components tab to your community, simply perform the following steps (see Figure 5-8 for an example):

1. Click the desired component.

2. Drag the component to the appropriate section and position on the page.

3. Place the component by "dropping" it (releasing from the click).

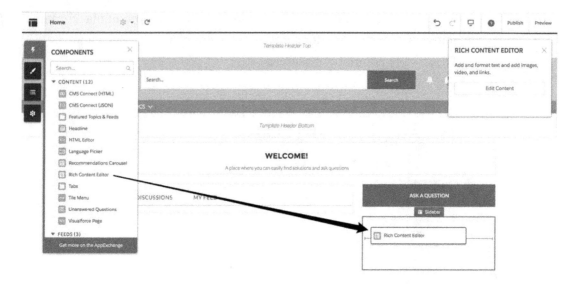

Figure 5-8. Dropping the Rich Content Editor component on a Lightning page

Don't worry; if a component is placed in the wrong section on the page, it can be easily moved later. I'll discuss the details of handling components following a drag and drop from the Components tab later; for now, I'll continue walking through the sidebar tabs within Builder.

Theme

While the Components tab focuses specifically on page-level content, the Theme tab generally provides sitewide configurability. Theme includes four distinct sections, as shown in Figure 5-9.

- Colors

- Images

- Fonts

- Theme Settings

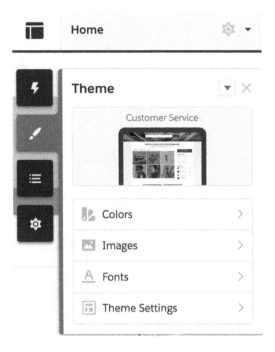

Figure 5-9. *The Theme tab*

Colors

The Colors section of the Theme tab defines the colors of specific elements on community pages. The settings in Colors apply to all community pages; as of the Spring '18 release from Salesforce, it is not yet possible to apply branding color settings to specific community pages or sections. Figure 5-10 shows the different color settings available and examples of where one can find them on an actual page (in this example, a Home page with minimal variance from the out-of-the-box configuration).

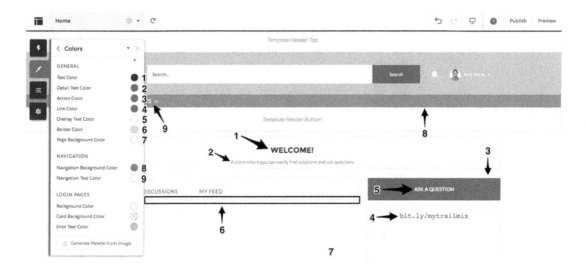

Figure 5-10. *Application of theme colors to a non-login page*

Login page colors are also controlled from Theme ➤ Colors. Figure 5-11 shows how the Background Color and Card Background Color settings impact the login page.

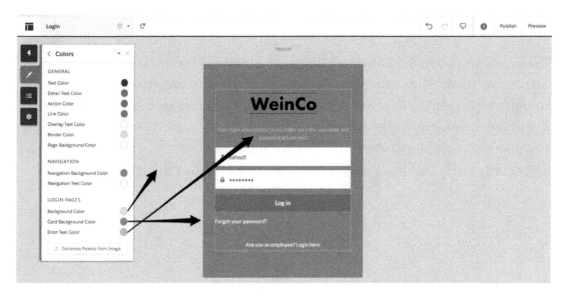

Figure 5-11. *Application of theme colors to a login page*

Images

The Images section impacts the standard header, which is included in all Salesforce-provided templates (other than Build Your Own), as well as the login page. Figure 5-12 shows Theme ➤ Images.

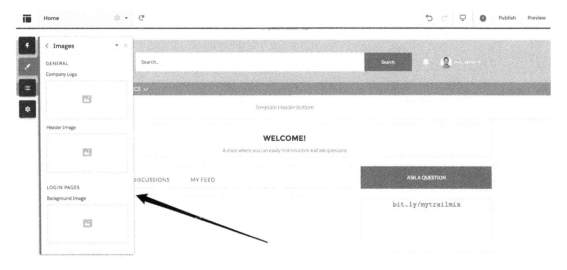

Figure 5-12. *Management of community theme images*

If the standard header is used (as opposed to replacing it with a custom header), two specific elements come into play that are updated in Theme ➤ Images.

- Company Logo

- Header Image

To add either a company logo or header image, click the placeholder image underneath the image type (e.g., Company Logo) and then identify an image. An image can be uploaded from the user's local computer or selected from Salesforce. External data sources that are configured will be displayed as well, allowing users to select images from sources such as Quip, Office365, or Google Drive, among others. See Figure 5-13 for a look at how uploading an image works.

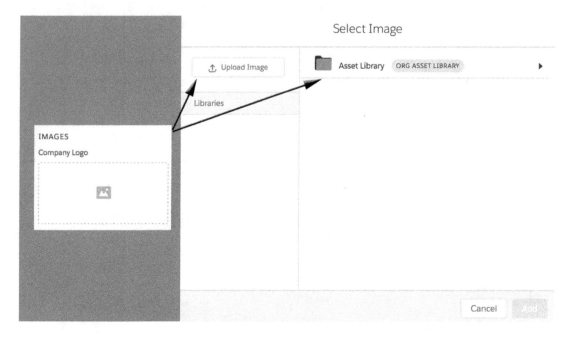

Figure 5-13. *Uploading or selecting an image*

Figure 5-14 shows the final result after uploading both a company logo and a header image.

Figure 5-14. *Uploaded images*

Figures 5-15 through 5-17 show three examples of how the header might look in the Customer Service (Napili) template.

Figure 5-15. *Header example 1*

Figure 5-16. *Header example 2*

Figure 5-17. *Header example 3*

The Images section also allows for the upload of the login background image, if desired. Figure 5-18 shows an example of an uploaded image for the login page.

Figure 5-18.   *Uploaded image*

One common area of confusion is the source of the logo on the login page. While it's not clear to me why this is the case, the login logo is managed in a different area. I'll dive into that area later, but I'll mention it now for context. It can be found in Workspace ➤ Administration ➤ Login & Registration ➤ Logo. See Figure 5-19 for a look at where you can modify the logo.

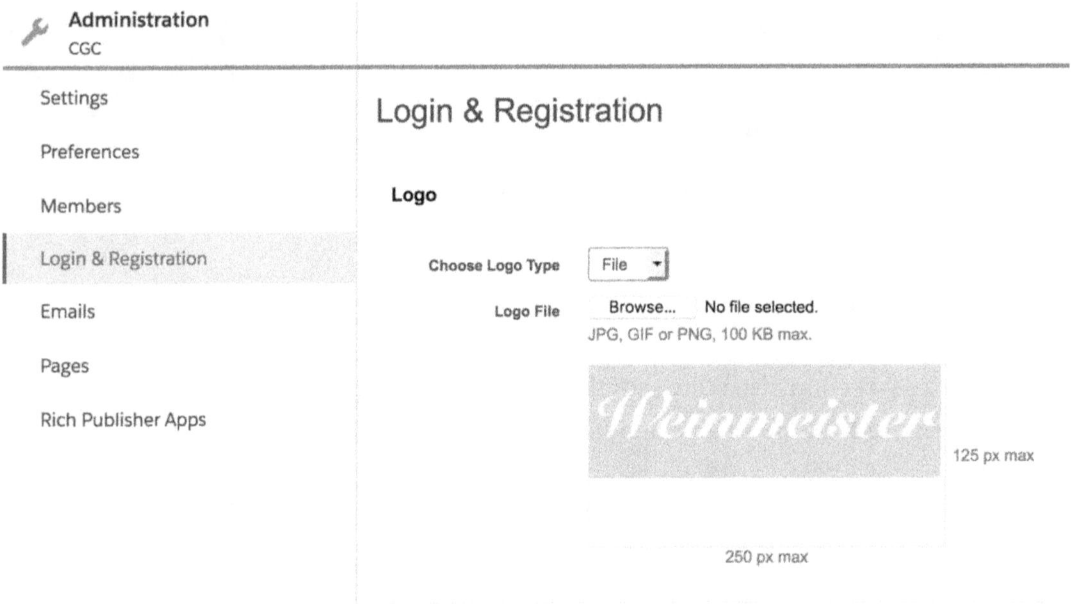

Figure 5-19.   *Use the Login & Registration section within Administration to modify the displayed logo on the login page*

> **Note** The images used for the header image and background image should web-optimized versions of high-resolution images. While it's ideal to have clear/vivid images, it's not ideal to "break the performance bank" by forcing a large image to load when the community is accessed.

With the right theme/branding settings, the login page can be transformed into a bright, welcoming page for community members. Figure 5-20 shows a Weinmeister-branded login page.

Figure 5-20. *Fun with the login page, thanks to a younger Weinmeister*

Fonts

The Fonts section impacts the font of all text that does not explicitly have a font already specified. An admin can modify the font for paragraph text (Primary Font) and header text (Header Font). Figure 5-21 shows an example of text impacted by the Primary Font setting.

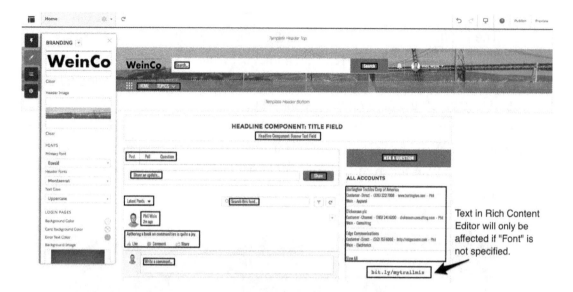

Figure 5-21. *This image shows a number of examples of how the primary font impacts the text on a community page (the Home page, in this case)*

Figure 5-22 shows an example of text impacted by the Header Font setting.

Figure 5-22. *This image shows a number of examples of how the header font impacts the text on a community page*

Additionally, the case of certain text can be configured via the Text Case setting, allowing an admin to set text formatting as Uppercase, Lowercase, or Capitalize, or to leave it unformatted. Figure 5-23 shows the text impacted by this setting.

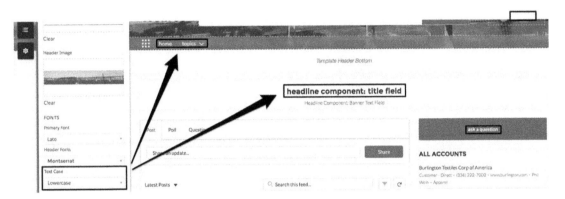

Figure 5-23. *This image shows how the text case impacts the text on a community page (in this case, with lowercase text)*

Theme Settings

The fourth section within the Theme Branding tab is Theme Settings. This allows for modification of some community-wide settings of the theme that apply to all pages. There are four settings available, as shown in Figure 5-24.

- Hide the header region and navigation (includes header image, search box, user profile, and navigation menu)

- Hide Notifications icon in community header

- Search Component (allows replacement of the standard search component with a custom component)

- User Profile Component (allows replacement of the standard user profile component with a custom component)

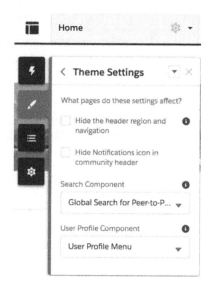

Figure 5-24. *Theme Settings section*

Prebuilt Community Themes

With the Summer '18 release, new themes come "preloaded" within communities. Previously, each Salesforce-provided community template had only one standard theme option (e.g., the Customer Service theme for the Customer Service template). However, it is now possible to select a prebuilt theme that significantly expands what is possible with the declarative Community Cloud UX. See Figure 5-25 for the Change Theme page.

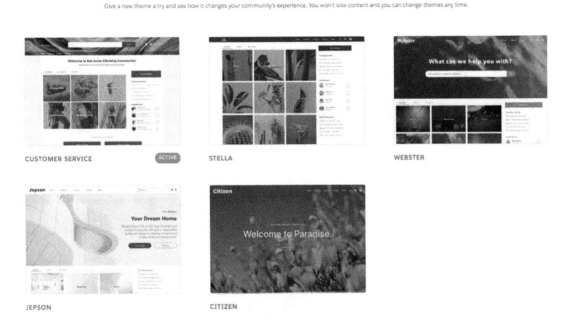

Figure 5-25. *Out-of-the-box community themes*

Administrators should confirm the latest themes available by checking the release notes website (https://releasenotes.docs.salesforce.com).

Note   Technically, branding sets live within the Theme tab, as well. However, this tool is really about audience targeting; I will discuss branding sets in Chapter 12.

Page Structure

Unlike the three other tabs within Community Builder, the Page Structure tab is purely informational; no actions can be performed from the tab. Page Structure displays two types of data.

- Each layout section that is present on the page currently being displayed

- All Lightning components present within each of those layout sections

Figure 5-26 shows an example of the Page Structure tab contents for a community Home page.

Figure 5-26. *Page Structure tab*

I want to point out a few specific items within the Page Structure tab in the example shown in Figure 5-25.

- *Empty sections*: Some content sections may be empty. This is not a problem; it's common to have a completed page with multiple page sections that do not contain any components.

- *Lock icon*: While the template header shows three components, these components are locked. This means that admins cannot manually remove components within this group through standard means (clicking an X to delete a component). The Napili header, in particular, can be removed by navigating to the theme settings (to be described later in this chapter).

- *Hidden components*: Some components will not show up at all if the corresponding feature is not enabled or set up. Some examples of components that won't initially display for this reason include Reputation Leaderboard and Recommendation Carousel. Other components, like Trending Topics, are dependent on data and won't appear until corresponding data exists.

Admittedly, I access the Page Structure tab the least of the four tabs on the left of Community Builder. Since no actions can be performed, it's not necessary to ever use it. However, I do see value from the Page Structure tab. It allows administrators to confirm page contents. Whether a component is hidden or simply hard to distinguish, it can help to verify exactly what is in a specific section. Additionally, it is useful for confirming whether a specific component is present on the page at all.

Settings

The Settings tab within Community Builder hosts a multitude of configurations that broadly impact your community, as opposed to correlating directly to a specific page or component. The Settings tab includes seven sections.

- General

- Theme

- Languages

- Advanced

- CMS Connect

- Updates

- Developer

I will review each section and explain its purpose and how to manage it.

General

The General section serves as a hub to consolidate key community-wide information. It includes two primary subsections, Community Detail and Topics.

The Community Detail section houses four pieces of information.

- Community Template
- Community Title
- Published Status
- Guest User Profile

The Community Template setting is purely informational; it is useful for confirming whether the template being used has certain functionality available as well as for troubleshooting an issue that emerged around the time of a new release or a template upgrade. Figure 5-27 shows this setting.

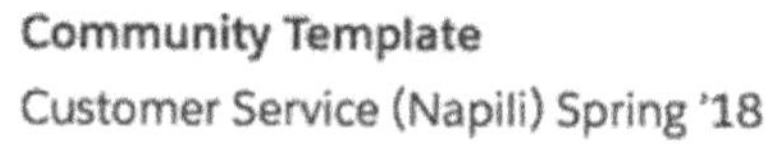

Community Template
Customer Service (Napili) Spring '18

Figure 5-27. *The Community Template field in a Spring '18 org*

Public Access is an important setting that, surprisingly, was not available for quite some time after communities were initially released. This setting allows you to open up access to your community to guest users (i.e., public, unauthenticated users who have not logged in). By default, a community does not allow public access; unless settings are changed from the default, anyone trying to directly access a page in the community would be redirected to a login page.

Note   Here are two key points about public access. First, visibility can be controlled at the page level as well. Even if the community as a whole is restricted, a page can be opened up to guest users. Second, making the community public means that guest users are granted access to all asset files on a public page; you can restrict this in Administration ➤ Preferences (see Chapter 7).

Community Title displays the title of the current community.

Published Status is purely informational and lets you see one of two statuses: "Not published" or "Published". A "Published" status is followed by the URL of the community's Home page.

Guest User Profile is also informational and allows you to access the guest user profile (the profile used by unauthenticated users) much more easily than following the traditional page via administration settings. See Figure 5-28 for the aforementioned four settings.

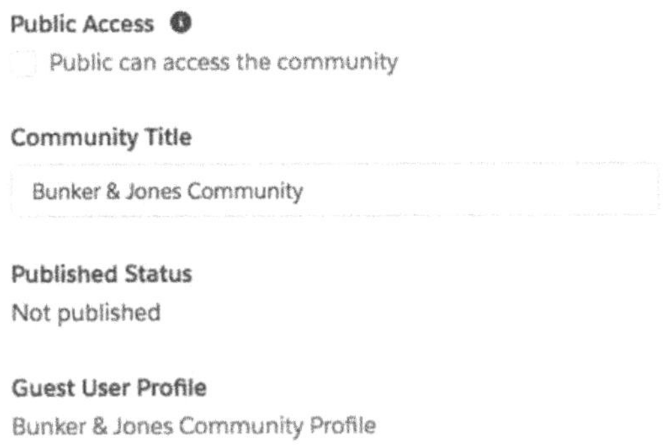

Public Access ⓘ
   Public can access the community

Community Title

   Bunker & Jones Community

Published Status
Not published

Guest User Profile
Bunker & Jones Community Profile

Figure 5-28. *Public Access, Community Title, Published Status, and Guest User Profile settings /fields*

In the second section of General settings, the Navigational Topics and Featured Topics links are displayed. See Figure 5-29 for a view of this.

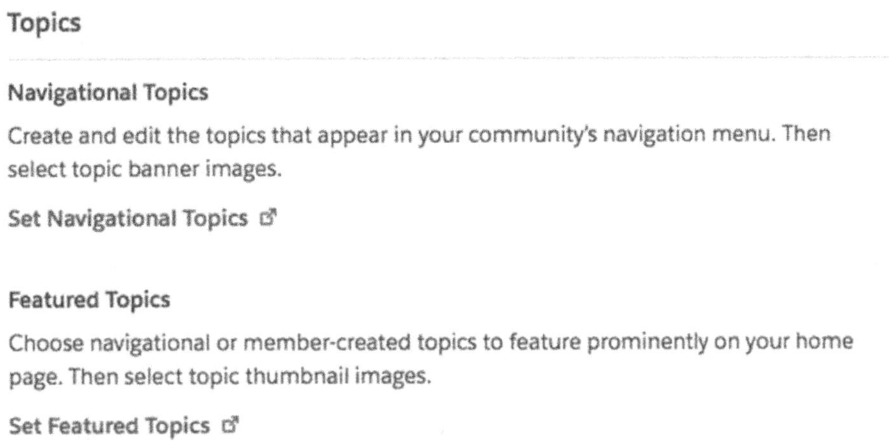

Topics

Navigational Topics

Create and edit the topics that appear in your community's navigation menu. Then select topic banner images.

Set Navigational Topics ⤢

Featured Topics

Choose navigational or member-created topics to feature prominently on your home page. Then select topic thumbnail images.

Set Featured Topics ⤢

Figure 5-29. *Community topics*

Theme

The Theme section within Settings impacts the look, feel, and usability of a community. On this page, a community administration can assign and configure the Theme Layout components associated with a particular theme layout. Community themes can be an area of some confusion because of how they are managed and configured. To help clarify how theme layouts and Theme Layout components work with pages, see Figure 5-30.

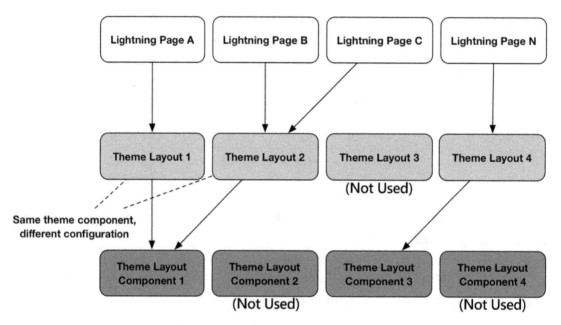

Figure 5-30. *An overview of how Lightning pages, theme layouts, and Theme Layout components work together in a Lightning community*

I'll walk through Figure 5-30 starting with the Theme Layout component. Three sources exist: Salesforce (to use an included Theme Layout component such as Customer Service), one's own development team (to build a homegrown theme), and a third-party provider. All communities use what is provided by Salesforce by default, so that will always be an option. If that is not sufficient, an organization may consider building its own custom Theme Layout component. The Theme Layout component is literally just that: a Lightning component. It has to be developed intentionally for this purpose; it may include an interface, a design resource, and a CSS resource. I won't dive down into code-level details in this book, but that information can be found at `http://developer.salesforce.com`. Alternatively, a custom Theme Layout component could be obtained from a third-party provider and installed for use.

Once the appropriate Theme Layout components have been installed or identified within the community's org, a community admin would determine how the Theme Layout component (or components) should be applied to specific pages; this is where theme layouts come into the picture. Two different theme layouts most commonly leverage different Theme Layout components. However, this is not a given; the same Theme Layout component could be used in different theme layouts but just configured differently. Figure 5-31 shows two configurations of the same Theme Layout component, manifested as two different theme layouts.

Figure 5-31. *Note that these two theme layouts use the same Theme Layout component but with a different configurations*

As part of setting up theme layouts, individual Lightning pages within the community will need to be mapped to a specific theme layout. Figure 5-32 shows an example of how a specific community page (in this case, Quip Docs Related List) could be configured. To modify the associated theme layout, the setting "Override the default theme layout…" must be checked; that will reveal theme layout options below.

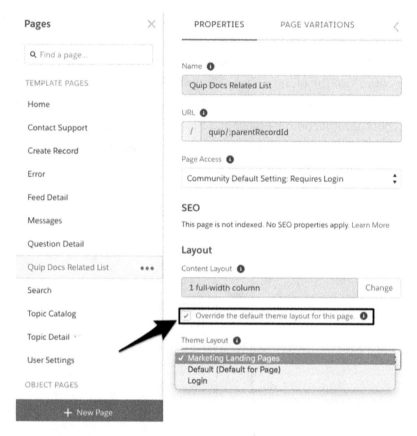

Figure 5-32. *Setting the theme layout for a page*

In Figure 5-33, a custom theme is displayed. This is an example of what is possible when shifting from the standard, out-of-the-box theme that is included with standard community templates.

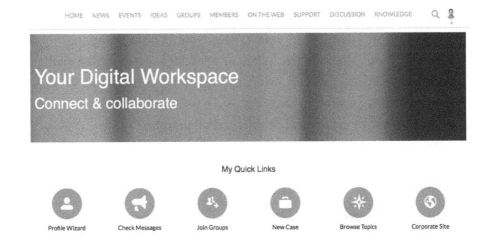

Figure 5-33. *A custom theme. Custom themes can be applied to any bolt/template, as long as the theme has been made available for it*

Languages

Language setup within Salesforce is not exclusive to communities; it is a platform activity that touches various parts of an org. I won't dive terribly deep into all things language within Salesforce, but I do want to at least cover the aspects specific to communities here.

For quite some time after the inception of communities, the only way to configure languages for a community was to navigate to the well-hidden Site.com settings and make changes there. Fortunately, for Lightning communities, that is no longer the case. The languages for your community can be configured by navigating to the Languages section of the Settings tab.

First, the default community language can be established, along with the label of that language. Figure 5-34 shows this setting. To modify the display label, simply click "Edit display label" and change the text.

Default Community Language

| English (US) ▾ | Edit display label |

Figure 5-34. *Default Community Language setting*

The bottom section of the page allows an admin to do the following:

- *Add languages*: Establish additional languages to be used within the community, whether the default or a secondary language. Once added, the display label and fallback language (if the language is unavailable) are both configured, as is a setting to activate the language for the community. See Figure 5-35 for details.

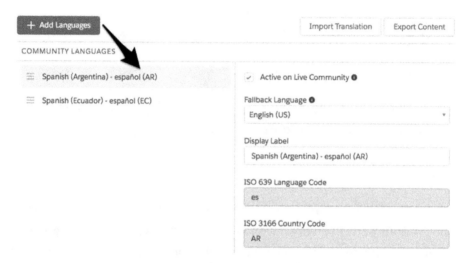

Figure 5-35. *Adding a language*

- *Import translations*: Bring in properly formatted translations as XML to use for a specific language being used within the community. See Figure 5-36 for the modal that is displayed to allow a user to import content.

Import Translated Content

Import overwrites the current translation values in your community. Ensure the XML file matches the expected format and is well formed. Learn more

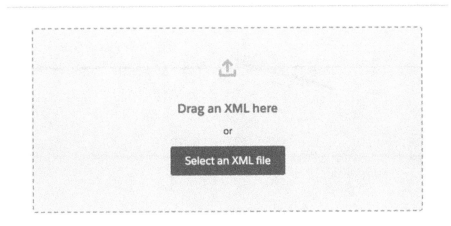

Drag an XML here

or

Select an XML file

Figure 5-36. *Importing language content*

- *Export content*: Export existing translation content for a specified
  language to be used externally (see Figure 5-37)

Export Content for Translation

Select All   Deselect All

English (US)

Spanish (Argentina) - español (AR)

Spanish (Ecuador) - español (EC)

Save as:

Languages   .xml

Cancel   Export

Figure 5-37. *Exporting language content*

Associating multiple languages with your community will impact the top navigation within Community Builder, introducing one additional button/control (shown in Figure 5-38) to manage your languages.

Figure 5-38. *Language management within Builder*

Advanced

The Advanced section on the Settings tab allows the ability to enable and gather additional analytics and to control the head markup of all pages within the community.

For an organization that isn't yet set on a web analytics tool for its Salesforce community, I highly recommend using Google Analytics. The reason is not a secret; Salesforce supports Google Analytics out of the box with ease. An admin can simply create a new Analytics property and then enter the corresponding Google Analytics Tracking ID in Builder. See Figures 5-39 and 5-40.

Figure 5-39. *Obtaining your Google Analytics Tracking ID*

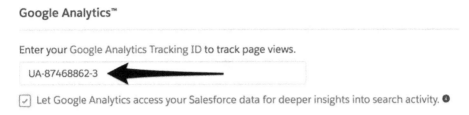

Google Analytics™

Enter your Google Analytics Tracking ID to track page views.

UA-87468862-3

☑ Let Google Analytics access your Salesforce data for deeper insights into search activity. ⓘ

Figure 5-40. *Entering your Google Analytics Tracking ID*

After setting up Google Analytics for Salesforce communities, an admin will need to wait for community activity to occur. Once that happens, the analytics will start to come to life. Figure 5-41 shows an example of what this might look like.

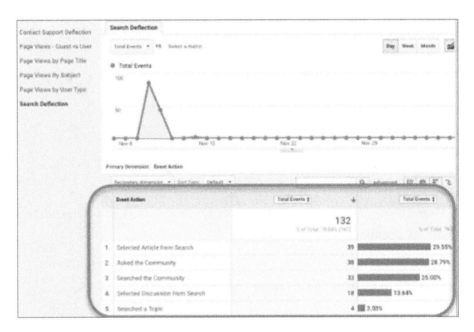

Figure 5-41. *Google Analytics in action*

While Google Analytics tracking doesn't change your community itself in any way, the Head Markup section does. This section is primarily to help inform search engines and browsers how to label, report on, and present a community, but some markup can actually change its behavior and the user experience. The markup set here is applied to each page within your Lightning community. Entire books are dedicated to this topic, so I won't be covering it in much more detail here. However, it is important to understand what is allowed within the head markup; see Figure 5-42.

Allowed Tags	Allowed Attributes
<base>	href, target
<link>	as, charset, crossorigin, disabled, href, hreflang, id, import, integrity, media, rel, relList, rev, sheet, sizes, target, title, type
<meta>	charset, content, http-equiv, name, property, scheme
<script>	
<title>	None allowed

Figure 5-42. *Allowed head markup in a Salesforce community*

Here is an example of what the head markup could look like:

```
<base href="https://philwein.my.force.com/s/" target="_blank">
<link rel="stylesheet" type="text/css" href="theme.css">
<link rel="icon" type="image/png" href="https://weinforce.files.wordpress.
com/2017/08/phil-new-pic.png">
```

This markup provides the following results:

- Establishes `https://philwein.my.force.com/s/` as the base URL for all relative links

- Uses `https://philwein.my.force.com/s/theme.css` as a stylesheet for the overall community

- Sets `https://weinforce.files.wordpress.com/2017/08/phil-new-pic.png` as the icon for the community

Two additional sections reside on the Advanced page. An admin can reveal all components on all pages. This is not recommended, as incompatible components may appear on specific pages and cause some confusion for the community administrator. However, scenarios may exist where this is helpful. The last section is Performance; this is basically a link to the Chrome extension Community Page Optimizer. This extension provides additional analytics on component performance to help organizations better consider and act on existing performance when managing a community. Navigate to `http://bit.ly/2ABtIGF` to learn more about this tool.

CMS Connect

The CMS Connect section of the Advanced section on the Settings page allows for a few communitywide settings from CMS Connect to be applied. I will dive into CMS Connect in general later in the book; for now, I'll address this area of Builder only. Specifically, an administrator can control the header and footer via CMS Connect using the Settings tab. Once a CMS Connection is set up, that connection, along with the corresponding URL, can be used to serve up a header or footer for the site. Figure 5-43 shows how the header might be set via CMS Connect.

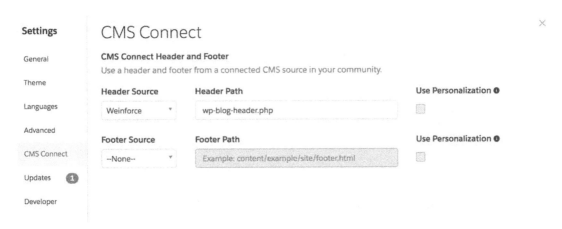

Figure 5-43. *CMS Connect within community settings*

Updates

The Updates section of the Settings tab provides information on template updates and allows upgrades to be performed from the same location. See Figure 5-44 for an example of a pending update. If no update is available, a message will appear formatted like this: "You're already using the latest version of your template: [Template/Bolt] [Release Name]."

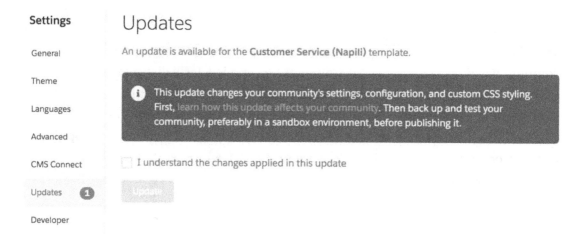

Figure 5-44. Presentation of a pending template update

After selecting "I understand…" and clicking Update, a warning message appears. See Figure 5-45 for the message.

Update community?

You can't reverse the update. Some parts of the community can be reverted if you've exported a backup. Make sure you understand all the implications before continuing. Learn More

Figure 5-45. Template update warning

Developer

In my opinion, the naming of the Developer section of the Settings tab is a bit of a misnomer. This page could be leveraged by individuals in a variety of roles, not just developers. Currently, the page allows for exporting solutions (i.e., Lightning Bolts) and Lightning pages. Figure 5-46 shows the initial view of the Developer section; the template/bolt export page is in focus by default.

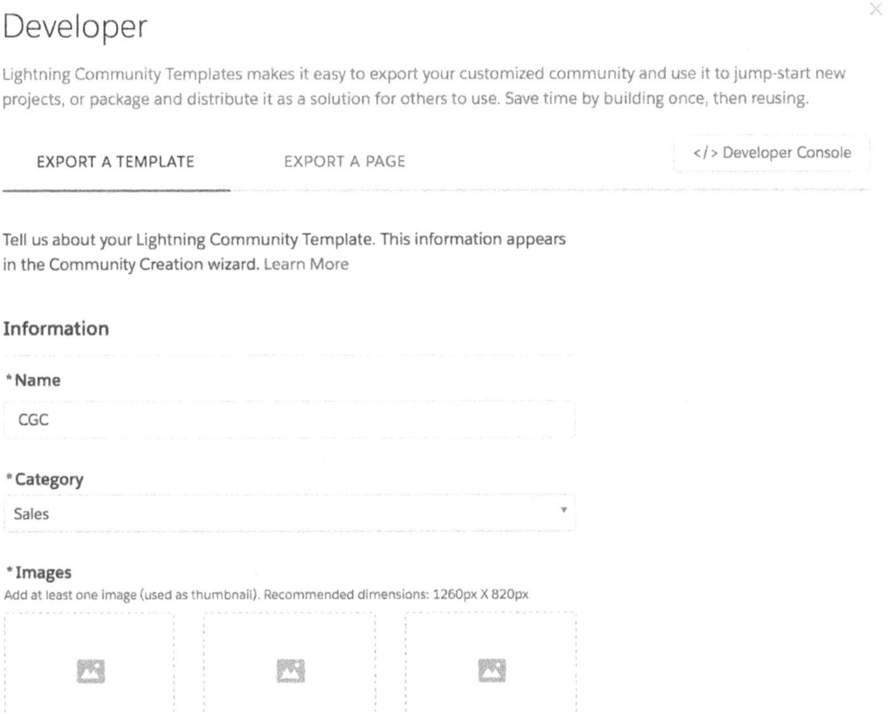

Developer   ×

Lightning Community Templates makes it easy to export your customized community and use it to jump-start new
projects, or package and distribute it as a solution for others to use. Save time by building once, then reusing.

EXPORT A TEMPLATE   EXPORT A PAGE   </> Developer Console

Tell us about your Lightning Community Template. This information appears
in the Community Creation wizard. Learn More

Information

*Name

CGC

*Category

Sales   ▾

*Images

Add at least one image (used as thumbnail). Recommended dimensions: 1260px X 820px

Figure 5-46. *The Developer section of the Settings tab in Community Builder*

Both templates and pages significantly speed up community configuration, as they
offer preconfigured community elements that can be used in place of multiple manual
steps. I will dive into templates, or Lightning Bolts, in granular detail in Chapter 13. Here,
I'll explain the second tab (Export a Page). This allows an administrator to essentially
copy a page in the existing community, including the layout, component placement,
component configuration, and metadata associated with that page. The administrator
can immediately reuse that page quickly within the existing community or another
community in the same org. Additionally, that page can be exported, via Change Set,
package, or IDE, to another org; this allows the use of that page template within any
community in that destination org. See Figure 5-47 for a look at this tab.

Developer

×

Lightning Community Templates makes it easy to export your customized community and use it to jump-start new projects, or package and distribute it as a solution for others to use. Save time by building once, then reusing.

EXPORT A TEMPLATE   EXPORT A PAGE   < / > Developer Console

After you export a page, it appears in the New Page dialog.

Select a page to export:

| Messages ▾ | Export |

Figure 5-47. *Exporting a Lightning page from a community*

Do keep in mind that this page, when exported, is not actually connected to a community. It is a page template, essentially, that can be used to create a new page in a specific community. Figure 5-48 provides another view of the contents included in a page export.

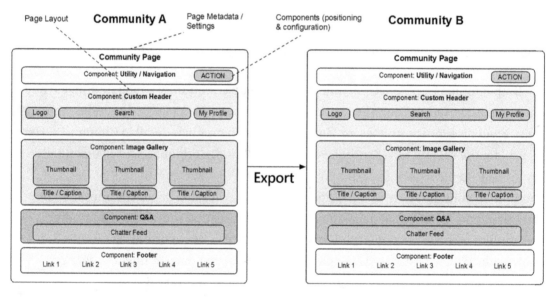

Figure 5-48. *Exporting a page allows the page contents, including layout, component positioning, and component configuration, to be leveraged within another community*

Top Navigation Bar

While the left sidebar is a major focus for activity within Community Builder, the top navigation bar also boasts a number of commonly used controls, menus, and actions. It contains the following elements:

- Community menu (community navigation/control center)
- Pages menu (page management)
- Builder controls
- View Mode
- Help
- Builder Mode

Figure 5-49 shows where each of these elements is located.

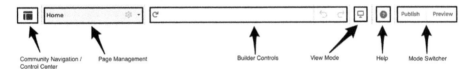

Figure 5-49. *The top navigation bar within Community Builder*

Note   The Languages button is introduced if multiple languages are configured for the community.

Community Menu

The Community menu allows for navigation not only to all administrative areas of the current community in focus but to all other communities within the org. There are three main sections.

- Top-level navigation
- My Workspaces
- My Communities

Figure 5-50 shows the panel with each section clearly delineated.

Figure 5-50. *The Community menu within Community Builder*

Top-Level Community Navigation

The top-level community navigation section provides three common "quick links" for the following purposes:

- Viewing the community "live" (i.e., as a user in production).

- Accessing the workspaces page for the community in focus.

- Navigating to the All Communities page in the standard Salesforce setup menu. Figure 5-51 shows the destination pages for a community named Self-Service Community.

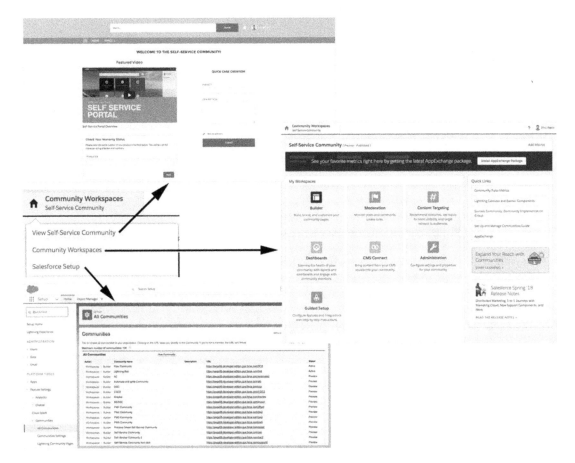

Figure 5-51. *A look at the destinations of each of the links in the top section of the Community menu*

My Workspaces

This area of community administration is relatively new, being introduced in 2017. It involves a modular approach to administration, segmenting different key areas that drive community functionality. There are currently seven modules, yet I expect that number to grow over time as new administrative elements are added. As of the Summer '18 release, the following modules are available:

- Builder

- Moderation

- Content Targeting

- Dashboards

- CMS Connect

- Administration

- Guided Setup

See Figure 5-52 for a view of the community workspace screen.

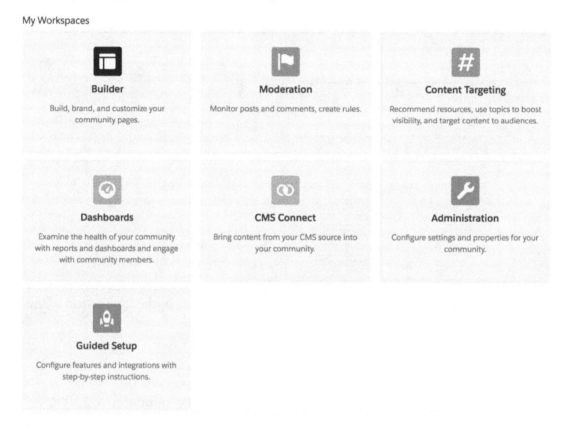

Figure 5-52. *Community workspaces*

I will cover each of the workspaces in more detail later in this book.

Note   The specific workspaces that appear may differ, depending on the template being used and the version of that template.

My Communities

In the third and last section of the community navigation/control center, users will find a list of all communities, whether Tabs + Visualforce, Lightning, preview, active, or inactive. You'll see something like the list shown in Figure 5-53.

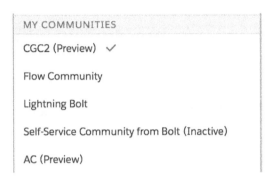

Figure 5-53. *My Communities, a list of all communities in the org*

Pages Menu

The Pages menu allows for quick access to all pages associated with the community. Figure 5-54 shows a standard view of the menu for a newly created Customer Service (Napili) community.

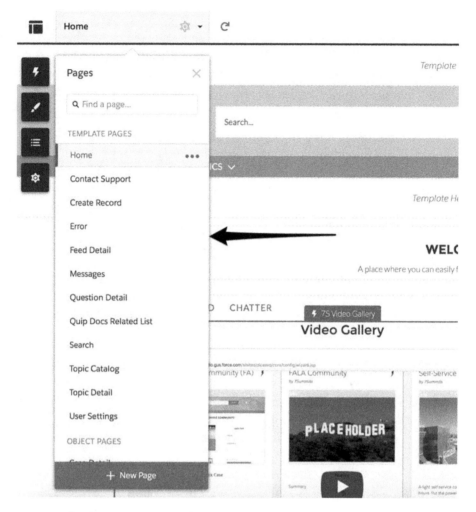

Figure 5-54. *The Pages menu*

This menu does not prioritize pages based on a page's prominence on the site or criticality within the standard community navigation; it simply lists every page that exists in that community, whether or not the page is technically being used. The menu does, however, categorize pages into multiple sections.

- *My Pages*: Custom pages (i.e., pages not created by Salesforce). These might be created manually, come with a Lightning Bolt, or originate from a page that was individually exported for use in the community.

- *Template Pages*: Any pages that are available with the selected template that don't fall into any of the three following categories. Some examples include Home, Messages, Search, and User Settings.

- *Object Pages*: Object-specific pages. These come in three flavors: Detail, List, and Related List. They include objects such as Cases, Groups, and Dashboards.

- *Generic Record Pages*: Pages to handle records for objects that do not have an object page. For example, viewing an opportunity when an Opportunity Detail page is not existent would instead leverage the generic record detail page.

- *Login Pages*: Login-specific pages, including Check Password, Forgot Password, Login, Login Error, and Register.

I will dive into the page setup screen/interface in detail in the next chapter (shown in Figure 5-55).

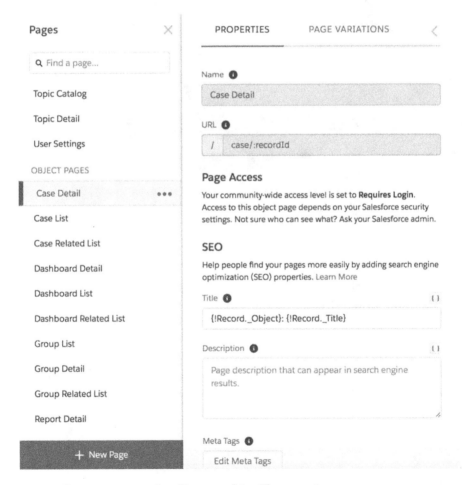

Figure 5-55. *Page setup, to be discussed in Chapter 6*

Builder Controls

Builder controls, as I refer to them, allow a community administrator to perform some basic actions to assist with community development. First, a Refresh button allows for back-end updates to be reflected in Builder. Let's say that Salesforce data has changed four records that are being displayed on the community page shown in Builder; those updates won't automatically be reflected within Builder. However, clicking Refresh will display the latest, most up-to-date version of the applicable community page. See Figure 5-56 for the button location.

Figure 5-56.   *The Refresh button, useful for updating a page based on data changes*

The additional controls are Undo and Redo. Admittedly, I rarely use these controls. However, they could be of significant value for community builders. For example, let's say a component with a large number of property editor configurations is deleted. The community administrator then realizes that he or she made a mistake and actually does need the component. With one click, the component can be re-inserted on the page in the same position and with the same configurations. See Figure 5-57 for a view of the Undo and Redo controls.

Figure 5-57.   *Undo and Redo buttons*

View Mode

The View mode that is built into Community Builder is extremely useful for community managers or builders to determine what the community looks like on a variety of device types. Specifically, three options are provided.

- Mobile

- Tablet

- Desktop

With one click, the view can be adjusted to validate the responsiveness and positioning of components within the community. Figures 5-58, 5-59, and 5-60 show the same community page in all three modes to convey how the view mode changes the display.

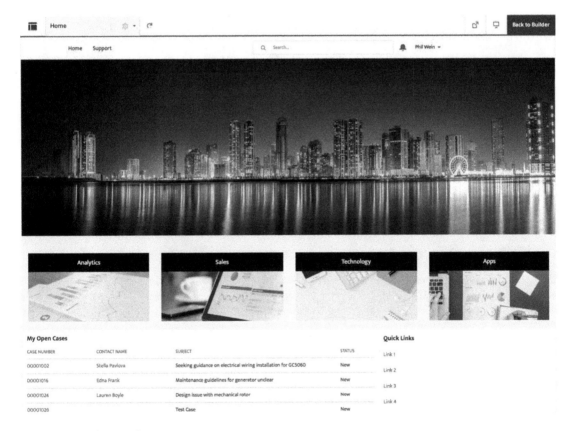

Figure 5-58. *Desktop view*

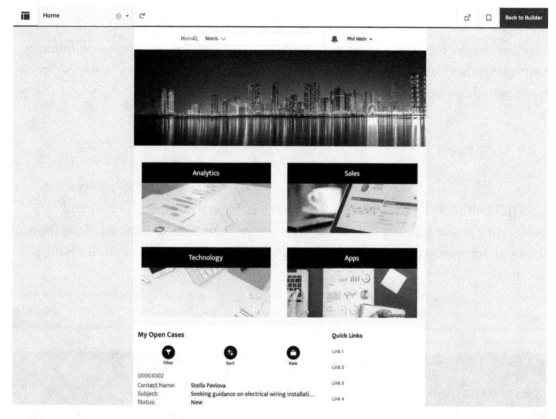

Figure 5-59. *Tablet view*

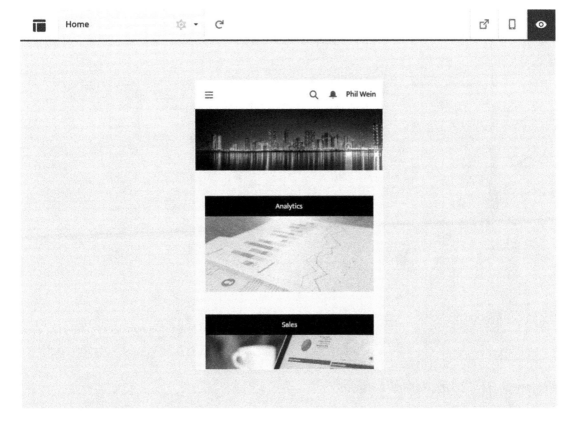

Figure 5-60. *Mobile view*

It's great to see the different responsive views, but don't miss what's actually happening with the page display. The "algorithm" to determine the view is structured and logical, making it easy to build a community with different views in mind. For example, let's take a look at a specific page layout (Figure 5-61).

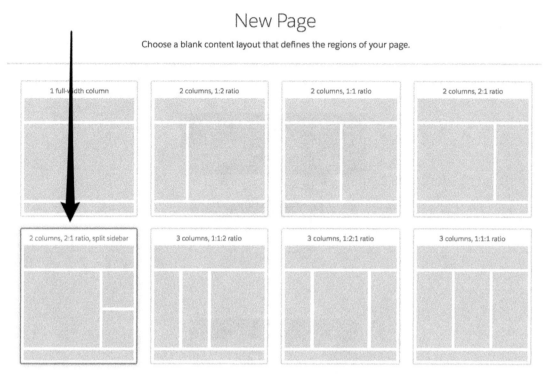

Figure 5-61. *2:1 ratio, split sidebar*

To clarify what's happening, I set up one component in each section below the header—the Rich Content Editor component. In each instance of the component, I display the name of the page section. See Figure 5-62 for the desktop view.

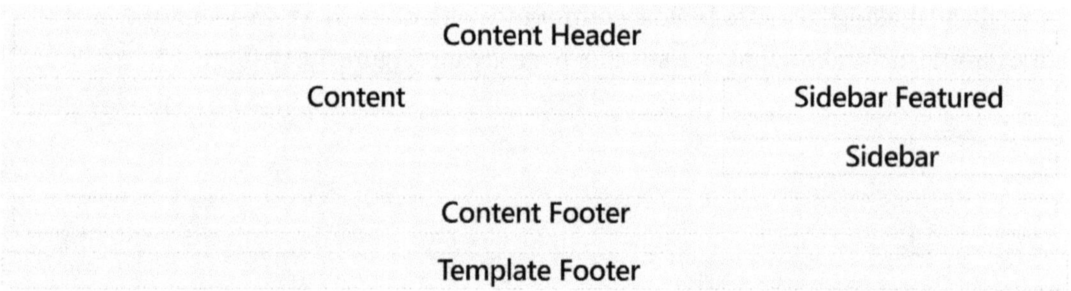

Content Header	
Content	Sidebar Featured
	Sidebar
Content Footer	
Template Footer	

Figure 5-62. *Sections clearly labeled for the purpose of viewing sequence in a mobile view*

I take the desktop view and modify it to the mobile view to show how these sections are sequenced; see Figure 5-63.

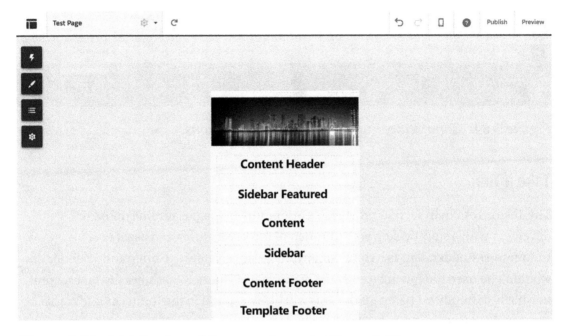

Figure 5-63. *Mobile view of the page shown in Figure 5-62*

The main takeaway here is the positioning of sidebar content relative to the main "content" section: Sidebar Feature comes first, followed by Content and, finally, Sidebar.

Help

Salesforce has you covered on help documentation relevant to Community Builder; even better, the available help documentation doesn't require that you exit Builder to read it. There are currently three help sections provided.

- Take a Tour
- What's New
- Help & Training

Figure 5-64 shows where these different areas of help can be selected.

Figure 5-64. *Community Builder help has three sections*

Take a Tour

The Take a Tour help section provides a community manager, administrator, or developer with a step-by-step walk-through of the key features and aspects of Community Builder. This is helpful for anyone relatively new to Community Builder but wouldn't be used too much by veterans in the space. Figure 5-65 shows the first screen in what is currently a 14-step guide. This will likely expand in the future, as additional communities features are added to Salesforce.

Figure 5-65. *Take a tour of Salesforce Community Builder*

What's New

The What's New section within help provides a "bullet list" overview of some significant enhancements and changes delivered in the most recent of the tri-annual releases. Figure 5-66 shows what was made available via What's New in Spring '18.

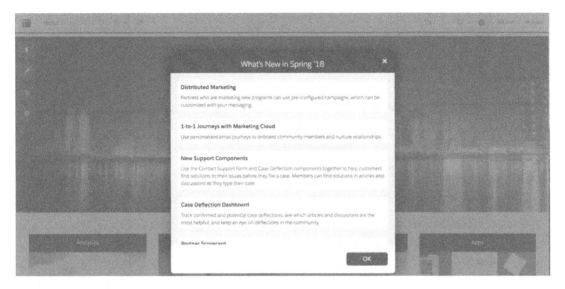

Figure 5-66. *What's New shows what came out in the last Salesforce release related to communities*

Help & Training

The Help & Training links take users to the standard Salesforce help documentation and, specifically, to the Community Builder Overview article. Figure 5-67 shows the article that appears.

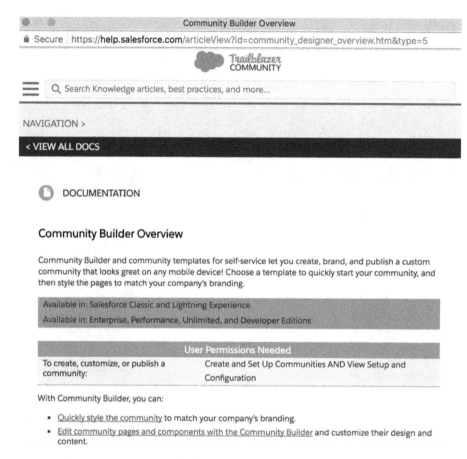

Figure 5-67.   Community Builder help

Builder Publication and Modes

The final area of the top navigation menu within Community Builder allows administrators the ability to perform two key actions.

- *Publish*: Publish the community

- *Preview/Back to Builder*: Toggle between preview and Builder modes

Publish

With the exception of changes made to the navigation menu, no Builder changes are immediately/directly exposed to external users. To make site changes visible to end users, the community must first be published. Clicking Publish (Figure 5-68) does the following:

- Pushes "live" any changes since the last publication of the community; the user-facing version of the community will reflect what is in Builder as of that moment

- Sends an email to the publisher notifying him or her that the live community has been updated

- Eliminates any undo/redo cache

Figure 5-68. *Publish a community to push draft changes to the community's audience.*

Figure 5-69 displays the three-step process that occurs once an administrator clicks the Publish button.

1. The administrator is presented with an information modal before proceeding by clicking another Publish button.

2. The progress indicator is shown (or "No changes to publish" is shown).

3. Notification of publication completion is displayed.

Figure 5-69. *Steps involved in publishing a community*

Preview

While it is true an admin can fairly easily view the live community from Builder (referenced earlier in the chapter), those live changes might not reflect the latest changes made in Builder. To quickly view those changes as a user would actually see them in a production-like environment, the admin can click Preview at the top right (see Figure 5-70).

Figure 5-70. *Preview a community*

Preview will remove all section indicators, minimize controls, and provide an easy toggle back into Builder. Figure 5-71 shows that the Preview button is replaced with once entering Preview mode.

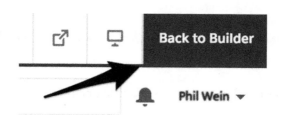

Figure 5-71. *When previewing, an admin is provided with an option to return to Community Builder.*

Note   Preview is extremely useful for separate changes to multiple pages within a community in sequence. Make a change, preview, navigate to the next page, return to Builder, and repeat as often as needed. This process is much easier than navigating through the community within Builder.

Recap

This chapter on Community Builder was extremely lengthy, warranted by the high volume of content and detail associated with this powerful tool. I reviewed every aspect of the Community Builder user interface. The first major section covered was the left sidebar/tabs, which revealed multiple layers of functionality, starting with the Page menu, theme controls, page structure, and settings. Additionally, I walked through the top navigation bar, which houses the main community menu, page manager, and various Builder controls. You should feel fairly comfortable with how to navigate Builder and be able to start to construct a basic Lightning community.

CHAPTER 6

Pages and Components in Lightning Communities

For anyone planning to build a Lightning community on the Salesforce platform, understanding the creation and management of the corresponding pages and components (in the context of communities) is essential for success. In this chapter, I'll build upon the Community Builder framework that was covered in detail in Chapter 5 and provide insights on how to make the most of what comes out of the box in a Lightning community, as well as how to extend that with additional pages and components.

Before I jump in and walk through the ins and outs of page publication and component configuration, I want to make sure the concept of the journey—as it relates to Lightning pages and components—is abundantly clear. Let's first take a look at a starting point: a standard, Salesforce-provided community template. Figure 6-1 shows this starting point, which includes standard objects, standard Lightning pages, and standard Lightning components.

© Philip Weinmeister 2018
P. Weinmeister, *Practical Guide to Salesforce Communities*, https://doi.org/10.1007/978-1-4842-3609-3_6

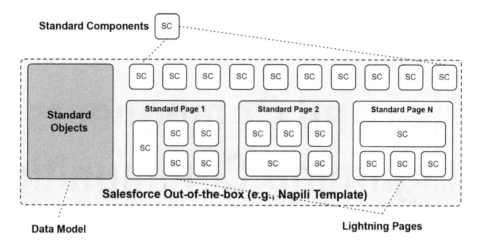

Figure 6-1. *The starting point for a Lightning community, based on a template, includes the data model, Lightning pages, and Lightning components*

Right out of the gate, Salesforce provides a slew of existing Lightning pages and components to work with. It's extremely likely, however, that a community administrator or developer will want to build upon this initial inventory of assets that are available to address requirements and use cases specific to his or her organization. Figure 6-2 provides the next high-level step, which is supplementing existing objects, pages, and components, as needed.

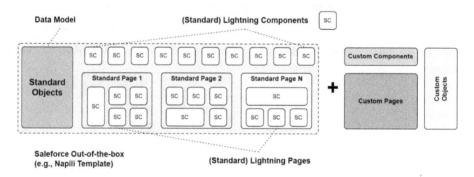

Figure 6-2. *The objects, pages, and components that are initially available in a Lightning community can—and usually should—be supplemented*

Assembly and configuration now follow as the final step in the implementation process. Once the conceptual "Lego pieces" are made available, they need to be put together and placed appropriately on the corresponding Lego boards. Figure 6-3 shows the final picture of a community, following the addition, placement, and configuration of relevant pages and components.

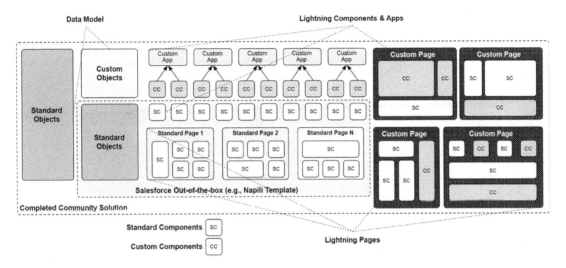

Figure 6-3. *Representation of a customized, configured Lightning community that has gone beyond the assets initially available at community creation*

Note   The Build Your Own template comes out of the box with pages and components, but they are minimal, providing only what is absolutely required for a basic Lightning community solution.

I will not be covering actual development of Lightning components in this chapter and, generally, will not be providing guidance on programmatic aspects of the platform. There are abundant resources on how to build custom components in the Salesforce ecosystem; I will be focusing on how to use these components within your Lightning community.

Lightning Pages

Before delving into Lightning components for communities, one must understand Lightning pages. Why? A component's utility is minimal (nonexistent in a purely declarative framework) without a Lightning page to actually house the component

within a community. To break down the details of a Lightning page, we will start at the
beginning with page creation.

Within Community Builder, an admin can access the Pages menu for anything and
everything related to the management of a Lightning page within a community. See
Figure 6-4 for a look at the Pages menu and, in particular, the "New Page" button at the
bottom of the menu.

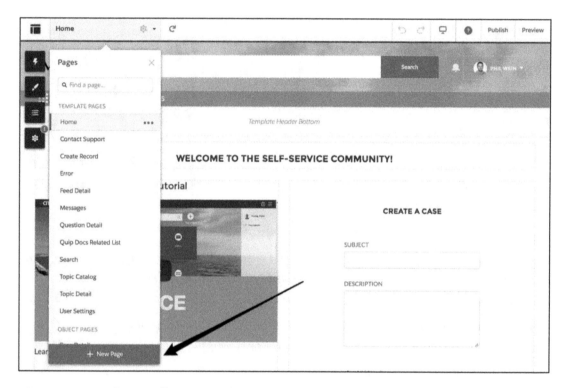

Figure 6-4. *Selecting "New Page" at the bottom of the Pages menu starts the page
creation process*

To create a new page, a community administrator clicks the "New Page" button. The
first step is a critical one: deciding whether the page will be a *standard page* or an *object
page*. Figure 6-5 shows the choices available when creating a new page.

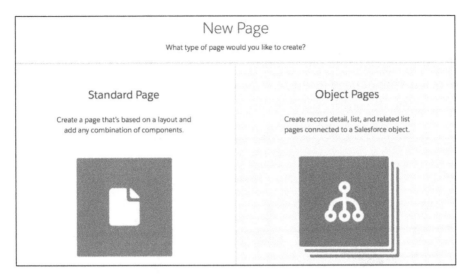

Figure 6-5. *The New Page dialog provides two choices: Standard Page or Object Page*

During page creation, the admin will need to determine whether the page will need to be bound to a specific object. If not, a standard page will suffice. If so, an object page will be needed. See Figure 6-6 for the thought process critical to making this decision.

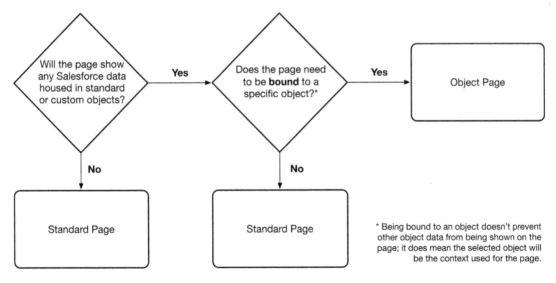

Figure 6-6. *Decision tree for creating a standard page or an object page*

When creating a standard page, the next choice is to determine whether to start from a preconfigured page or from scratch. The preconfigured pages that are available (Figure 6-7) are sourced from the "Export a Page" option on the Developer page within the Settings tab. Once a page is exported (and, if from a different org, imported), it will appear as a candidate starting point for any new page.

Figure 6-7. When creating a new page, an admin can select a blank page or select from available imported pages as a starting point

It is critical to understand what it means to create a page from an existing, preconfigured page, instead of creating a new, blank page. With a new, blank page, an administrator can select the page layout, but no content will exist on the page (with the exception of anything that is part of the overall theme). When a preconfigured page is selected, however, any components that are present on the selected page will be on the page at inception. Not only will the components be present, they will be positioned and configured exactly as they are on the selected page. Think of this as a page-level template. Figure 6-8 shows the process of the page creation process and the various selection points and activities.

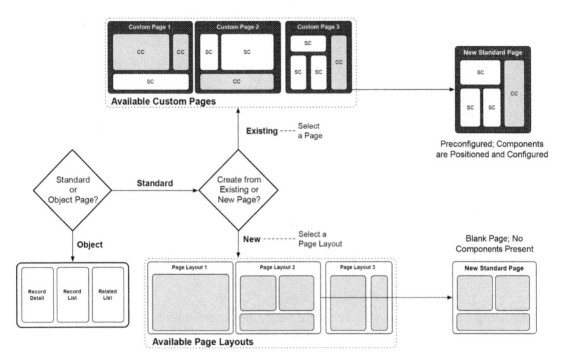

Figure 6-8. *Thought process and considerations for Lightning page creation*

For those selecting a new standard page, an option to select the page layout will appear. The layouts that are available will include a number of out-of-the-box layouts but may also include some that are custom. In Figure 6-9, a combination of both standard and custom layouts is shown.

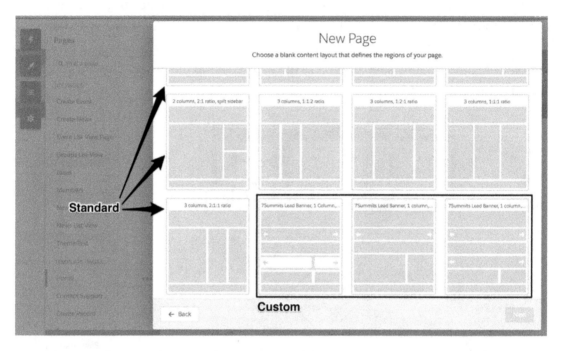

Figure 6-9. *The page layouts that are available during page creation can include a selection of custom page layouts*

Creating a new object page is fundamentally different from creating a new standard page. An object page actually results in three new pages, not just one.

- Record Detail
- Record List
- Record Related List

As an example, I'll create an object detail page for the product object (Figure 6-10).

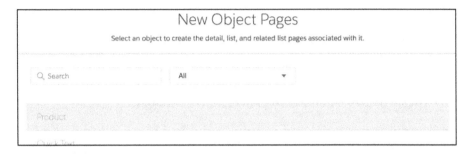

Figure 6-10. *Creating new object pages for the Product object*

Once completed, this action will result in the following activities being completed via automation for the product object:

- Page layout (one full-width column)

- Applied components (differs by page)

- Configuration of components (differs by page)

Figure 6-11 shows what the Product List page looks like without any additional configuration.

Figure 6-11. *New, unmodified Product List page following creation*

Navigation Menu Bar

The navigation menu bar that is available in Lightning communities goes hand-in-hand with Lightning pages. The navigation menu bar is a highly configurable component that drives the overall site navigation. While Lightning pages (standard or object) are the most common targets of menu items, the navigation menu bar supports a variety of destination types. Figure 6-12 shows the navigation menu bar.

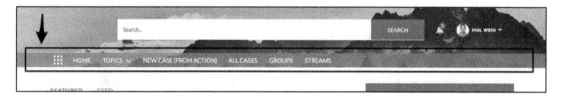

Figure 6-12. *Standard navigation menu bar*

The navigation menu bar has a couple top-level settings, relating to App Launcher and the home page, as shown in Figure 6-13. The App Launcher icon can be hidden, and the home page icon can be shown as text or a small house icon.

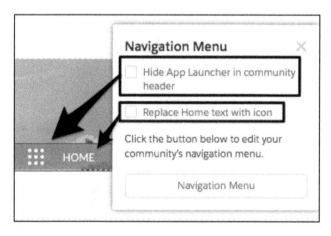

Figure 6-13. *Navigation menu bar top-level settings*

The Navigation Menu configuration settings provide significant flexibility for modifying the navigation menu items. Figure 6-14 shows the six types of menu items that can be added.

Figure 6-14. *Navigation Menu management interface*

To help with understanding all available options and suggested considerations, refer to Figure 6-15 for details on the navigation menu item types.

Type	Available Settings	Notes
Community Page	Page	Any standard or object page can be selected. The page must be published; otherwise, it will not show up as available.
	URL (for certain pages)	
	Publicly available	
External URL	URL	This can be used to point to internal URLs, as well, for exceptional situations. For example, if it was desired to point to a Visualforce page from a Lightning community, it could be done here.
	Open link in the same tab	
	Publicly available	
Global Action	Action	This menu item will open a modal, not direct the user to a page.
	Publicly available	
Menu Label	Publicly available	Non-functional item other than serving as a parent menu item. Other menu items can be added "underneath" it.
Navigational Topic	Type	This is included by default.
	Add the "More Topics..." link	
	Publicly available	
Salesforce Object	Object Type	Similar to selecting a Community Page that is an object page (vs. a standard page).
	Default List View	
	Publicly available	

Figure 6-15. *Navigation menu bar item types, settings, and considerations*

Note   As of the Summer '18 release, changes to the navigation menu can be saved in a draft state. Previously, any changes to the navigation menu had to be published immediately.

Lightning Components

I find it helpful to use metaphors in the context of Lightning communities (hence my previous example of referencing Legos). I'd like to use a slightly different one here. This time let's use a neighborhood as the example for a Lightning community. Lightning pages serve as the "slabs" under homes, and Lightning components equate to elements of the homes themselves that sit on the slabs. While both slabs *and* the houses are absolutely essential, owners of houses really don't care about the slabs too much; the slabs exist to support and provide a layout for the house, but they don't provide much functional value to the owners.

It's the same with Lightning components and pages; most users don't think too much about the page itself, but instead, they care about the content (components) on the page. See Figure 6-16 for a visualization of this concept.

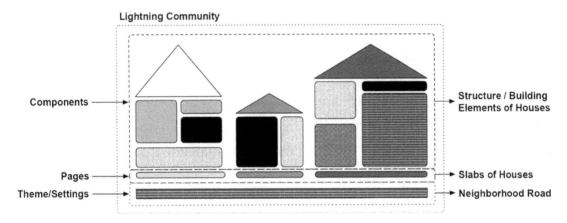

Figure 6-16. *Conceptualizing aspects of a Lightning community as neighborhood housing elements*

When we talk about Lightning communities, the components are at the core of the functional experience. In Chapter 5, I covered the Components tab within the left tab/sidebar and discussed the presentation of the components (with standard components being grouped functionally/logically and custom components being consolidated in their own group). Here, I will go a little deeper to help community administrators go from concept to application in their journey to create the perfect community, specifically at the point of determining what to do with the plethora of Lightning components that are available.

Understanding Components within Communities

Assuming a Lightning component is built properly for its intended purpose, the value of a component within a Lightning community is predicated on these three factors:

- Placement (Lightning pages on which the component is placed)

- Positioning (page section or sections in which the component is dropped)

- Configuration (configured settings of the component)

If any of these is not appropriately considered, the value of the component will decrease for community users. I'll briefly walk through each to ensure the concept is clear.

Component Placement

Before an admin can start configuring a component for its particular use, he or she must decide which page (or pages) it should be associated with. The absence of a high-value component on a particular page can be extremely impactful; similarly, the extraneous presence of a component on a page can be distracting and create a convoluted experience for a user. While many components can be placed anywhere within a community, it is critical to understand context and the fact that some components have a limited number of potential page homes. See Figure 6-17 for some examples of where and how components might apply to pages.

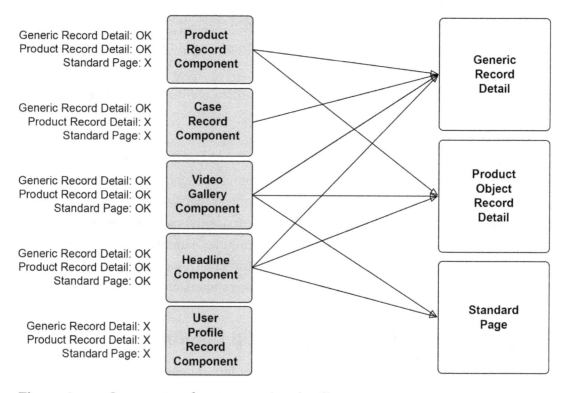

Figure 6-17. *Components have context and will not necessarily function on all Lightning pages*

Component Positioning

I discussed page sections in Chapter 5 and will let you revisit that section for corresponding details. Here, I want to help answer the question, where on a page should a component be placed? There is typically no shortage of options; see Figure 6-18 for an example of what a community admin might be faced with when choosing a component's positioning within a Lightning page.

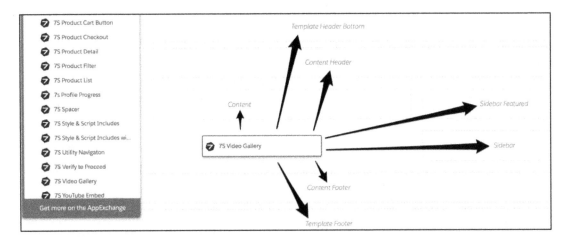

Figure 6-18.   *It is not always obvious where a component should be positioned*

I want to make sure that these factors are considered before a component is placed onto a page:

- What other components will reside on the page?

- What is the available "experience real estate," and how will the component be used in conjunction with other components?

- How will the component play a role in the expected user experience on the page?

- Is the component suitable for different page sections (i.e., has it been built to satisfactorily display in a single, full-width column on a desktop)?

It is quite easy to fall into the trap of going drag-and-drop crazy and letting user experience and context slip to the back of one's mind during a community build; community builders must fight against that potential slip and ensure that components are placed purposefully and intentionally within a specific page. If one asks these questions, successful positioning of the components will be much more likely.

Component Configuration

Even with the perfect placement and positioning of a Lightning component within your community, the component could render zero value if configured improperly. While this may seem obvious, a community administrator needs to know his or her Lightning components very well. By that, I mean that it's important to learn most, if not all, of the available configurations for a particular component. First, knowing the configurations means knowing the underlying functionality and not missing out on some potential value for your community. Second, it's all about the context. Many components are contextual, providing different functions or capabilities depending on where they are placed.

Consider context with the Headline component, for example. In my first example, I have the component on the Home page and simply set the Title property to "Welcome!" See Figure 6-19.

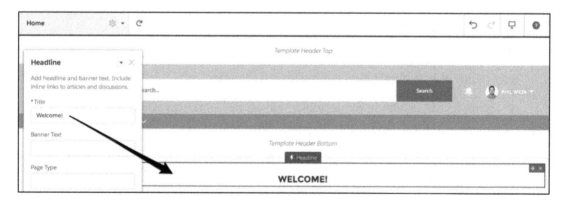

Figure 6-19. *Headline component on the Home page*

Now, I'll place the same component, configured similarly, on the Topic Detail page. I'll leave "Welcome!" as the title, but I'll make one change: setting the Page Type property to "topic" as shown in Figure 6-20.

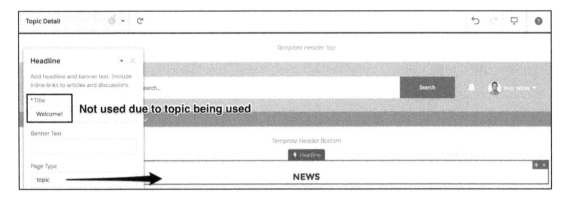

Figure 6-20. *Headline component on the Topic Detail page*

Notice that, although Title is set to the same value as it was on the Home page, "Welcome!" no longer appears. That has to do with the context and other settings. This is the Topic Detail page, so I want to show the name of the topic within the Headline component, not a static value that would show up on all topic pages. Once I set Page Type to "topic," the title "Welcome!" no longer shows up. The takeaway here is that community builders need to understand each of the properties available for their components, as well as how properties overlap and/or work together.

Note   With the Summer '18 release, progressive rendering is available. This allows administrators to assign top-level components a priority grouping to determine the sequence in which they appear when a particular page is loading.

A Real-World Example

If any standard community template (other than Build Your Own) is being used to create a community, the number of available Lightning components is significant. As of mid-2018, I count a number quickly approaching 100, and I would not be surprised if that milestone is eclipsed by 2019. As a result, it's not feasible for me to review all, or even most, of the available standard components available for communities. Instead, I will take a handful of components and use them as examples, walking through this select group to show possible configurations, and explain the different options and why one would select certain settings over others. I will leverage the following components:

- Headline

- Rich Content Editor

- Tabs

- Tile Menu

- Record List

- Create Case Form

These are not necessarily the most commonly used components for communities, but they are utilized fairly often. To best bring all of this life, I'll start with a new standard page. From there, I will add, position, and configure components to create a community experience. I'll use the "2 columns, 2:1 ratio" page layout, as shown in Figure 6-21.

Note   While most standard components are available in standard (Salesforce-provided) community templates, they are not all available in each. For example, Headline is not available in Customer Account Portal, at least through the Summer '18 release. The following Salesforce help page outlines which components are available in each template: `https://help.salesforce.com/articleView?id=rss_component_reference_table.htm`.

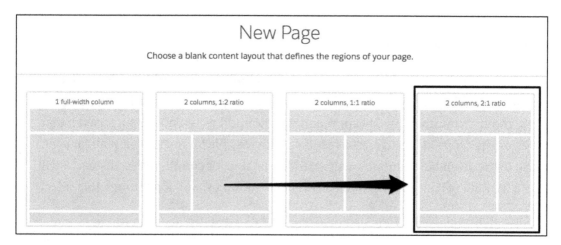

Figure 6-21. *The "2 columns, 2:1 ratio" page will be used for this example*

Figure 6-22 shows the blank canvas before any components are placed or configured.

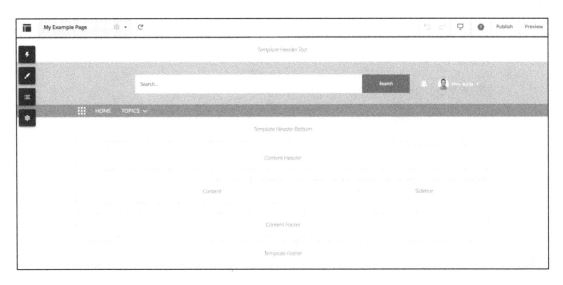

Figure 6-22. *Blank page, prior to the positioning of any components*

Headline

The first component I'll drop onto the new page that was just created is Headline. This component is located in the Content section on the Components tab. Figure 6-23 shows step 1 (placing the component on the page).

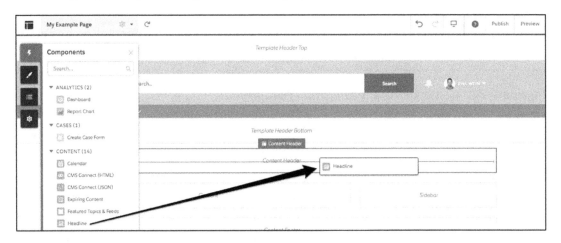

Figure 6-23. *Positioning the Headline component*

Headline is a fairly simple component that is useful for providing a text-based content header on a given page. The component configurations include the following:

- Title

- Banner Text

- Page Type

- Unique Name or ID

- Banner Text with Articles and Discussions

- Banner Text with Discussions

- Show Subtopics

The last five configuration settings here have to do with knowledge articles, topics, and discussions. This page won't include any of those, so the first two settings are the only two that require attention. I'll keep it simple and add explanatory text for each: "Chapter 6 Example Page" for Title and "Practical Guide to Salesforce Communities" for Banner Text. Figure 6-24 shows the configured component, after being placed in the Content Header section of the page.

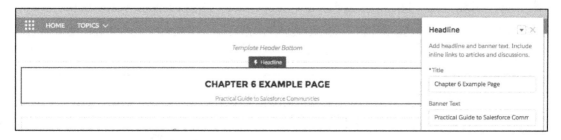

Figure 6-24. *Configuring the Headline component*

Rich Content Editor

Next, I'll focus on Rich Content Editor. Similar to the Headline component, this component allows for emphasized text; however, it handles much more. An admin can feature images, videos, links, and formatted text with Rich Content Editor. Also, unlike most other components, standard configuration settings do not exist; instead, a rich text/content editor is provided (see Figure 6-25).

Figure 6-25. *Configuring the Rich Content Editor component*

For this page, I will use the Video option, which is the rightmost button in the editor shown in Figure 6-25. Figure 6-26 shows the component settings and the page after the update, as placed in the Sidebar section.

Figure 6-26. *Configuring the Rich Content Editor component to show a video*

Tabs

The Tabs component is simple yet extremely useful. In the case that a community admin wants to support a significant amount of content or functionality on a single page without cluttering up the experience, tabs will allow for the content to be spread across "subpages" that keep the in-focus display simple. The options with the Tabs component are limited because it is basically a placeholder for other content; an admin can create, label, and sequence tabs. In addition, he or she can determine whether a tab will display on a public page (a page not requiring authentication). For the example page, I need to first place the component in the Content section (Figure 6-27).

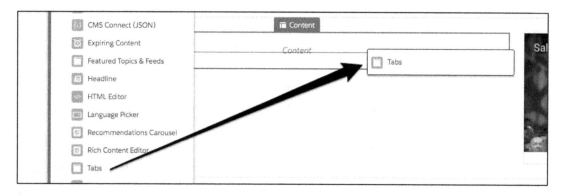

Figure 6-27. *Positioning the Tabs component*

To support the three remaining components for my example, I will configure the Tabs component accordingly; see Figure 6-28.

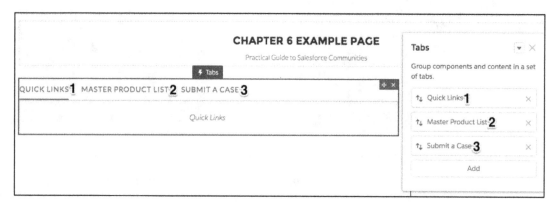

Figure 6-28. *Creating three tabs using the Tabs component*

Tile Menu

The Tile Menu component is relatively new, introduced in the Winter '18 release. This component allows for branded/stylized links to other pages or content. For my example page, I'll use it to point to various communities-focused pages in the Salesforce ecosystem. First, I need to place it in the first tab within the Tabs component I just set up (Figure 6-29).

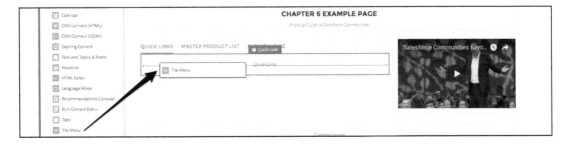

Figure 6-29. *Positioning the Tile Menu component within the first tab*

For each tile menu item, I configure the label, image, and destination URL. Figure 6-30 shows the settings for the first of the four tile menu items.

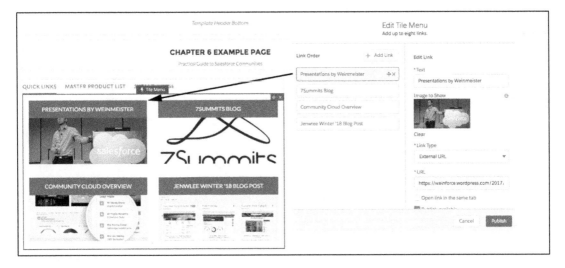

Figure 6-30. *Configuring the Tile Menu component*

Record List

Record List is a staple component within any community that leverages underlying CRM data. I would not say that is highly configurable, but it gets the job done. The following configuration options are available:

- Number of Records

- Layouts

- Object Name

- Filter Name

For this example, I will use a filter called Master List for the Product object. I will select the Standard layout to provide a less-cluttered look within the tab. See Figure 6-31 for a look at this component, as configured for this example page.

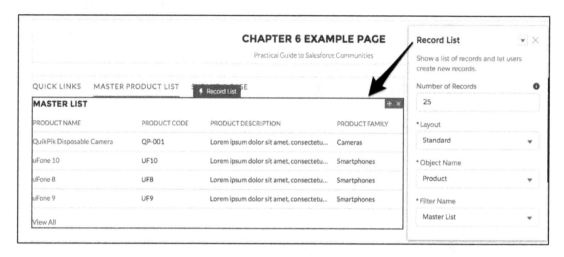

Figure 6-31. *Positioning and configuring the Record List component*

Create Case Form

If you need a simple way to submit a case, you can use the Create Case Form component. For this example page, I'll drop in the Create Case Form component (Figure 6-32) and configure it as needed.

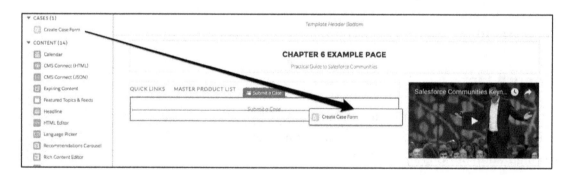

Figure 6-32. *Positioning the Create Case form on the third tab*

The Create Case component boasts a number of settings, but I will keep it simple in this example. Once I drop in the component, an alert that reads, "To create cases, an action must be specified by the administrator," is immediately displayed. (see Figure 6-33).

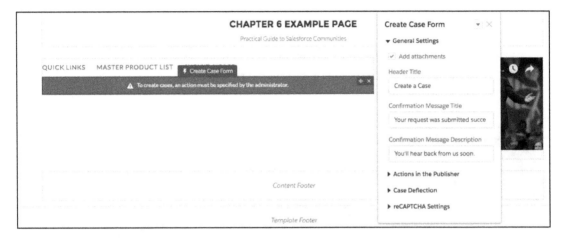

Figure 6-33. *The Create Case form will initially show an alert*

To address this, I will need to specify the action to be used. I created a custom global action to create cases in advance, and I will reference it here. See Figure 6-34 for a look at a configured custom global action in the Create Case Form component.

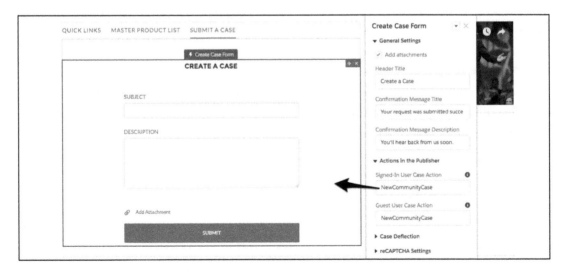

Figure 6-34. *Once an eligible action is specified, the Create Case form comes to life*

Review

Now that the page has been configured, I don't want to neglect the best part: seeing the page in action. Figure 6-35 shows a three-tab view of the new community page that has been set up. Note that the page is being displayed in a tablet view.

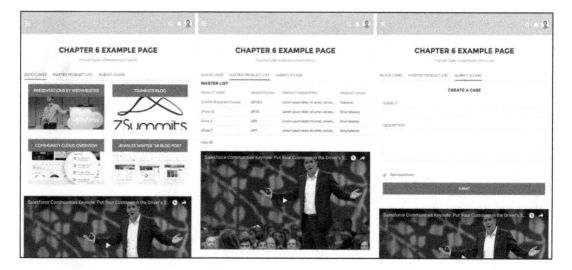

Figure 6-35. *Layout of each tab from a three-tab version of the Tabs component*

Recap

In this chapter, I transitioned from the Community Builder tool in the previous chapter to the Lightning pages and Lightning components that it supports. I provided an overview of how page creation and management works, along with the various options. I then dove into an example that featured a number of popular components, along with specific page placement and configuration, to provide a functional custom page within a community.

CHAPTER 7

Setup and Administration

The last few chapters have focused heavily on communities built with Lightning templates and not on tabs-based or Visualforce communities. In this chapter, I'll back things up and look at the knobs and controls that drive communitywide settings for *all* communities, regardless of template type. I'll group these configurations into two buckets.

- Setup (displayed as "Communities Settings")

- Administration

Setup

When thinking about building the first community within a particular org, an admin will need to start at the Communities Settings menu. The settings here not only control key functional aspects of the communities but also enable communities altogether. One important aspect of these settings that is critical to understand is that they apply to the entire org, not an individual community. The Administration workspace, as I will cover later in this chapter, is community-specific. Figure 7-1 shows the concept visually.

© Philip Weinmeister 2018
P. Weinmeister, *Practical Guide to Salesforce Communities*, https://doi.org/10.1007/978-1-4842-3609-3_7

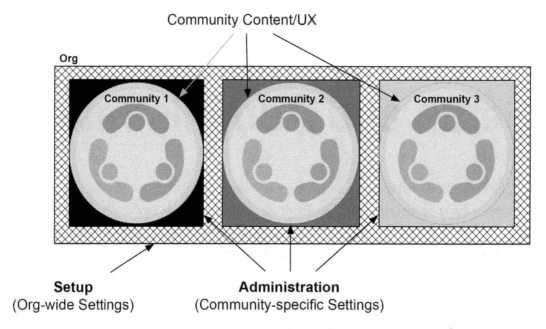

Figure 7-1. *The Communities Settings page (Setup) affects all communities; administration impacts a specific, individual community*

Initial Setup

The initial setup of communities within an org involves a few steps. Search for *Commu* in the Quick Find search box to filter down to a few choices and then select Communities Settings. The first step is simply to enable communities within an org. Figure 7-2 shows the corresponding checkbox.

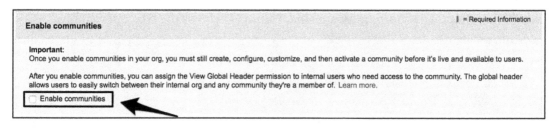

Figure 7-2. *Enable communities to allow the creation of a new community within an org*

Before saving and actually enabling communities for the org, an additional setting must be configured: selecting a domain name. This domain name will serve as the base/domain URL for all communities in the org. So, for example, if "pw-comm-guide" was selected, the domain in production would be `https://pw-comm-guide.force.com/s` for a community without a directory and `https://pw-comm-guide.force.com/support/s` for a community with a directory of `support`. Note that these examples assume a production org; the URL is different in trial or sandbox orgs. See Figure 7-3 for a view of the "Select a domain name" section once communities are enabled.

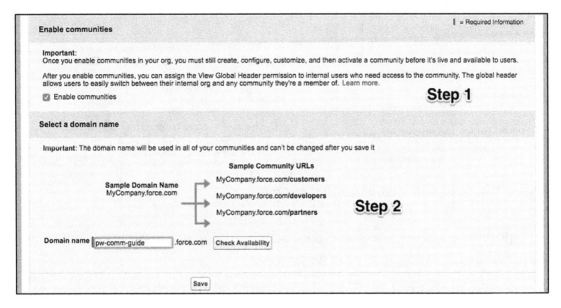

Figure 7-3. *A domain name must be selected when enabling communities*

While it is strongly advisable to select a domain name with permanence in mind, it can potentially be modified later. Although Salesforce doesn't allow an administrator to modify it directly, it is possible that Salesforce support will change it if a support case is submitted for that request.

Note   Before a Partner Central community can be enabled, one or more valid Partner community licenses must be present within the org. However, in Enterprise, Performance, and Unlimited orgs, up to 100 communities can be created without a license.

Additional Communities Settings

Once communities are enabled and a domain name is selected, a number of additional settings are exposed. See Figure 7-4 for these settings.

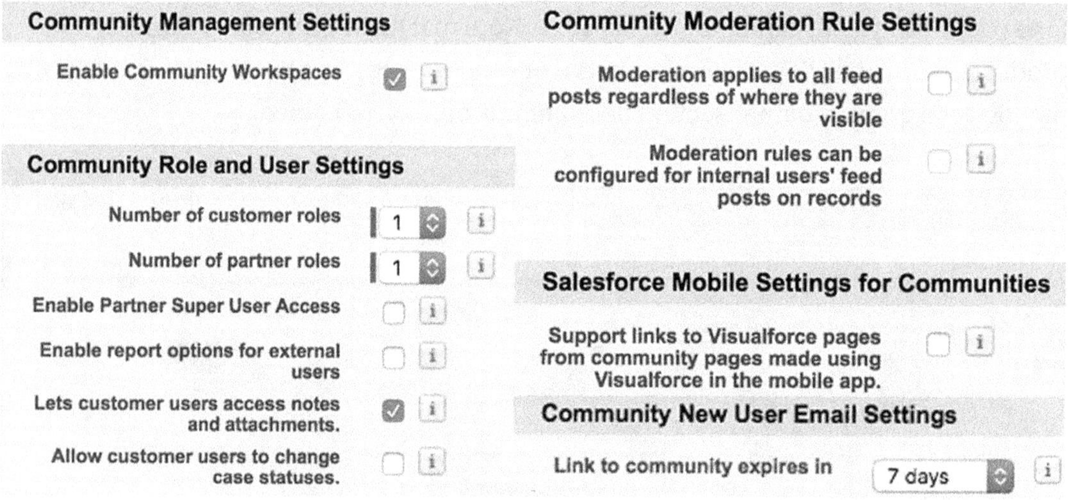

Figure 7-4. *Additional communities settings*

I will provide an overview of all of these settings, including my recommendation for the corresponding setting that works for most orgs.

- Enable Community Workspaces (recommendation = enabled)

    - This setting opens up a completely new community management interface. I highly recommend making the switch. There is no functionality lost, and it is the suggested approach moving forward, so get on board! Note that this is automatically enabled for new communities, as shown in Figure 7-5.

- Number of customer/partner roles (recommendation = 1)

    - This setting defines how many customer roles, for users with Customer Community Plus licenses, or partner roles, for users with Partner licenses, should be created. More roles may support additional use cases, but that is usually unnecessary, bringing extra complexity and potentially impacting performance. Increase this setting only if needed.

- Enable Partner Super User Access (recommendation = disabled)

    - This setting allows users individually identified as superusers to have visibility equal to other contacts on the same account. Truthfully, there is no immediate harm in enabling this setting. However, to be safe, leaving it disabled is probably ideal because it eliminates any risk of extraneous access being granted through this setting. Of course, if needed, use it.

- Enable report options for external users (recommendation = enabled)

    - For community users who have the ability to run reports, this setting will also allow them to view and modify reports for the purpose of summarizing and filtering them.

- Lets customer users access notes and attachments (recommendation = disabled)

    - This option allows customer community users to access notes and attachments on contact and account records. I suggest defaulting this to disabled for security reasons, unless required.

- Allow customer users to change case statuses (recommendation = disabled)

    - This allows users with Customer Community Plus licenses to modify the status on cases. Enable this only if necessary and consider the consequences of that access.

- Moderation applies to all feed settings regardless of where they are visible (recommendation = enabled)

    - This option allows posts to be moderated across communities. Specifically, if a post exists in multiple communities, this setting would allow a moderator of any of the related communities to flag the post. Leaving this as disabled means that only community-specific posts can be moderated.

- Moderation rules can be configured for internal users' feed posts on records (recommendation = enabled)

    - This is similar to the last rule but specific to internal users' posts. It allows those posts to be moderated in all corresponding communities where the post is visible.

- Support links to Visualforce pages from community pages made with Visualforce using the mobile app (recommendation = disabled)

    - Enabling this setting will retain the Apex prefix on all community URLs to ensure that Visualforce pages will properly load using the mobile app. Enable if needed.

- Link to community expires in (recommendation = 7 or 180 days)

    - Enabling this setting will set the community invitation link to expire in a certain number of days. The options are 1 day, 7 days, and 180 days.

Administration

I rarely access the Communities Settings menu once I enable communities and establish a domain. However, it's the exact opposite with administration, which is a different tool to control a community; it is critical to intimately know the corresponding configurations because they are guaranteed to come into play within your communities.

While the setup applies to *every* community in an org, the Administration menu is community-specific. If it's not clear why both exist, one can make a parallel with page-specific components versus a theme component. A theme component applies to the entire community and has settings that impact every page, while an individual component has settings that impact only that specific component.

Assuming workspaces are enabled (which I recommend), community administrators will find that "Administration" is one of the displayed workspaces. See Figure 7-5 for a view of the workspace.

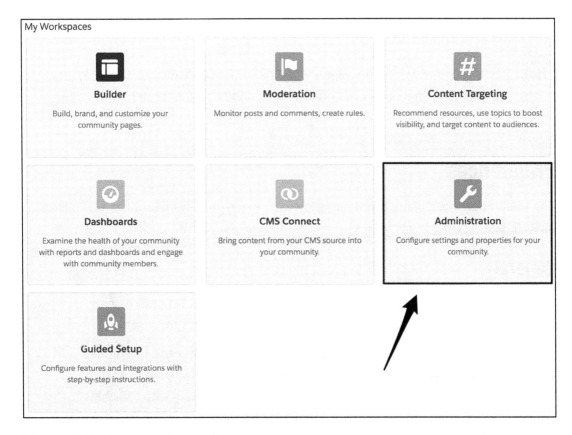

Figure 7-5. *Community workspaces*

As of the Spring '18 release, the following Administration sections exist:

- Preferences

- Members

- Tabs

- Branding

- Login & Registration

- Emails

- Pages

- Reputation Levels

- Reputation Points

- Rich Publisher Apps

I'll walk through the settings of each of these sections.

Note   Some of these settings appear only in certain contexts. For example, the Tabs and Branding sections correspond only to Tabs + Visualforce communities.

Preferences

The Preferences page of the Administration workspace provides a number of Boolean (on/off) settings that impact the associated community.

General

The General section in Preferences provides settings related to access, display, analytics, and more. Figure 7-6 shows the corresponding settings, which are described here:

- *Show nicknames*: Instead of displaying the user's first and last names within standard components, the value in the user's Nickname field will be displayed. Use this if you want to provide users with a visible identity without showing real names or if you want to allow users to self-identify by editing their own nicknames.

- *Give access to public API requests on Chatter*: Enabling this setting allows community administrators to display content in one or more public Chatter groups to guests (unauthenticated) users, along with any other public Chatter content that is served up.

- *Enable direct messages*: This allows users to send direct messages to other community members. Note that direct messages differ from private messages. Direct messages are an older feature typically associated with customization.

- *Users can send and receive private messages*: This allows users to leverage the Messages inbox for private communication. I highly recommend enabling this when there is a need for private, one-to-one communication within a community.

- *Let guest users view asset files on public and login pages*: This allows unauthenticated users to see certain resources on corresponding pages within the community. An example of this setting's impact is the login page background image; that image will not be accessible by guest users if this setting is disabled, instead showing a background color without an image.

- *Gather Community 360 data*: This setting allows for the capture and propagation of data within the community to be exposed to internal users within Lightning Experience through the Community 360 component.

- *Use custom Visualforce error pages*: This setting replaces the standard (and ugly) error pages with custom-built, Visualforce error pages.

- *Show all settings in Workspaces*: While I don't recommend enabling this setting, it allows admins to "force" the display of all community settings, even if some of the settings are not relevant to their community.

Settings	Preferences
Preferences	
Members	**General**
Tabs	✅ Show nicknames ⓘ
	✅ Give access to public API requests on Chatter ⓘ
Branding	✅ Enable direct messages ⓘ
	✅ Users can send and receive private messages ⓘ
Login & Registration	✅ Let guest users view asset files on public and login pages ⓘ
Emails	✅ Gather Community 360 data ⓘ
	✅ Use custom Visualforce error pages ⓘ
Pages	✅ Show all settings in Workspaces ⓘ

Figure 7-6. *General preferences*

Community Management

The Community Management section contains settings that directly impact a community member's experience or allowed functions. Figure 7-7 shows the corresponding settings, described here:

- *Allow members to flag content*: This setting enables members to flag content that they might consider to be inappropriate or a piece of spam. I recommended enabling this for communities with significant Chatter activity, but it is critical to understand that a resource must be available in the community to review the flagged content.

- *Allow members to upvote and downvote*: This setting, if enabled, will replace the Like button on questions and answers.

- *Enable setup and display of reputation levels*: This is a widely popular setting that essentially turns on gamification within a community. However, as the setting implies, reputation levels must be configured (i.e., set up) before they can be displayed.

- *Exclude contributions to records when counting points toward reputation levels*: In a community that includes significant operational activity via Chatter on records, the distribution of reputation points/levels can become extremely skewed based on those operational requirements. To center gamification around pure community activity, enable this setting.

- *Enable knowledgeable people on topics*: This setting allows users to identify users as "knowledgeable" on topics, enabling a self-managing expertise identification network. Admins should carefully assess the impact first, however; if users will not take the "nominations" seriously, the results may not be representative of true subject knowledge.

- *Suggest topics in new community posts*: This setting will result in certain topics being suggested after a post is made; the suggested topics are derived from the post content itself.

- *Show number of people discussing suggested topics*: This setting shows a statement such as "100 people are discussing this topic" following a post that contains a topic. In a community with lighter traffic or a smaller user base, this may inadvertently discourage community members; think carefully before enabling this in a small community.

Community Management

☑ Allow members to flag content ⓘ

☑ Allow members to upvote and downvote ⓘ

☑ Enable setup and display of reputation levels ⓘ

☑ Exclude contributions to records when counting points toward reputation levels ⓘ

☑ Enable knowledgeable people on topics ⓘ

☑ Suggest topics in new community posts ⓘ

☑ Show number of people discussing suggested topics ⓘ

Figure 7-7. *Community Management preferences*

Files

While not discussed heavily, this section is quite handy. Administrators can limit the types of files allowed for Chatter upload, as well as the maximum file size allowed. It is a great thing that Salesforce allows such large files via Chatter, but a scenario may arise (i.e., limited storage space) in which a reduced maximum file size would be beneficial. The maximum file size must be between 3 MB and 2,048 MB. See Figure 7-8.

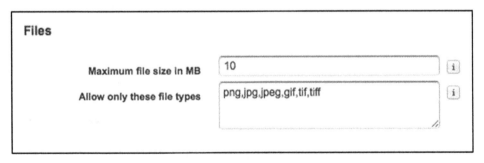

Files

Maximum file size in MB   10   ⓘ

Allow only these file types   png,jpg,jpeg,gif,tif,tiff   ⓘ

Figure 7-8. *Limit the file size and type of files that can be uploaded in a community*

Figure 7-9 and Figure 7-10 show the result of each of these settings as they appear to end users.

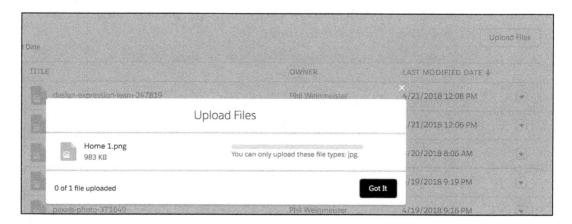

Figure 7-9. *A .png file is blocked when allowed file types are limited to .jpg files*

Figure 7-10. *A 16.3 MB file is blocked when the maximum size is set to 3 MB*

Uploading a file via Chatter takes these limits into consideration, as well, although the reason for the blocked file is not displayed. See Figure 7-11.

```
┌─────────────────────────────────────────────────────────────────────┐
│  Add Topic                                                          │
│  ┌──────────────────────────────────────────────┐                  │
│  │ ⚠  Picture5a-Home              (2.3MB)  ✕    │                  │
│  └──────────────────────────────────────────────┘                  │
│                                                                     │
│  ⊘                                                  ┌──────────┐   │
│                                                     │  Share   │   │
│                                                     └──────────┘   │
└─────────────────────────────────────────────────────────────────────┘
```

Figure 7-11. *Blocked file through Chatter*

Note   The Files settings do not impact standard attachments; they are specific to files.

Members

In the Members section, an administrator can establish who is allowed to log in to a specific community. Specifying "log in" versus access is important, as a public community or Lightning page technically allows anyone access to the public portions of the community. Member access is granted in these two ways:

- Associating a profile with the community

- Associating a permission set with the community

This approach allows for a significant amount of flexibility for both users and communities. If a user is included in a profile or permission set that is associated with a community, the user can be authenticated for it. Since neither profiles nor permission sets are limited to being associated with only one community, users can be part of multiple communities within the same org. The permission sets allow for extremely granular access, even down to an individual user.

Additionally, on the community side, communities can be associated with multiple profiles and permission sets, allowing administrators to configure the authorized community audience with ease. Figure 7-12 provides a visual of how access might work within an org that has multiple communities, profiles, and permission sets.

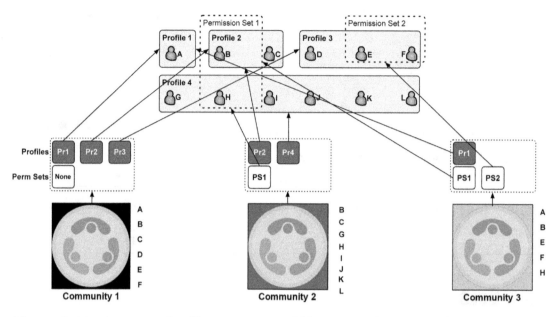

Figure 7-12. *An example of how access could be granted using profiles and permission sets*

Figure 7-13 shows the profile selection menu, and Figure 7-14 shows the permission set selection menu.

Select Profiles

Search: [All ▾] for: [_____]   [Find]

Available Profiles		**Selected Profiles**
Authenticated Website		System Administrator
CCU2		
Chatter Free User		
Chatter Moderator User		
Contract Manager	**Add**	
Cross Org Data Proxy User	[▶]	
Custom: Marketing Profile		
Custom: Sales Profile	[◀]	
Custom: Support Profile	**Remove**	
Customer Community Login User		
Customer Community Plus Login User		
Customer Community Plus User		
Customer Community User		
Customer Portal Manager Custom		

Figure 7-13. *Community profile selection menu*

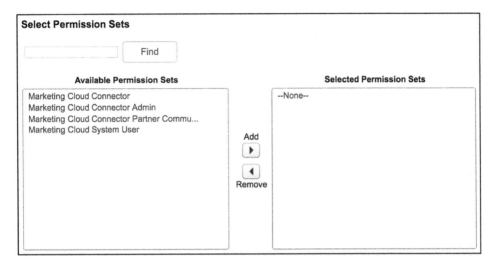

Figure 7-14. *Permission set selection menu*

Tabs

Tabs is a straightforward administration area. This menu allows community administrators to add tabs to a community, causing them to appear in a Tabs + Visualforce community. Also, this panel will impact the objects that appear in a Salesforce1 community (even if within a Lightning community). See Figure 7-15 for a look at the settings, and see Figure 7-16 for the result.

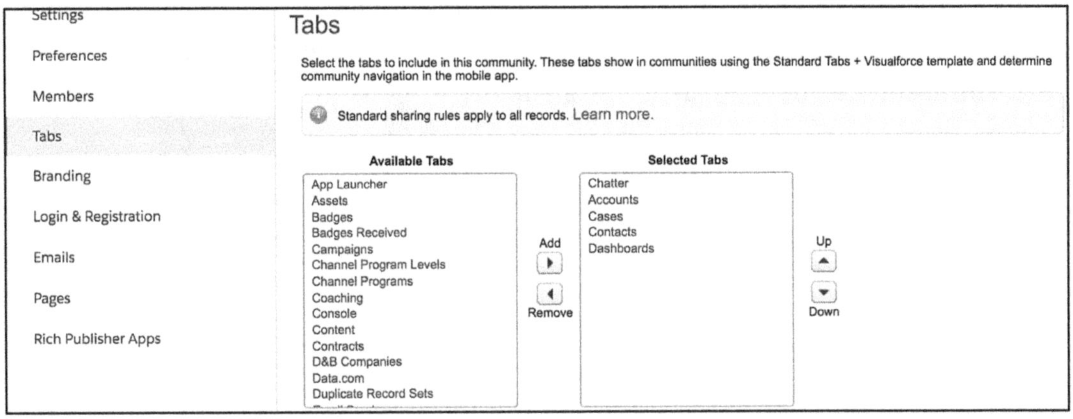

Figure 7-15. *Tabs settings*

Figure 7-16. *Displayed tabs, as configured in Figure 7-15*

Branding

For Tabs + Visualforce communities, which do not use Community Builder, defining the branding colors is done within the Branding page of the Administration workspace.

Header and Footer

In this subsection, the community header and footer are defined. An administrator must first upload a file as a document and then reference the document from the Branding page. The header can be configured with an upload of a JPEG, GIF, PNG, or HTML file, but the footer can be HTML only. Also, administrators should be aware that if the HTML file is uploaded for the header, they will need to include a custom search field within that HTML file. See Figure 7-17 for the settings, and see Figure 7-18 for the impacted area of the community.

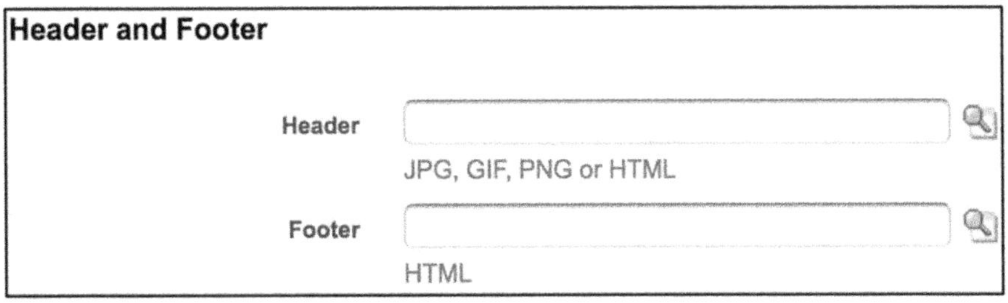

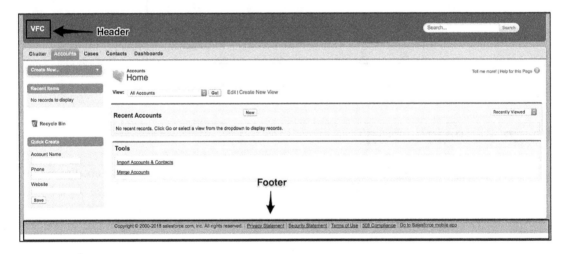

Figure 7-17. *Header and footer settings (for a Tabs + Visualforce community)*

Figure 7-18. *The page areas impacted by the header and footer settings*

Colors

Community administrators of a Tabs + Visualforce community can control branding colors. See Figure 7-19 for the different settings.

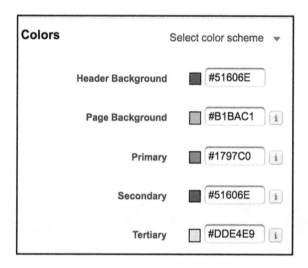

Figure 7-19. *Branding color settings for a Tabs + Visualforce community*

Login & Registration

The Login & Registration settings provide administrators with the ability to configure how users authenticate and register within a community.

Logo

The Logo section houses the settings to configure a community logo. This logo will be used on the login page, whether the community is Tabs + Visualforce or Lightning-based. An administrator will first need to determine the logo type. That setting will determine the second setting. If File is selected for Logo Type, the administrator will click Browse to upload a file from the local computer. See Figure 7-20.

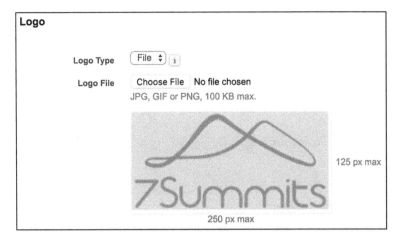

Figure 7-20. *A file or URL can be used to display a logo on the login page*

If URL is selected, a URL-based image can be used for the logo on the login page. One little-used feature is dynamic branding on the login page, set up by entering a dynamic URL. Search for *Dynamic Branding with Login Pages* to learn more. With this feature, an organization can show different login logos based on an audience.

Colors, Right-Side Content, and Footer

The following settings will further allow configuration of the login page:

- *Colors*: Configure the background color or the button color on the login page.

- *Right-Side Content*: This is a way to configure an image on the right half of the login. To add personalization, apply a dynamic URL to change the logo based on a particular audience.

- *Footer*: Footer text on the login page.

See Figure 7-21 for an example of these settings, and see Figure 7-22 for what a login page might look like, based on the settings.

Colors

Background	☐ #B1BAC1 ⓘ
Login Button	☐ #1797C0 ⓘ

Right-Side Content

Right Frame URL   https://upload.wikimedia.org/wikipedia/commons ⓘ

Footer

Footer Text   www.weinmeister.com

Figure 7-21. *Login page settings*

Figure 7-22. *A login page with configured right-side content*

Login

The login settings, while typically fairly straightforward, are critical to community success and can require some focused attention. In total, there are three login settings.

- Login page

- Direct community login for internal users

- Login options

The first setting is the configured login page. Three types of login page are available: default, Community Builder page, and Visualforce page. See Figure 7-23 for a view of the login page options.

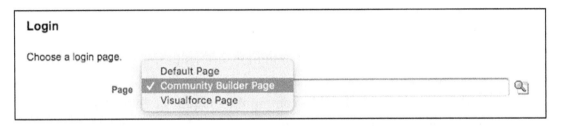

Figure 7-23. *Login page options*

These are my suggestions for various desired scenarios and the corresponding settings that should be selected:

- *Lightning community/standard login page*: Select Community Builder Page and "login."

- *Lightning community/custom Lightning login page*: Select Community Builder Page and then select a Lightning page.

- *Lightning community/custom Visualforce page*: Select Visualforce Page and then select a Visualforce page.

- *Tabs + Visualforce community/standard login page*: Select Default Page.

- *Tabs + Visualforce community/custom login page*: Select Visualforce Page and then select a Visualforce page.

A community admin will then decide whether internal users should be allowed to log in directly to the community. This is typically turned off, encouraging internal users to log in to the "standard" Salesforce org before toggling to the community. However, there is no inherent issue with enabling this setting. It's important to make sure that the login process aligns with company procedures and rules, but it's a legitimate option, especially if users exist who rarely log in to the main org. See Figure 7-24.

Figure 7-24. Allow users to log in to the community without first logging in to the "internal" org

The final login option involves single sign-on settings and authentication providers. Simply put, this is where an administrator would configure access to authenticate using something other than the standard community username and password. The first option, and often the only option selected, is the standard login method using the username and password. However, many communities require additional options. I won't go into detail on how to set up authentication providers, but I will show an example of how an administrator might set these up to drive community login options. See Figure 7-25 for a look at some configured providers.

Auth. Providers

A | B

			New
Action	Name ↑	URL Suffix	Provider Type
Edit | Del CoveoAuth		CoveoAuth	Open ID Connect
Edit | Del DocuratedAuth		DocuratedAuth	Open ID Connect
Edit | Del Facebook		Facebook	Facebook
Edit | Del Twitter		Twitter	Twitter

Figure 7-25. Configured authentication providers

In Figure 7-26, the four configured authentication providers now appear in the Login section.

Select which login options to display ⓘ

- ☑ Capricorn Consulting username and password
- ☑ Facebook
- ☑ Twitter
- ☐ DocuratedAuth
- ☐ CoveoAuth

To configure more login options, go to Single Sign-On Settings or Auth. Providers. ⓘ

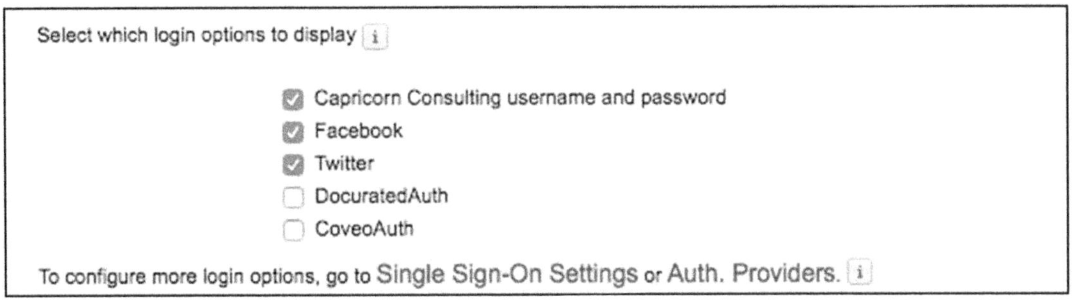

Figure 7-26. *The authentication providers from Figure 7-25 appear in the Login section on the Login & Administration page*

In this case, Facebook and Twitter are configured. Figure 7-27 shows the result of this on the actual community login page.

Figure 7-27. *A login page with Facebook and Twitter configured as login options*

Logout

Salesforce provides one option for customizing the page that is displayed following a logout by a community member: the URL of the desired page. Even if an administrator wants to point to a Community Builder page or a Visualforce page, the full URL needs to be configured. See Figure 7-28 for the Logout settings.

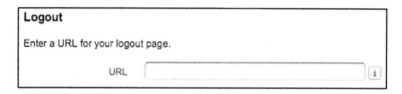

Figure 7-28. *An admin can enter a URL for the desired post-logout page*

Password

While I recommend using the default pages, if possible, Salesforce communities support custom pages to communicate a forgotten password and to change a password. The options are as follows:

- Forgot Password
  - Default Page
  - Community Builder Page
  - Visualforce Page
- Change Password
  - Default Page
  - Visualforce Page

See Figure 7-29 for a view of these options.

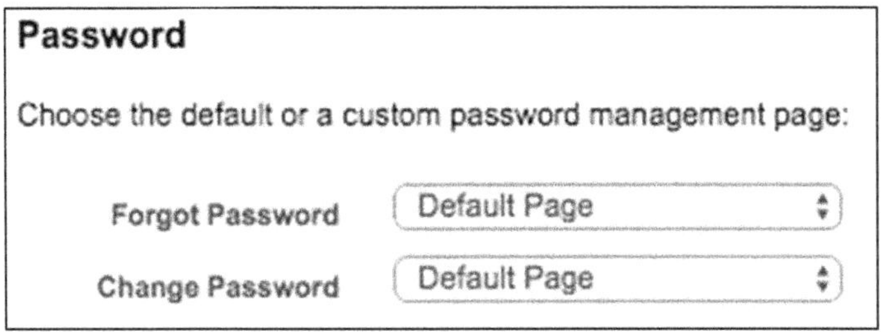

Figure 7-29. *Community settings for password-related pages*

Registration

Thankfully, Salesforce provides the ability to enable self-registration within communities. This is most relevant to customer communities since partners and employees will most commonly be identified as users by the organization that owns the community. Figure 7-30 shows the self-registration settings.

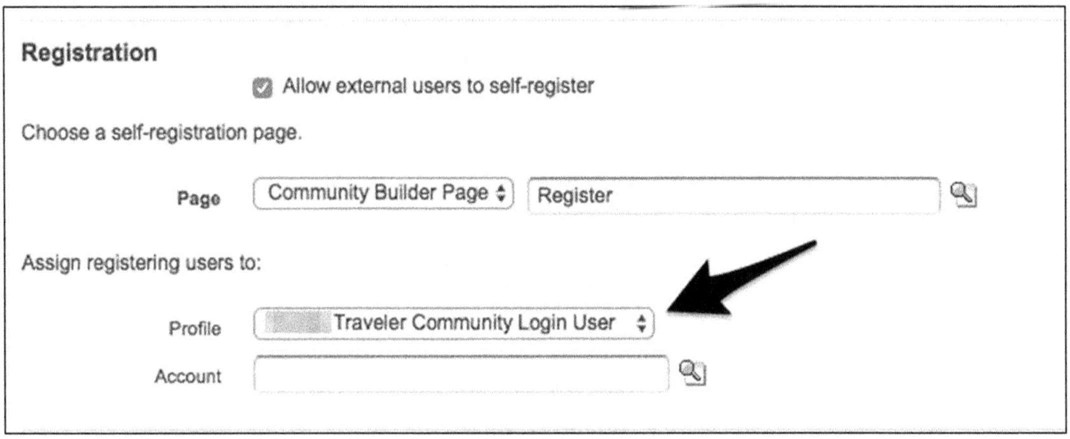

Figure 7-30. *Self-registration settings*

The first step in establishing self-registration within a community is enabling the "Allow external users to self-register" setting. This opens up a few additional settings, including the registration page. Select an existing (standard) page or point to a custom-built registration page, as needed. Also, a profile and account need to be configured since users will not determine their own profile or account.

Emails

Although standard email functionality (templates, alerts) within the classic or Lightning Experience interface is absolutely compatible with communities, some community-specific email settings are critical. Those settings are stored in the Emails section of the Administration workspace (see Figure 7-31).

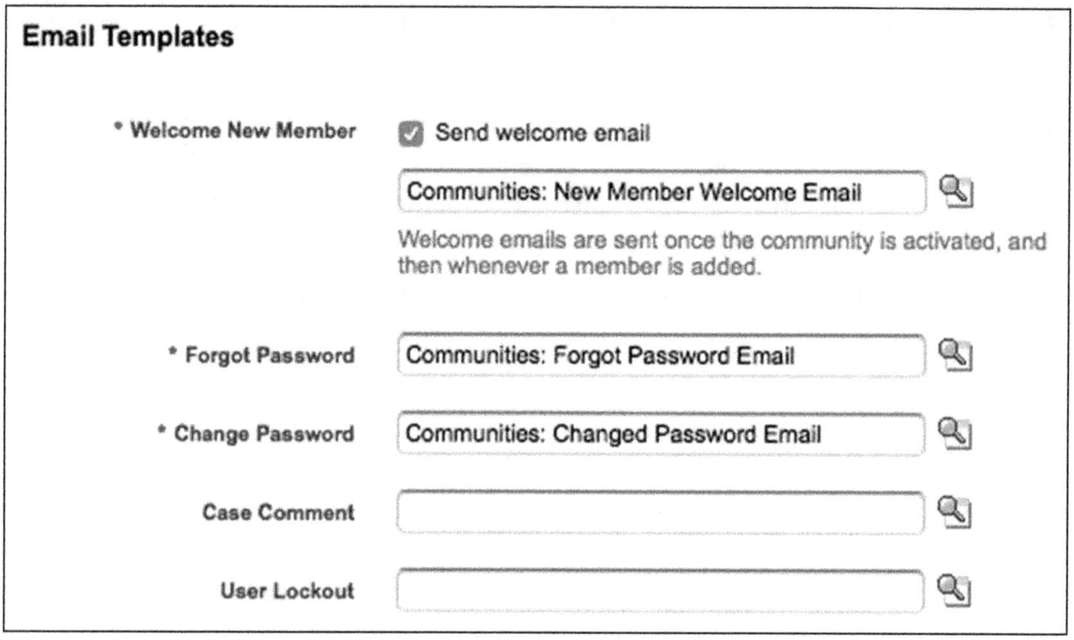

Email Templates

* Welcome New Member   ☑ Send welcome email

Communities: New Member Welcome Email

Welcome emails are sent once the community is activated, and then whenever a member is added.

* Forgot Password   Communities: Forgot Password Email

* Change Password   Communities: Changed Password Email

Case Comment

User Lockout

Figure 7-31. *Email settings for communities*

Four configurable community email templates exist.

- Welcome New Member

    - *Ability to disable this email template*: Yes

    - *Default template*: Communities: New Member Welcome Email

- Forgot Password

    - *Ability to disable this email template*: No

    - *Default template*: Communities: Forgot Password Email

- Change Password

    - *Ability to disable this email template*: No

    - *Default template*: Communities: Changed Password Email

- Case Comment

    - *Ability to enable/disable sending of email*: Yes

    - *Default template*: N/A (none)

- User Lockout

    - *Ability to enable/disable sending of email*: Yes

    - *Default template*: N/A (none)

It is absolutely supported to change any or all of these emails to add branding or modify content. However, an admin should check all available merge fields carefully to ensure that no functionality is lost when transitioning to a different email alert.

Note   For admins working on a community who want to absolutely ensure that no emails are inadvertently sent out to potential members of the community, I recommend temporarily unchecking the "Send welcome email" checkbox. It's easy to re-enable and can save some major headaches.

Pages

The Pages section is probably the least straightforward or self-explanatory of all Administration sections. Yes, it does relate to pages, but that doesn't exactly provide the full picture. See Figure 7-32 for a view of the Pages section.

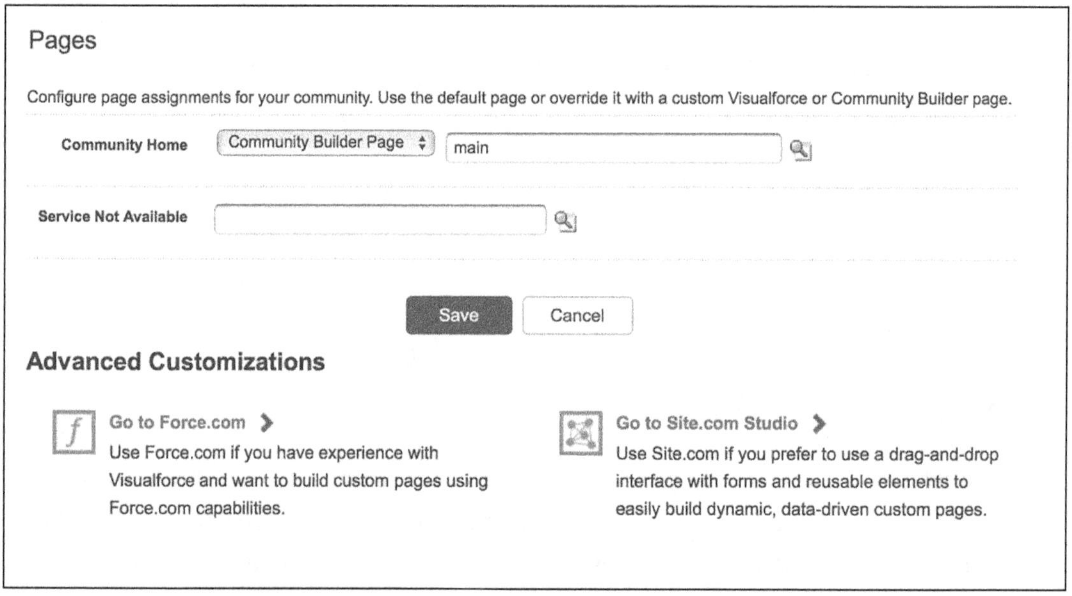

Figure 7-32. *The Pages section of the Administration menu*

Community Home and Service Not Available both allow a community administrator to override standard pages with a custom page. However, the greatest value on this page is found within Advanced Customizations, namely, the Go to Force.com link. Numerous settings exist that allow custom Visualforce pages to be swapped in to replace certain standard community pages. Quietly residing on the Force.com page are Guest User Profile controls. From here, an admin can configure exactly what guest users have access to. Note that this is just like any profile, allowing configuration of object access, field access, and much more.

Also on the Force.com page are certain related list sections, such as available Visualforce pages. These sections allow Visualforce pages, Apex classes, and more to be made available within the community. This is useful to apply when all users need the same level of access to a specific element within the community. See Figure 7-33 for an overview of the Force.com Pages menu.

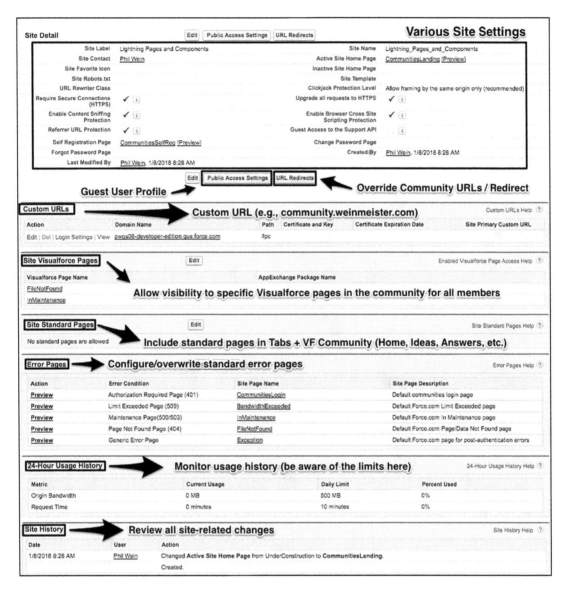

Figure 7-33. *Force.com Pages screen*

Reputation Levels

Once the setup of reputation levels and points has been enabled, an administrator can configure both of those new sections. See Figure 7-34 for a look at the Reputation Levels section.

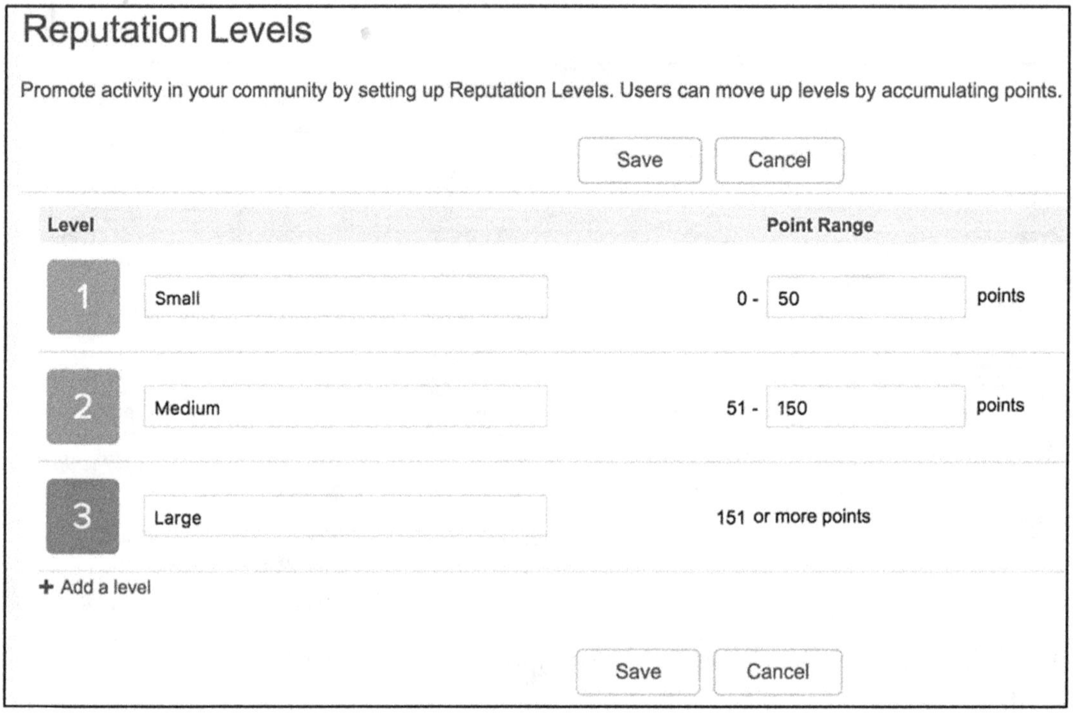

Figure 7-34. *Reputation Levels settings*

There are four steps to setting up reputation levels, shown here:

1. Determine the desired number of levels. The default number is 10, but this should be tailored to the needs of each community. To remove levels, an administrator can click the X icon by the last level until reaching the desired number of levels. To add levels, an administrator can click the "+Add a row" link and repeat until complete.

2. Configure the point range for each level. I recommend starting at level 1 and working up from there.

3. Name each level. A community administrator will want to know the audience to determine whether to come up with fun names or more serious/professional ones.

4. Upload a badge/level icon for each level.

Reputation Points

Reputation points directly relate to reputation levels, as each level is bound by a range of points. The number of points per contributing activity can be modified. It is critical to understand what might warrant a change in the number of points configured for a specific activity. I suggest the following as valid reasons, among others:

- Increased emphasis on particular activities

- Decreased emphasis on particular activities

- "Right-sizing" of points to make them better align with overall community trends

- Elimination of spam-supporting behavior (e.g., removing points for a "like" when users are liking every community record they can get to)

Figure 7-35 shows the Reputation Points menu.

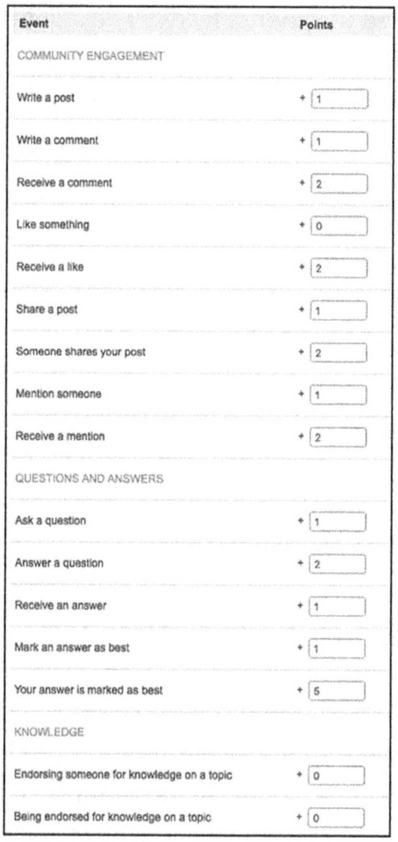

Event	Points
COMMUNITY ENGAGEMENT	
Write a post	+ 1
Write a comment	+ 1
Receive a comment	+ 2
Like something	+ 0
Receive a like	+ 2
Share a post	+ 1
Someone shares your post	+ 2
Mention someone	+ 1
Receive a mention	+ 2
QUESTIONS AND ANSWERS	
Ask a question	+ 1
Answer a question	+ 2
Receive an answer	+ 1
Mark an answer as best	+ 1
Your answer is marked as best	+ 5
KNOWLEDGE	
Endorsing someone for knowledge on a topic	+ 0
Being endorsed for knowledge on a topic	+ 0

Figure 7-35. *Reputation Points settings screen*

Figure 7-36 shows an example of the standard Leaderboard component once reputation levels and points have been configured.

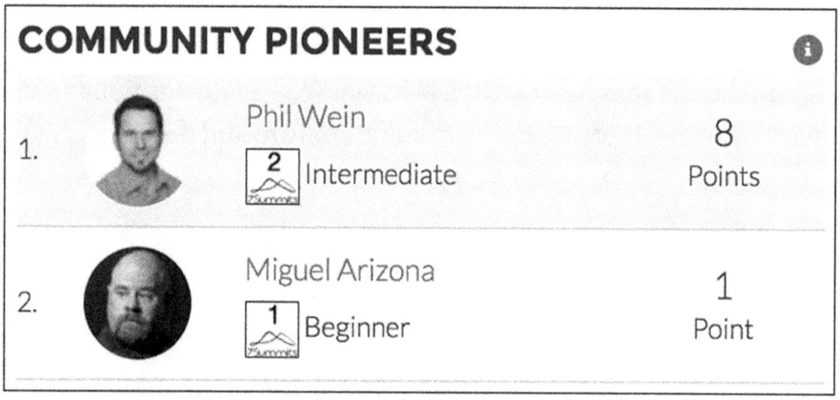

COMMUNITY PIONEERS

1. Phil Wein
   2 Intermediate
   8 Points

2. Miguel Arizona
   1 Beginner
   1 Point

Figure 7-36. *Leaderboard component with reputation levels and points configured*

174

Rich Publisher Apps

Rich publisher apps are a newer feature that can be used within communities. These apps allow for a payload to be accessed from and associated with a specific Chatter post within the community. Once the Lightning components (Composition and Render) and the Chatter extension that are part of the rich publisher app have been created, the app can be associated with a community (see Figure 7-37).

Figure 7-37. *Move publisher apps to Selected Apps to enable them within a community*

Once apps are enabled within a community, the icons will show up within the Feed Publisher component (see Figure 7-38).

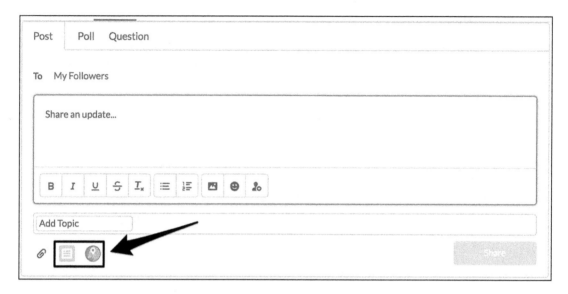

Figure 7-38. *Two rich publisher apps within the Feed Publisher component*

These apps allow for the selection of cases and Trailhead modules, respectively. See Figure 7-39 and Figure 7-40 for the presented modals when each of the icons is clicked.

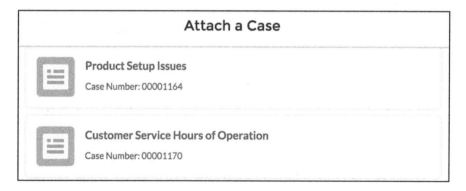

Figure 7-39. *Attach a case to a community feed item using a rich publisher app*

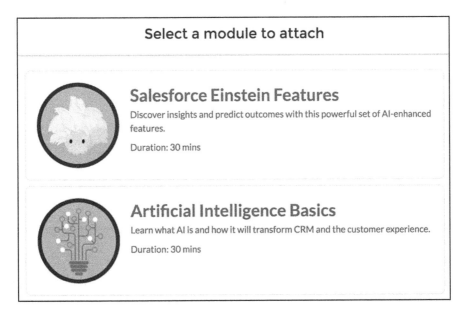

Figure 7-40. *Attach a Trailhead module to a community feed item using a rich publisher app*

When all is said and done, a community user can associate various data/content with a post within the community. See Figure 7-41 for an example of a post associated with a case and a Trailhead module.

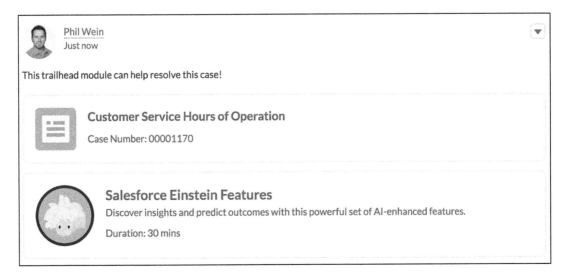

Figure 7-41. *View of a feed with an associated case and Trailhead module*

Recap

While I wouldn't exactly call the world of setup and administration glamorous or exhilarating, it is an absolute necessity on the path to success with a Salesforce community. In this chapter, I walked through each of the separate Communities Settings and Administration menus (and explained the difference between the two), covering areas such as preferences, email, login, registration, reputation, and more.

CHAPTER 8

Access, Sharing, and Visibility

I would assume all airlines list safety as their first corporate priority. The customer experience, while important, does not equate to the criticality of customer health. In the technology world filled with 1s and 0s, data security takes on a role analogous to that of airline passenger safety. Anyone would agree that user functionality and experience are of extremely high importance to Salesforce users; yet, the corresponding satisfaction from those factors will never outweigh the need for a secure system that provides access to those in need and prevents access from those who should be excluded. In other words, it's a great thing to have a powerful, useful application at one's fingertips, but if that application does not appropriately guard private or confidential data, its added value is likely eliminated.

Just as access, sharing, and visibility are key considerations in Sales Cloud and Service Cloud, they are critical factors to consider when building a community. I will walk through each area that I consider a key factor in establishing a foundation for appropriate access, sharing, and visibility within a community. I will not rehash the entire Salesforce security model, however, since there are security-related areas outside of communities that might warrant a completely separate book. Check out Trailhead for some relevant modules or my previous book, *Practical Salesforce.com Development Without Code*, to learn more about sharing capabilities for the platform as a whole. I will focus on four specific areas in this chapter.

- Community authentication and access
- Object and field access
- Organizationwide sharing (customer community versus other user types, external sharing model, communities sharing settings)
- Sharing sets/share groups

© Philip Weinmeister 2018
P. Weinmeister, *Practical Guide to Salesforce Communities*, https://doi.org/10.1007/978-1-4842-3609-3_8

Community Authentication and Access

Before anything else is discussed about a particular user's object access in a community or the visibility of a record on a community page, a community administrator must decide who should even be able to access the community. This is a two-part process, involving authentication and access settings.

Authentication (Private vs. Public)

By default, communities are private, meaning that authentication is initially required for any and all access to a community. However, that access can be opened up rather easily in one of two ways.

- Community-wide publicity
- Page-specific publicity

To modify the default setting, navigate to Settings ➤ General within Community Builder and select the checkbox shown in Figure 8-1.

Figure 8-1. *Communitywide Public Access setting*

All page-level default settings are inherited from here. In other words, if this is set to Public, then each page would, by default, be set to Public unless manually updated in Page Access, as shown in Figure 8-2.

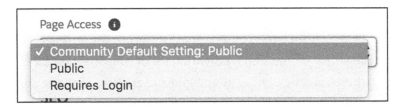

Figure 8-2. *The community-wide setting drives the Page Access values*

To make the picture clearer, I will step back and look at multiple communities that are configured differently. Take a look at Figure 8-3. In this diagram, I lay out three communities.

- *Community 1*: Private, with page settings all set to default

- *Community 2*: Private, with some pages manually set to public

- *Community 3*: Public, with some pages manually set to private

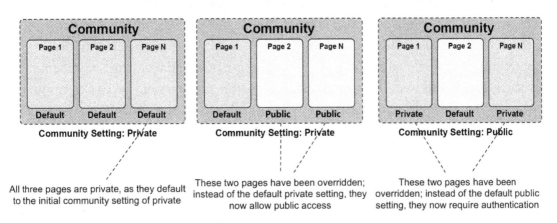

Figure 8-3. *Three scenarios involving communitywide publicity setting and different page-specific settings*

Community Member Access

To access any authenticated page (or functionality) within a community, a user must be provided access through the provisioning of a user profile or a permission set. I described the process in detail in Chapter 7 and won't repeat all of that, but this is a basic premise that needs to be understood when establishing community access; regardless of the scope of access and permissions individual users have through their profiles or a permission set, they will only be considered guest users (i.e., allowing consumption of public content only) without being added to the community. This goes for system administrators, too; be careful with removing that profile from a community.

Object and Field Access

The next critical area when establishing the proper security model for a community is the corresponding object and field access. The great news here is that this a standard platform activity; there's nothing community-specific to learn. For those who happen to have a copy of my 2015 book *Practical Salesforce.com Development Without Code*, a chapter is dedicated to this topic in detail.

I won't go through what is a fairly standard topic for the Salesforce platform, but I will provide a few examples to help illustrate the impact of these settings. First, consider a community that uses cases with customers for self-service purposes. Within the community, both a global action and a record list are provided within the navigation menu. Figure 8-4 shows a case record detail page from the point of view of a community user with Read, Create, and Edit access to cases and field-level security (FLS) visibility to all case fields.

Figure 8-4. *View of a case for a user with full case object access*

There are four aspects to note in Figure 8-4.

- A case global action in the navigation menu

- A case list in the navigation menu

- A displayed case page

- Three available actions at the top right: Edit, Change Owner, and Clone

If this user no longer has Create or Edit access, the available actions immediately disappear, as shown in Figure 8-5.

Figure 8-5. *Users may no longer see certain actions at the top right if they do not have Create or Edit access*

In Figure 8-6, I have served up the same page for a user with no case access.

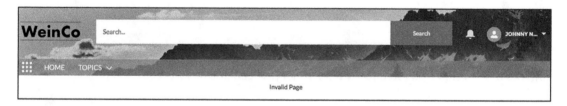

Figure 8-6. *A user without any case access sees neither the case record nor the case-related tabs in the navigation menu*

In Figure 8-6, I show the following conditions:

- The case global action does not appear in the navigation menu.

- The case list does not appear in the navigation menu.

- The case page does not load.

This is valuable because it's built completely on the existing Salesforce security model; administrators can set up the access for community users as they do for internal users, and all of the object and field permissions will carry through to the community fluidly.

Record Sharing

Object and field permissions are pretty straightforward (for example, whether or not a particular user can edit/update Case records). Record sharing, however, isn't so black and white. Record sharing is essentially the determination of who can see which records and in what capacity. In some orgs, it can get pretty complex. I'll cover a few areas specific to record sharing to help explain how to approach the subject for communities.

To get started, take a look at Figure 8-7. This shows how the layers discussed in this chapter so far provide access and visibility within a community.

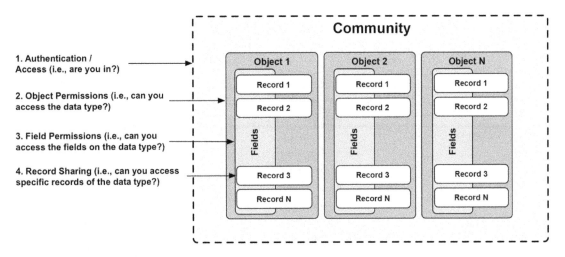

Figure 8-7. *A view of multiple visibility-related settings*

Like some of the other security-related areas, sharing is a general construct of the Salesforce platform. Still, although it's not specific to communities, there are some communities-specific aspects of sharing to consider.

Organizationwide Sharing and External Users

Just as with an "internal" Salesforce implementation, organizationwide sharing settings are critical to consider in a community implementation. These settings determine the base-level visibility to records of different object types. Three settings are available.

- *Public Read/Write*: All records are shared with all users and can be viewed and/or edited by those with proper object access.

- *Public Read Only*: All records are shared with all users and can be viewed by those with proper object access. The records can be edited based on additional sharing means.

- *Private*: Records are not automatically shared with all users. The records can be viewed and/or edited based on additional sharing means, depending on user object access.

Initially, within a Salesforce org, one setting per applicable object exists. However, an external sharing model can be enabled, allowing more granular sharing capabilities. Admins should note that access granted to external users cannot exceed that which is granted to internal users. So, for example, if the User object is shared as Public Read Only internally, it can only be shared as Public Read Only or Private; Public Read/Write cannot be selected because it would grant external users more visibility than internal users. See an example view of external settings in Figure 8-8.

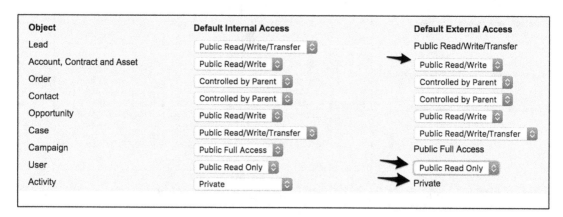

Figure 8-8. *External sharing (organizationwide sharing settings)*

It is important to understand that sharing visibility through these settings only goes as far as an individual user has access. Take accounts from Figure 8-7, for example. They are Public Read/Write. That does not mean all users can necessarily edit all accounts in the system; each user must have the appropriate object and field-level access to make that happen. See Figure 8-9 for a diagram of how this works.

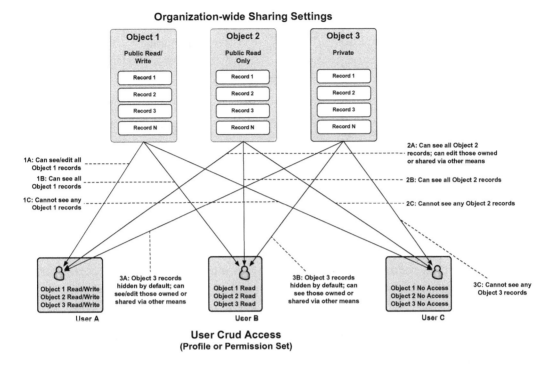

Figure 8-9. *A scenario with three users with varying object access and how sharing settings impact each of their access/visibility*

Customer Community vs. Other Community Licenses

As far as sharing goes, there is really only one community license type that one needs to be aware of: Customer Community (whether login or named user). Why? Because that type is considered "high-volume" and does *not* use the standard sharing model (see Figure 8-10). That's a major consideration for building a community solution; do users need full record sharing or not?

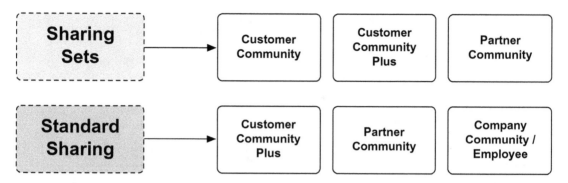

Figure 8-10. *Customer Community users do not use standard Salesforce sharing*

The concept here is that "high-volume" users will typically have very transactional needs that fit into one or a few narrow use cases (i.e., their activity and the corresponding records needed will be fairly predictable). Additionally, it assumes that the data the Customer Community license uses falls into one of the following buckets:

- It is shared directly with the user and no other external users (e.g., the user is the owner).

- It is shared with the user's organization (account).

- It is public read-only or read-write; all users can access it.

If a solution requires anything more complex for the group of users assigned to the Customer Community license, a reassessment of the chosen license types needs to be performed.

Sharing Sets

So, what exactly are change sets? I'll provide an overview and then dive into some examples.

Overview

To help explain sharing sets, let me first provide a hypothetical scenario for reference as I walk through the configuration options.

- License type of community users (Customer Community)

- The community includes the Case object.

- A customer-created case is always assigned to an internal user.

- The customer who created a case is set as the contact on the case.

- All contacts from the same account should be able to edit any case submitted by a colleague.

The first area to address here is organization-wide defaults. Organizationwide defaults do apply to customer community users. Whether an object's default is set to Private, Public Read Only, or Public Read/Write, that sharing model will extend to customers. Of course, some level of create/read/update/delete (CRUD) access to the object will need to be provided for it to be relevant; if a user cannot access an object, a sharing default of Private versus Public Read/Write will have no bearing on that user.

In theory, Public access could be granted to everyone for Cases and Contacts. However, doing that would almost never make sense for an organization. Think about it—that would provide each customer with visibility into all contact and case records for all other customers. Assume the organization-wide default for both objects to be private. See Figure 8-11 for these settings.

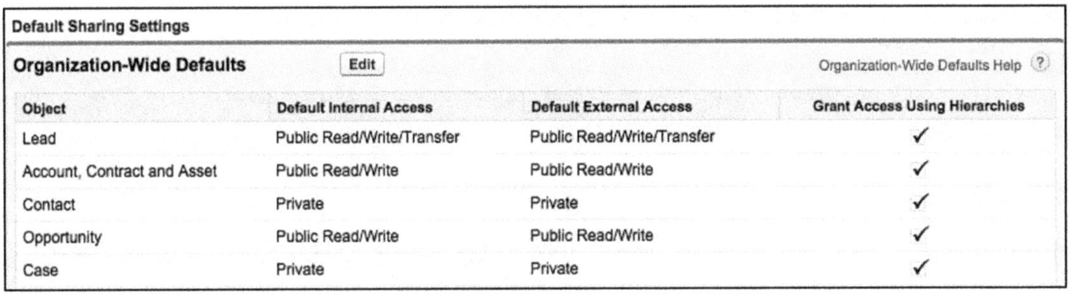

Default Sharing Settings

Organization-Wide Defaults	Edit		Organization-Wide Defaults Help (?)
Object	**Default Internal Access**	**Default External Access**	**Grant Access Using Hierarchies**
Lead	Public Read/Write/Transfer	Public Read/Write/Transfer	✓
Account, Contract and Asset	Public Read/Write	Public Read/Write	✓
Contact	Private	Private	✓
Opportunity	Public Read/Write	Public Read/Write	✓
Case	Private	Private	✓

Figure 8-11. *Organization-wide settings*

In an internal org, an administrator can easily create a custom sharing rule based on ownership or defined criteria to extend the ability to view or edit records to additional users or groups of users (see Figure 8-12). This is available in communities with Partner licenses.

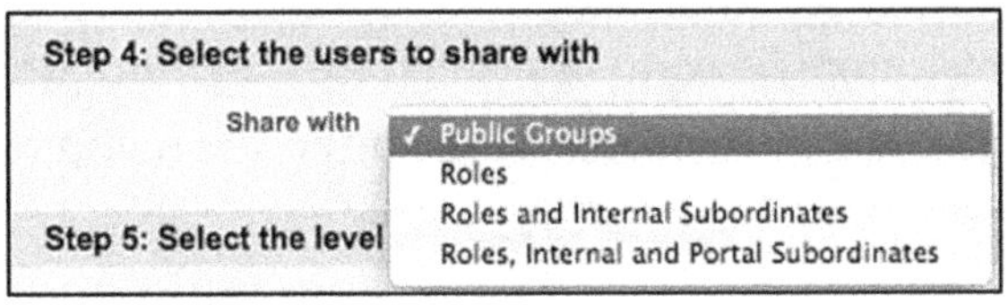

Step 4: Select the users to share with

Share with	✓ Public Groups
	Roles
	Roles and Internal Subordinates
Step 5: Select the level	Roles, Internal and Portal Subordinates

Figure 8-12. *Standard sharing (not available for Customer Community users)*

However, the administrator cannot create sharing rules in a Customer Community. Users with Customer Community licenses do not have roles and cannot be added to public groups. This results in an incompatibility between sharing rules and customer community users; see Figure 8-13 for an example of this.

Figure 8-13. *Role is not accessible on Customer Community user records*

To mitigate the deliberate but potentially debilitating gap in the sharing functionality between customer and partner communities, admins can create one or more sharing sets. The first key piece to understand about how sharing sets work is that no more than one sharing set can be created for each available profile. An administrator cannot create multiple sharing sets that provide different access and apply both to the same profile.

Once admins set the label and description for a sharing set, they will select one or more applicable profiles for this sharing set (Figure 8-14).

Sharing Set Edit   Save   Cancel

Label   Customer Access

Sharing Set Name   Customer_Access   i

Description   Sharing set to provide specific Case and
                   Contact sharing access to customers.

Select Profiles

Available Profiles   **Selected Profiles**

High Volume Customer Portal   Customer Community Profile
Authenticated Website

Figure 8-14. *Sharing sets can be created for Customer Community users*

On to the fun part. Here, the administrator will need to select the applicable object. In this case, the administrator will want to select Case and move it to Selected Objects. Once the admin has clicked Set Up next to Case, the access mapping for that object will appear (Figure 8-15).

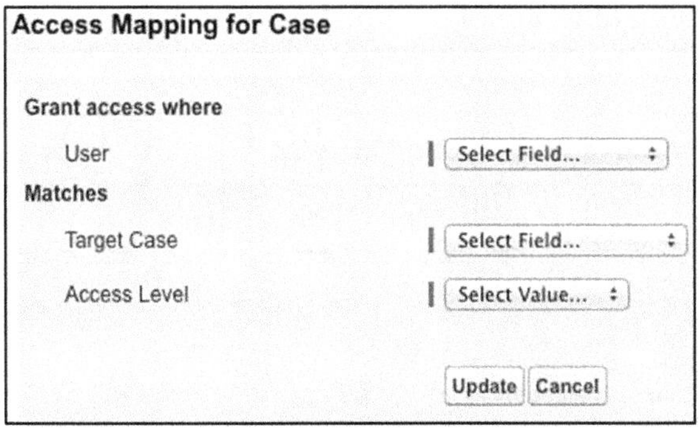

Access Mapping for Case

Grant access where

    User   [Select Field... ‡]

Matches

    Target Case   [Select Field... ‡]

    Access Level   [Select Value... ‡]

                                [Update] [Cancel]

Figure 8-15.   Access mapping (part of sharing sets)

As I stated earlier, the assumption is that the admin wants to provide read-write access to all of the submitting contact's colleagues. To do this, the admin will want to share the cases to which all contacts on the submitting user's account has access. In other words, the administrator will provide access to all contacts where User.Contact. Account = Case.Account. See the configuration in Figure 8-16.

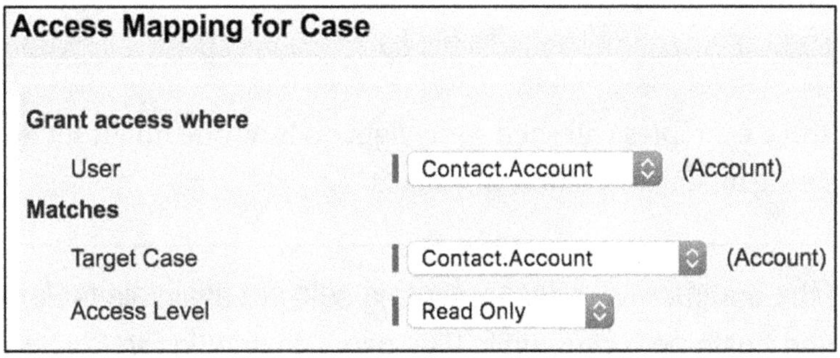

Access Mapping for Case

Grant access where

    User   [Contact.Account ⬍] (Account)

Matches

    Target Case   [Contact.Account ⬍] (Account)

    Access Level   [Read Only ⬍]

Figure 8-16.   Sharing users from an account with all other users on that account

Figure 8-17 provides a diagram of the finished product.

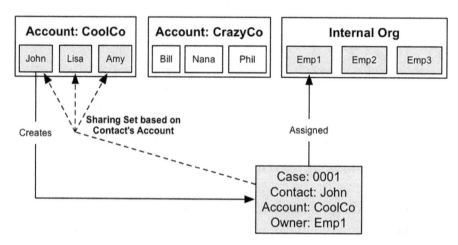

Figure 8-17. *This sharing set allows all external users associated with CoolCo to see the case created by John*

Success! We can see that this sharing set provides access to all of John's colleagues.

Examples

The following three examples will shed some light on how one might set up sharing sets to provide a sharing model for community users.

Note   As of the Summer '18 release, sharing sets are available to Partner Community and Customer Community Plus users, in addition to Customer Community users. This significantly expands the potential reach of sharing sets and means that anyone building a community with external users should be familiar with this tool/feature. The examples that follow will assume a Customer Community user.

Example 1: Sharing a Custom Object

Here are the scenario details:

- *Object*: Project (custom object)

- *Sharing Settings*: Private

- *Owner*: Customer user associated with an account

- *Sharing requirement*: Share with all other users who are on the same account

See Figure 8-18.

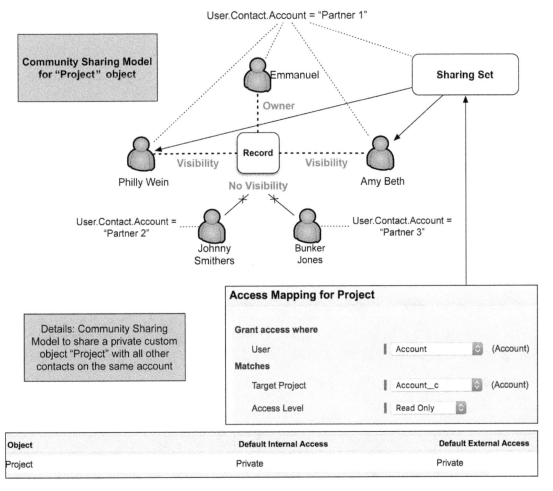

Figure 8-18. *Diagram of Example 1*

Example 2: User Visibility Based on Account

Here are the scenario details:

- *Object*: User

- *Sharing Settings*: Private

- *Sharing requirement*: Allow all users on the same account to see each other (i.e., have access to each other's user records)

See Figure 8-19.

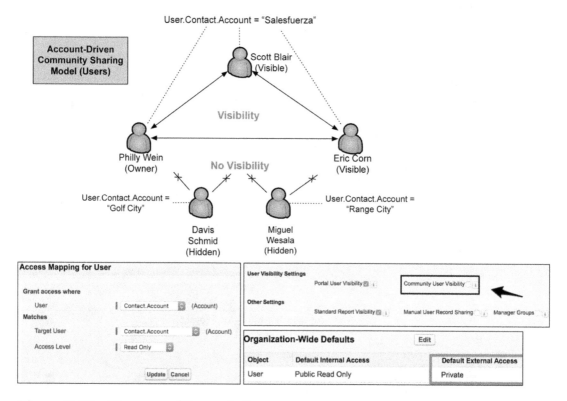

Figure 8-19. *Diagram of Example 2*

Example 3: User Visibility based on Custom Field

Here are the scenario details:

- *Object*: User

- *Sharing Settings*: Private

- *Sharing requirement*: Allow all designated/flagged users to see each other (i.e., have access to each other's user records); do not use the standard account field, as each user has a different account

See Figure 8-20.

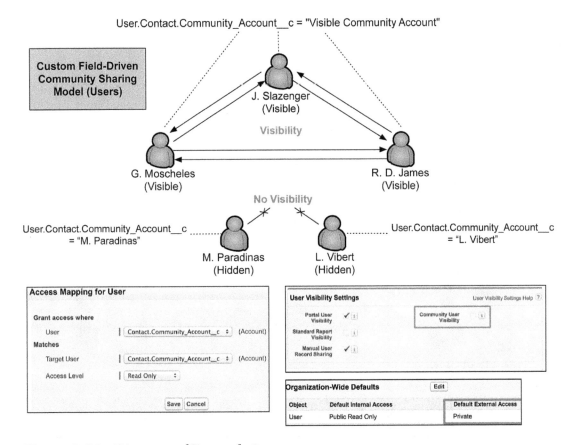

Figure 8-20. *Diagram of Example 3*

Share Groups

Since Customer Community users do not use the standard Salesforce sharing model, they can't be accessed when building a sharing rule. For example, an administrator would not be able to create a rule to share a record owned by a customer community user with a role or group or users who had full licenses.

This scenario is why Salesforce created share groups, which automatically share all records owned by high-volume portal users (e.g., Customer Community users) with specified users who are not of the same (e.g., Partner users, full internal users, etc.). To set up a share group, one must first create a sharing set. Once that is complete, a Share Group Settings tab appears on the Sharing Set page (see Figure 8-21).

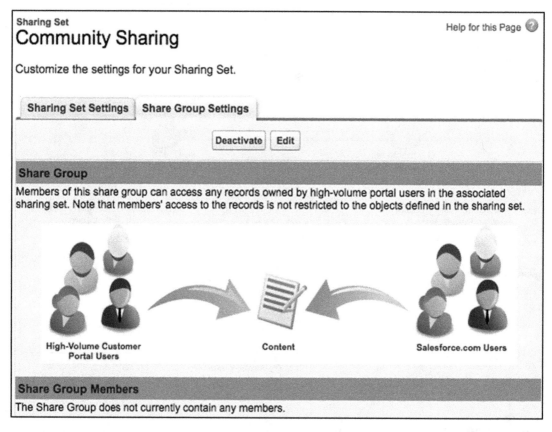

Figure 8-21. *Use a share group to share records owned by Customer Community users with internal users*

To add members, an administrator clicks the Edit button and moves the available members to Selected Members (use the Search drop-down to change the user type). See Figure 8-22.

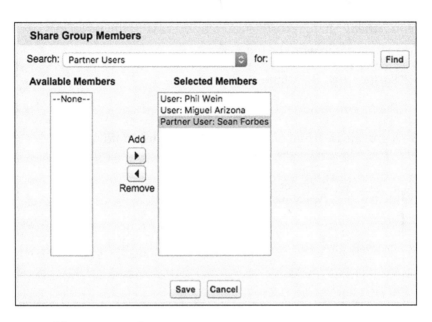

Figure 8-22. *Add users to a share group*

Upon adding the desired members, the users to whom records owned by the corresponding Customer Community users will be listed (see Figure 8-23).

Share Group Members	
Action	**Name**
Remove	User: Miguel Arizona
Remove	User: Phil Wein
Remove	Partner User: Edge Communications: Sean Forbes

Figure 8-23. *Share group members*

Let's wrap up the share group discussion by looking at an example. Here's the scenario:

- *Customer Community with two profiles*: WeinCo Customer and MeisterCo Customer

- *Requirement*: Share records owned by users with the WeinCo Customer profile with the following:

  - *Partner user*: R. D. James

  - *Public group*: Super Clique

Figure 8-24 provides a visual of how this share group would work.

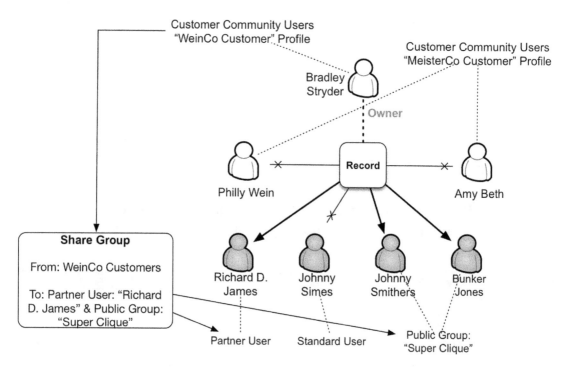

Figure 8-24. *A look at a share group*

Recap

In this chapter, I examined some key considerations for communities that impact security, access, and visibility. While a significant portion of the security model for communities leverages standard Salesforce platform mechanisms (e.g., object/field access), some aspects are specific to communities themselves (e.g., authentication, community membership, sharing sets, share groups, etc.). Make sure to thoroughly review and test your community for security requirements before launching to make sure that all users who need access have appropriate access and any users who should not have access are correspondingly restricted.

CHAPTER 9

Topics in Communities

Topics are quite interesting entities in Salesforce. While they have been around for years, they aren't extensively used in "internal" Salesforce (e.g., classic or Lightning Experience) outside of Chatter. In Chatter, users can associate topics with feed items to tag posts, polls, questions, and more; this helps users to quickly find related discussions. Figure 9-1 shows a view of a Chatter post in the classic and Lightning Experience interfaces.

Figure 9-1. *Topics in classic and Lightning Experience*

In communities, however, topics take on much more central roles in the lives of administrators, community members, and internal users. While not every community leverages discussion-style chatting, topics apply to a number of other areas, including questions, articles, and contextually driven experiences. In this chapter, I will cover the following as related to topics within communities:

- Overview/purpose

- Topic types (standard, navigational, featured)

- Internal versus community topics

- Other considerations for topics within communities

201

© Philip Weinmeister 2018
P. Weinmeister, *Practical Guide to Salesforce Communities*, https://doi.org/10.1007/978-1-4842-3609-3_9

Overview/Purpose of Topics in Communities

As I said in the introduction, topics apply broadly to communities and can serve as a central element in overall community interactions. I like to describe topics as the "glue" in communities because they introduce cohesion between different entities that would otherwise be disparate, disconnected items. Figure 9-2 shows how this happens, conceptually.

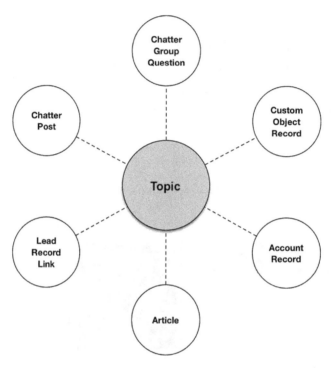

Figure 9-2. *Topics are the "glue" to join unrelated items*

At their core, topics are all about context. As shown in Figure 9-2, it is a topic that allows for a connection between an account and an article, a Chatter group question and a link posted to a lead record, a custom object record and a Chatter post, and so on. For a closer look at how this works, I will need to dive in to the data model.

Topic Data Model

At the center of a fairly simple data model that drives topics sits the Topic Assignment object. The Topic Assignment object is a junction object between the Topic and Target objects (see Figure 9-3).

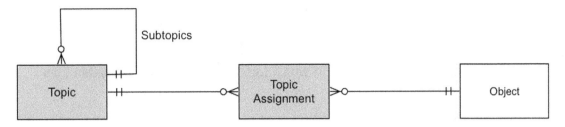

Figure 9-3. *Topic data model*

Let's take this a step further and make it specific with a real-life scenario. A few years ago, I helped to design a Salesforce community for a church. Custom objects were used to capture data such as sermons and church events. In this example, I'll show how topics can be intertwined with that data to create context and useful associations within the community. See Figure 9-4 for a visual representation of the following bullet points:

- Community (online church community/website)

- Topic (grace)

- Objects for which grace-related records exist: Sermon (custom), Event (standard), News (custom)

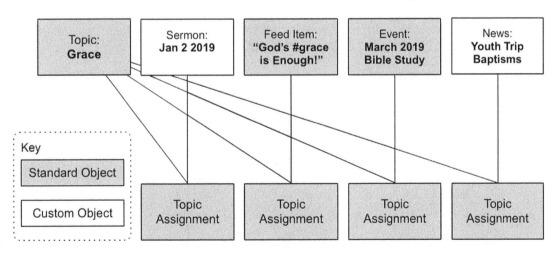

Figure 9-4. *An example of how a topic might be used in an online church community*

Note Topics must be enabled for objects before they can be associated with that object. In the Setup menu, under Topics for Objects, administrators must make sure to enable the objects with which topics will be associated within their communities.

Topic Presentation/UI

Within communities, a dynamic topic page exists that allows for related records (via topic assignments) to be displayed. On this page, two object types are displayed out of the box: discussions (feed items) and knowledge articles. Other object types can be displayed, but custom components are required. Figure 9-5 shows a topic detail page with related records from custom objects (via custom Lightning components), along with a feed item that shares the topic.

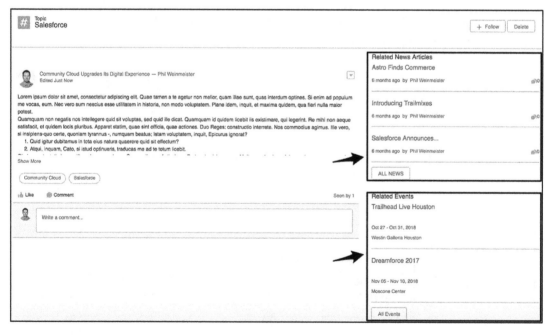

Figure 9-5. *Custom components on a topic page showing related content*

Figure 9-6 shows another example of how topics can be applied. In this instance, topics are used for filtering and categorizing custom records.

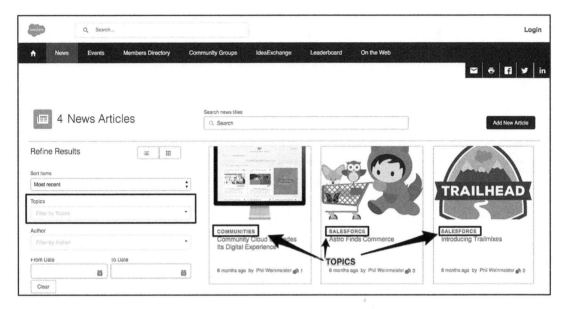

Figure 9-6. *Topics, as featured within custom components*

Topic Types

Within communities, three types of topics exist.

- Standard topics

- Navigational topics

- Featured topics

Each type has a special purpose and a different creation method. I will walk through each.

Standard Topics

Standard topics are really just topics; *standard* is a word I am adding to emphasise that they are not referencing navigational or featured topics. Standard topics are created through the Topic Management section of the Content Targeting workspace, as shown in Figure 9-7.

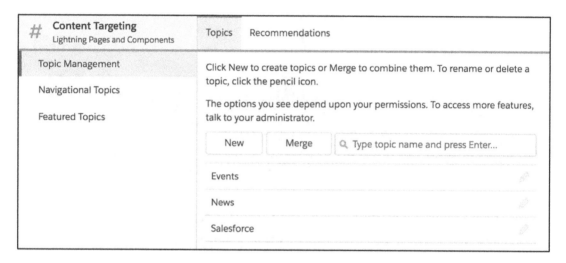

Figure 9-7. *Topic Management menu within content targeting*

Here, administrators can create a new topic or merge topics. For this example, I will create a new topic, as shown in Figure 9-8.

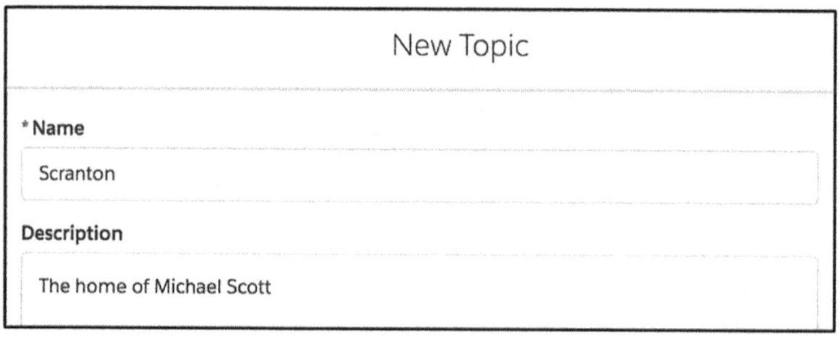

Figure 9-8. *New topic creation*

Creation is fairly straightforward. If an existing topic is too close to the new topic to warrant distinction, the two topics can be merged. In this case, I am going to merge the existing topic Scranton PA with my new topic, Scranton. Any feed item or record with the topic Scranton PA will now show Scranton. See Figure 9-9.

Merge Topics

Enter up to 5 existing topics you want to merge.

Scranton PA

QUICKLY ADD SEVERAL BY USING COMMAS

Merge the selected topics into the following existing topic.

Scranton

Merge   Cancel

Figure 9-9. *Merge Topics page*

Once the new topic is created, I will see it as an option (depending on my permissions) when creating a new feed item. See Figure 9-10.

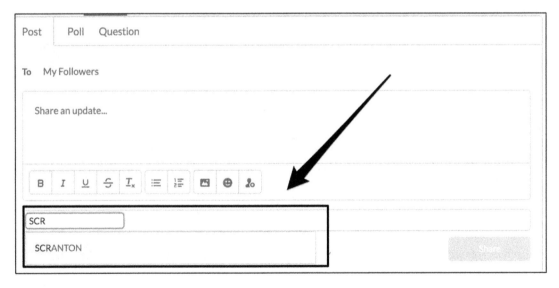

Figure 9-10. *Adding an existing topic to a feed item*

Navigational Topics

Navigational topics have additional, separate purposes on top of what standard topics bring to the table. First, navigational topics are, as one might expect, a part of the navigation menu. The Topics tab is, by default, included in the navigation menu and displays all navigational topics. See Figure 9-11 for an example of a community that has Products and Services as navigational topics.

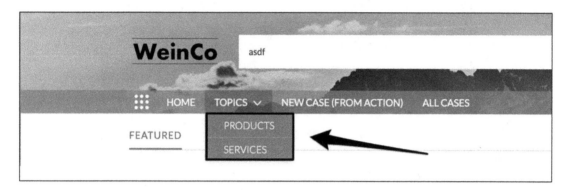

Figure 9-11. *Navigational topics in the navigation menu*

Additionally, when a user searches in a community and can't find what they want, they have the option of "asking the community." See Figure 9-12.

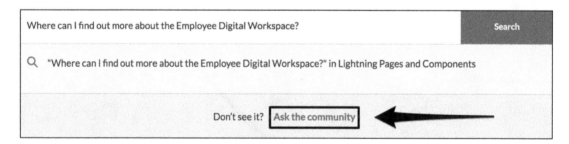

Figure 9-12. *Asking the community will leverage navigational topics*

Upon clicking "Ask the community," the community member will have to select one of the two navigational topics when the question is submitted. See Figure 9-13.

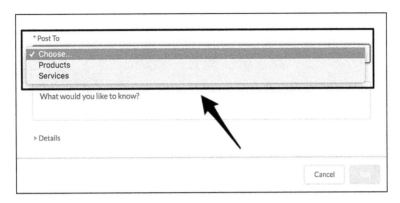

Figure 9-13. *Navigational topics within the ask modal*

With navigational topics, community administrators can configure a different header image to be displayed. Administrators can click to upload an image, as shown in Figure 9-14.

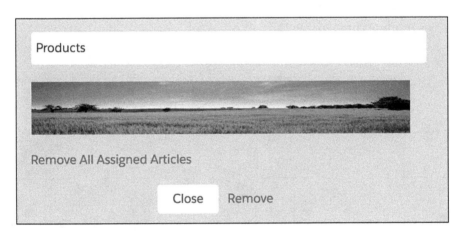

Figure 9-14. *Adding an image to a navigational topic*

Figure 9-15 shows what the updated topic page looks like.

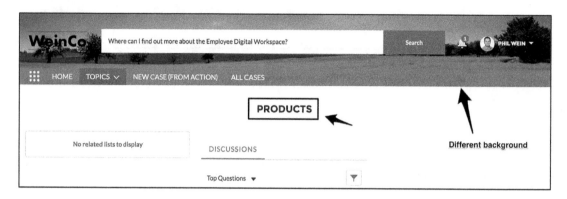

Figure 9-15. *Navigational topic page with a background image*

Navigational topics can go to an even deeper level with subtopics. This allows for a robust navigation experience based on areas of interest or relevance. I've put together an example of what a topic catalog might look like for a company that is building online communities products in Figure 9-16.

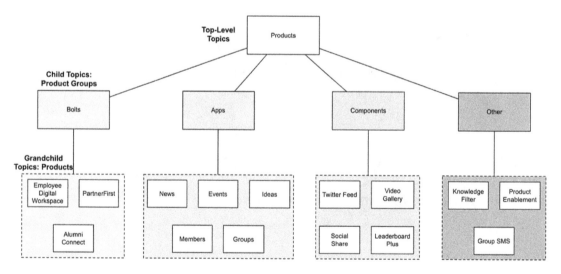

Figure 9-16. *A potential topic catalog design, with subtopics*

By creating subtopics, the overall community experience can be enhanced by guiding community users intuitively. See Figure 9-17 for an example of a topic that has subtopics associated with it.

Figure 9-17. A topic page for a topic that has subtopics

Featured Topics

Featured topics are basically standard topics that are identified or flagged as featured. Once identified as featured, they can be dynamically showcased to community members to promote collaboration or interaction around those particular topics. To create a featured topic, an admin must first create a standard or navigation topic. See Figure 9-18 for an overview of topic creation prerequisites and dependencies.

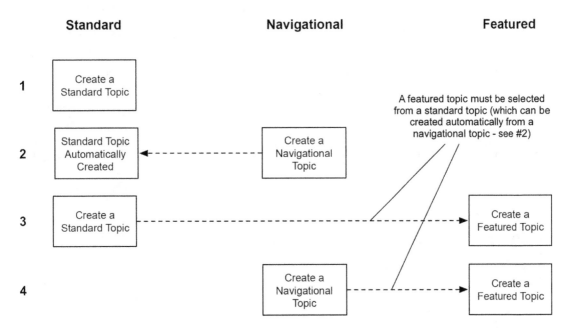

Figure 9-18. An overview of topic creation dependencies and prerequisites

Once a topic exists, it can be selected on the Featured Topics menu page during the creation process. In Figure 9-19, examples of existing topics are shown when a new featured topic is being configured.

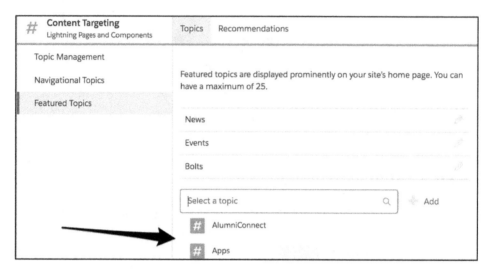

Figure 9-19. *Examples of existing topics when a new featured topic is being configured*

Similar to navigational topics, images can be associated with featured topics. However, instead of an image showing up in a header, it appears in the Featured Topics component that is available within Community Builder. Figure 9-20 shows an example community with three featured topics with one of the three having an image.

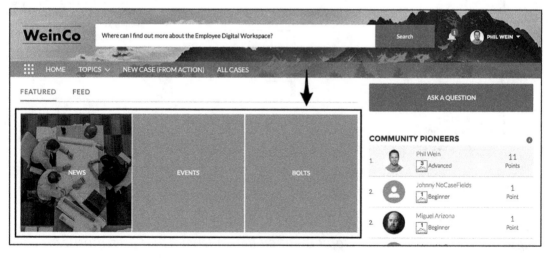

Figure 9-20. *Featured Topics component on the Home page*

Other Topic Areas

A few other areas exist in the world of topics that community administrators need to understand. I will walk through each at a high level.

Internal vs. Community Topics

For communities that expose records, it is important for administrators to understand that a topic applied to a record in classic or Lightning Experience is automatically exposed within a community that shows that record. Each topic assignment (the junction object between the Topic and Target objects) has a NetworkID field. For internal use, this field is blank. However, for a community, this field is populated with the network ID of the community; this creates a unique topic assignment that will not appear in classic or Lightning Experience. Sure, topic assignments can be cloned or duplicated to ensure that the same topics are leveraged across the community and the internal org, but there is nothing out of the box to make that happen.

In Figure 9-21, I provide an example where the same topic of Products is applied an Account record in both a community and the internal org.

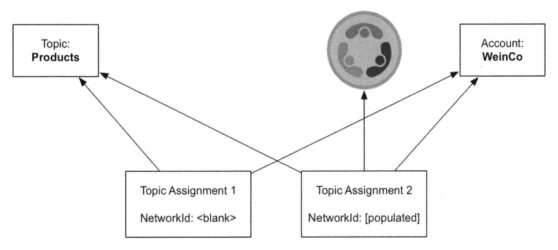

Figure 9-21. *Two topic assignments for the same topic*

Unlisted Chatter Groups

Currently, topics are not supported within unlisted Chatter groups. The Salesforce platform does not currently have a way to handle topics for these ultra-secure collaboration groups that would not potentially expose some data to unauthorized users.

Topics and Articles

Articles and topics overlap within communities quite a bit. I will go into more detail on how topics work with articles in the next chapter.

Management within Community Builder

There is an option to directly access Community Builder. Navigate to Settings (via the tabs on the left), click General, and scroll down. See Figure 9-22.

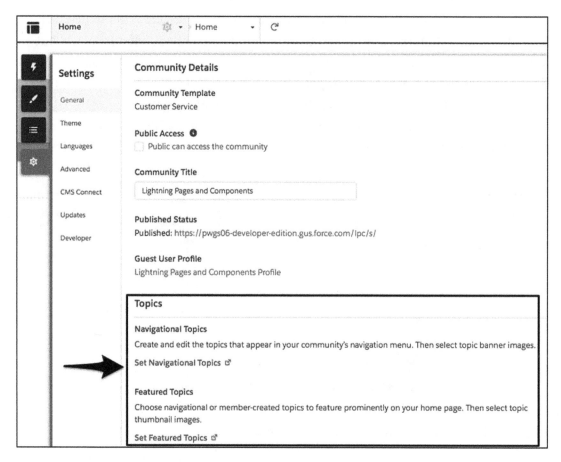

Figure 9-22. *Managing topics from Community Builder*

Recap

In this chapter, I focused on topics within communities and how they can be leveraged to enhance the community user experience. I dove into some of the nuances around topics that are critical for administrators to understand when managing a Salesforce community and explained the different types of topics—standard, navigational, and featured—and their purposes.

CHAPTER 10

Community Knowledge (Articles)

Since the inception of Community Cloud, Salesforce Knowledge has been a cornerstone in many of the communities that have been built on the Salesforce platform. Whether for customers looking for self-service troubleshooting help, partners needing documentation on a process, or employees seeking information on release notes for their own product, knowledge articles have often been the means to provide relevant information to community members.

For those who have managed an internal knowledge base in classic or Lightning Experience, much can be reapplied to communities. However, it is important to understand that articles do boast some community-specific functionality and capabilities (mostly around topics). In addition to covering those items, I will walk through the Salesforce Knowledge prerequisites and basic setup/administration to help developers, administrators, and managers get up and running with Salesforce Knowledge in their communities.

Prerequisites and General Setup

Before a community manager can work with Knowledge in a community, certain prerequisites must be satisfied, and Knowledge must be properly configured.

Licensing/Permissions

The first step in setting up Knowledge for communities is obtaining one or more Knowledge licenses for the org that houses the corresponding community. The Company Information section (in the Setup menu) shows the number of licenses for the org under Feature Licenses. See Figure 10-1.

217

© Philip Weinmeister 2018
P. Weinmeister, *Practical Guide to Salesforce Communities*, https://doi.org/10.1007/978-1-4842-3609-3_10

Feature Licenses				Feature Licenses Help ?
Feature Type	Status	Total Licenses	Used Licenses	Remaining Licenses
Marketing User	Active	2	1	1
Apex Mobile User	Active	2	1	1
Offline User	Active	2	1	1
Knowledge User	Active	2	1	1
Service Cloud User	Active	2	1	1

Figure 10-1. *A Knowledge User license must be available for Knowledge to be enabled*

Once a Knowledge User license is provisioned, it must be applied to a specific user. Navigate to a user record and select the Knowledge User checkbox to allow a user to manage Knowledge. See Figure 10-2.

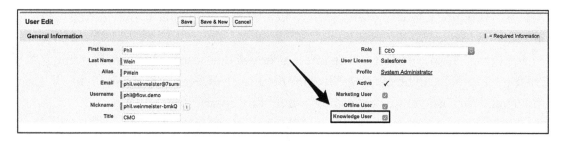

Figure 10-2. *A user who will manage Knowledge articles in any way (i.e., not simply viewing the articles) will require a Knowledge User license*

Once a user has been granted the Knowledge User license, the user can access the Knowledge-related settings within the Setup menu. After enabling Knowledge, an administrator will see various settings that can be configured. Those are not specific to communities and should be examined as an organization rolls out Salesforce Knowledge. Figure 10-3 shows a sample of Knowledge settings that are available.

General Settings

✓ Allow users to create and edit articles from the Articles tab

☐ Activate Validation Status field

✓ Allow users to add external multimedia content to HTML in the standard editor

Lightning Knowledge Settings

☐ Enable Lightning Knowledge

☐ Enable automatic loading of rich-text editor when editing an article

Article Summaries

Show article summaries in article list views

☐ Internal App

☐ Customer

☐ Partner

Figure 10-3. Knowledge settings

Lightning Knowledge

It is worth noting that Lightning Knowledge now exists, in addition to the standard/ classic Knowledge that has been available for years. The key difference between standard Knowledge and Lightning Knowledge is that the former employs article types, while the latter leverages record types (based on one object). See Figure 10-4 for the setting that enables Lightning Knowledge.

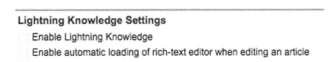

Lightning Knowledge Settings

☐ Enable Lightning Knowledge

☐ Enable automatic loading of rich-text editor when editing an article

Figure 10-4. Lightning Knowledge can be enabled from the standard Knowledge Settings screen

---

Note   It will be assumed that standard/classic Knowledge (not Lightning Knowledge) is used throughout the rest of this chapter.

Knowledge Administration

While not specific to communities, article types and data categories are critical to proper Knowledge administration. I will cover each at a high level to help community managers get the ball rolling.

Article Types

Article types help to distinguish knowledge that is fundamentally different in content and desired presentation. These are some examples of article types:

- FAQ

- Troubleshooting Guide

- Tutorial

- Release Notes

- Product Manual

Each of these could have completely different fields and page layouts; as a result, they are different article types. By default, each org has an article type called Knowledge, which will suffice if only one article type is needed. See Figure 10-5.

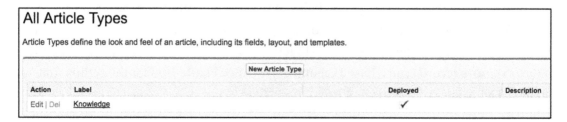

Figure 10-5. *The default Knowledge article type that exists upon enabling Knowledge*

Data Categories

Data categories are also critical within the world of Salesforce Knowledge. To best understand their purpose, it's probably easiest to think of data categories in the context of searching. When one users want to find one or more articles, data categories will help users to categorize, group, or filter article search results. Data categories can be set up hierarchically, with child data categories; Figure 10-6 shows a data category called Location with two subcategories.

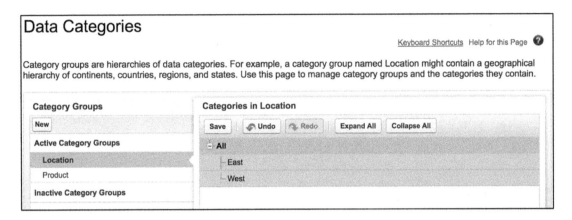

Figure 10-6. *Data category setup menu*

I will use the structure shown in Figure 10-7 for the examples in this chapter. This diagram shows two "top-level" data categories and multiple "child" data categories that roll up to the top-level categories.

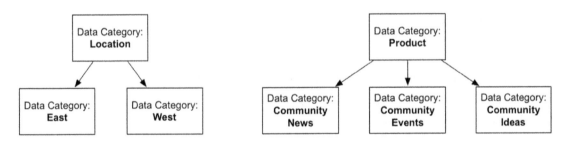

Figure 10-7. *An example of data category setup. Community News, Community Events, and Community Ideas are apps that are available for use within Lightning communities*

Note   Profiles and permission sets can be used to control the visibility of articles based on data categories.

Articles in Communities

A few items must be considered within the context of communities regarding articles.

- Article visibility

- Articles and topics

- Articles in global search (for communities)

Article Visibility

When creating articles, a Knowledge manager or author can associate an article with zero to many channels. A channel determines whether the article is potentially visible at all for a particular group of users. The following are the available channels:

- Internal App

- Public Knowledge Base

- Customers

- Partners

Regardless of the permissions of users in these channels, they will not be able to see articles if the corresponding channel is not enabled. In Figure 10-8, an article is set to be visible to customers and partners.

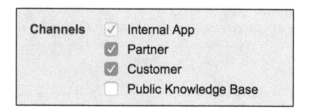

Figure 10-8. *Channels are used to control visibility of articles in communities*

While it may be fairly intuitive, it is critical to note which license types map to the applicable channels. Figure 10-9 shows the association between the two entities.

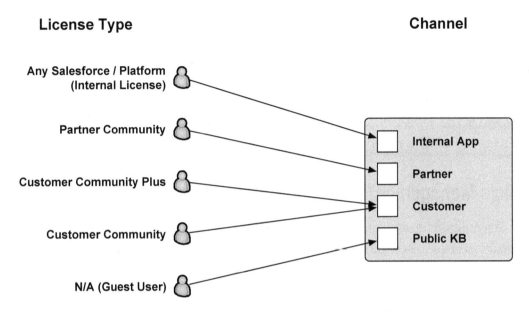

License Type   **Channel**

Figure 10-9. *Mapping of license type to Knowledge channel*

Articles and Topics

A key area for Knowledge managers to be aware of is the interplay between articles and topics. This overlap comes into play a few ways, through standard components and relationships between articles and topics and between data categories and topics.

Topics for Articles

Before topics in communities can be used with articles, topics must be enabled for the applicable article types from the Topics for Objects settings within the Setup menu. Figure 10-10 shows the page from which topics are enabled for articles.

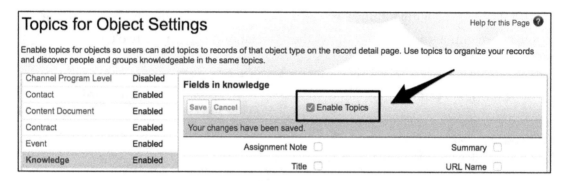

Figure 10-10. *Topics must be enabled on all applicable article types to allow for full usage of articles in a community*

Article Management in Communities

The first method to associate Knowledge articles with community topics is a direct association of an existing article with an existing topic. Figure 10-11 provides a view of what happens from a data model/schema perspective.

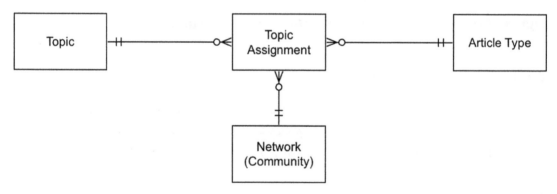

Figure 10-11. *Data model of articles and topics within communities*

Within the Content Targeting workspace, the Article Management menu allows articles to be selected for topic assignment. See Figure 10-12. In this example, an article is associated with three related topics.

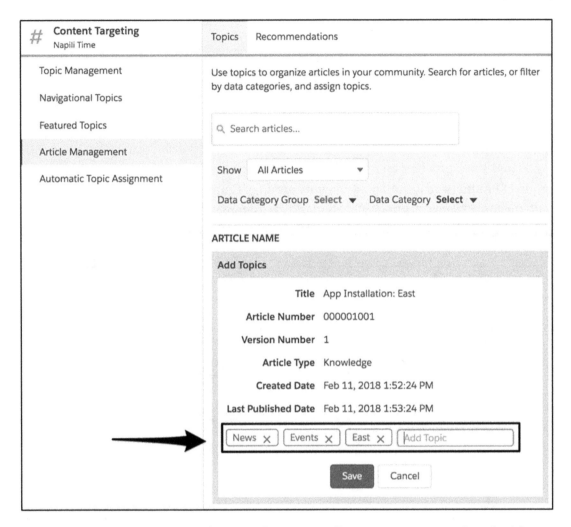

Figure 10-12. *Here, an article named App Installation: East is associated with three topics: News, Events, and East*

Note   While this feature absolutely has value in some scenarios, direct association of topics with articles is not dynamic and will require manual administration for any changes to corresponding topics.

Automatic Topic Assignment

A relatively new capability that is extremely handy is the ability to automatically associate topics with articles. This is done by identifying one or more topics that should be assigned to topics based on a data category. The function can apply to existing articles and will automatically associate any newly created article that has the applicable data category with the selected topics.

Figure 10-13 provides an example. Here, all articles with a parent data category group of Product and a child data category group of Community Events are associated with the topic Events. Additionally, the "Add above topic(s) to all existing articles in the data category" setting means that any existing articles will be updated.

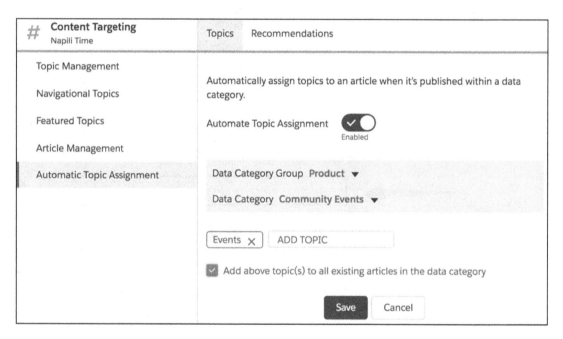

Figure 10-13. *Articles in communities can automatically be associated with topics, based on article data categories*

Article Display

Once everything is set up, a community manager can enjoy the display of articles related to a topic from a topic detail page. In Figure 10-14, two articles are dynamically listed on the topic detail page for the News topic.

Figure 10-14. *A topic page showing two related articles, based on associated topic*

Articles in Global Search

By default, articles that are exposed in the community will appear in the type-ahead results in the global search from the standard header. See Figure 10-15.

Figure 10-15. *Articles will show up in the global search type-ahead results by default*

The default setting is typically recommended, but there may be scenarios where an administrator wants to hide those results. To do so, access the property editor settings for the component and click the X next to Articles in the Objects in Autocomplete Results section. See Figure 10-16.

Figure 10-16. *Articles can be removed from autocomplete results*

Similarly, articles can be repositioned on the full search results page. However, this is a different setting. This can be accessed on the search page in Community Builder by clicking the Global Search Result component and modifying the appropriate settings in the property editor. See Figure 10-17.

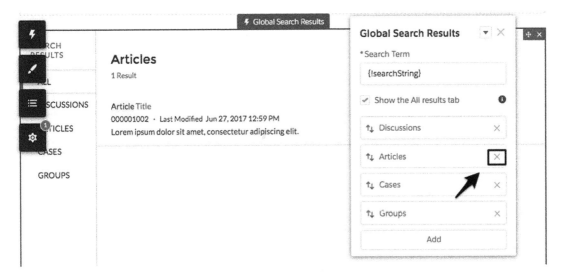

Figure 10-17. *Removing articles from the search results page*

Recap

Salesforce Knowledge is a large, platform-spanning topic. A plethora of documentation exists to help users become experts in Knowledge. In this chapter, I strictly focused on the intersection of articles and communities. I covered the basics of Knowledge setup, walking through prerequisites and "core" Knowledge administration (article types and data categories). Additionally, I dove into community-specific areas of Knowledge, including channels, topics for objects, article management, and automatic topic assignment.

CHAPTER 11

Process Automation in Communities

There is significant power and value to be found within the world of Salesforce communities that isn't necessarily obvious to those who see Community Cloud as an isolated, stand-alone product or are relatively new to Salesforce overall. It lies in the platform, whose inception came almost 15 years before communities were born and has been rapidly expanding with new features and capabilities ever since. Much of what has been discussed in this book so far has focused on community-specific functionality. However, in my opinion, one of the most exciting areas for communities lies in the intersection between declarative community-building capabilities and innovative business process automation (BPA).

Salesforce offers three BPA tools: Workflow, Flow (also known as *visual workflow*), and Process Builder. While there are few community-specific elements among these three tools, all three have notable potential overlap with communities. Figure 11-1 shows a diagram similar to the one from Chapter 1 detailing the overlap between the Salesforce "clouds." This diagram shows the overlap found in Salesforce BPA tools with communities.

© Philip Weinmeister 2018
P. Weinmeister, *Practical Guide to Salesforce Communities*, https://doi.org/10.1007/978-1-4842-3609-3_11

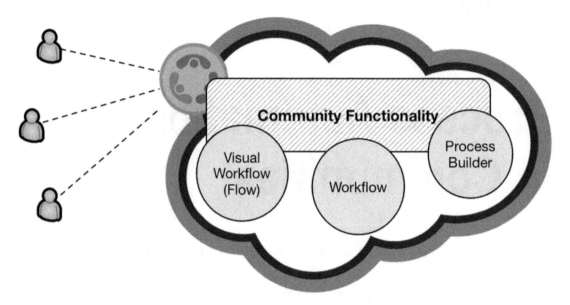

Figure 11-1. *A large amount of Salesforce community functionality can be automated with platform tools*

In this chapter, I will look at this overlap, giving guidance on how to leverage each tool and providing specific examples with each tool.

Note   This chapter is not intended to provide comprehensive instruction on Flow, Workflow, and Process Builder for individuals not already familiar with those tools. For detailed guidance on Workflow, readers can reference my first book on Salesforce, *Practical Salesforce.com Development Without Code.* For in-depth information about Process Builder and Flow, see *Salesforce.com Lightning Process Builder and Visual Workflow.* Both books are available at www.apress.com and www.amazon.com.

Workflow

While it no longer receives noteworthy enhancements and definitely isn't the sexiest application available to administrators, Workflow is the oldest and most predictable of the BPA tools on the Salesforce platform. By "predictable," I mean just that— admins know what they are going to get when they use it. The premise of Workflow is straightforward; certain actions can be automated based on the creation of or update to a record of a particular object. Workflow can trigger four types of actions, but two most directly apply to Salesforce communities: sending email and updating fields. Since many field update scenarios can be addressed arguably more comprehensively via Process Builder, I will focus on automated email distribution in this section.

As addressed in Chapter 7, the community Administration page allows some basic configuration of four emails that can be sent to community members based on certain actions: member welcome, forgotten password, reset password, and case comment. However, depending on community context and communication needs, many other types of emails could come into play. Here are a few examples of email automation within communities that clearly add value and efficiency:

- Case creation (community-specific emails)
- Community group membership

Community Case Creation Notification

The first example of a common scenario for communities would be case-related email automation or cases created or modified within a community. In this case, I will show how to create a custom workflow rule for cases created via a community.

The first step is to update the Case Origin field on the Case object to allow the identification of the community as the case's source. See Figure 11-2 for a new picklist value added to Case Origin.

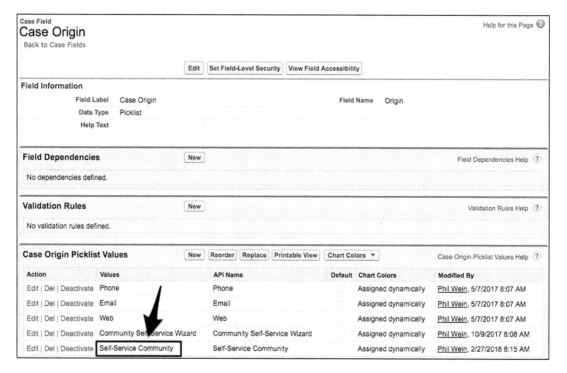

Figure 11-2. Leverage a new case origin picklist value in a community-specific workflow

Once the Case Origin field has been updated, the workflow rule can be created. In this case, the workflow rule will be evaluated upon creation only and will use the Case Origin field and newly added picklist value for the corresponding criteria. See Figure 11-3.

Workflow Rule
Self-Service Community Case Created
« Back to List: Workflow Rules

Help for this Page

Workflow Rule Detail   Edit Delete Clone Activate

Rule Name	Self-Service Community Case Created	Object	Case
Active	☐	Evaluation Criteria	Evaluate the rule when a record is created
Description			
Rule Criteria	Case: Case Origin EQUALS Self-Service Community		
Created By	Phil Wein, 2/27/2018 8:19 AM	Modified By	Phil Wein, 2/27/2018 8:19 AM

Workflow Actions   Edit

Immediate Workflow Actions

Type	Description
Email Alert	Send Case Creation Email for Community

Figure 11-3. *A workflow rule to be used within a community*

For the related actions, I create a new email alert that sends the actual email to the creator of the case. Figure 11-4 shows an overview of the process.

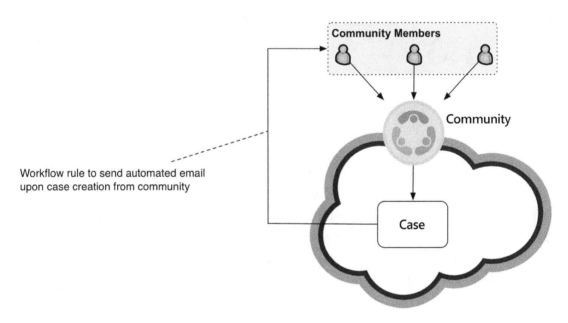

Figure 11-4. *Overview of the community-related email scenario being automated*

Note   When adding email automation, it is important to step back and assess the entire suite of emails that are being automated to ensure that existing automation does not duplicate an alert. In this case, a duplicate would cause two alerts to go out to the Contact (creator) of the Case record, which is obviously not ideal.

Community Group Membership Notification

The first example of a common scenario for communities involves membership within a Chatter group. In this case, I will create a custom workflow rule associated with new members within community groups. Figure 11-5 provides an overview.

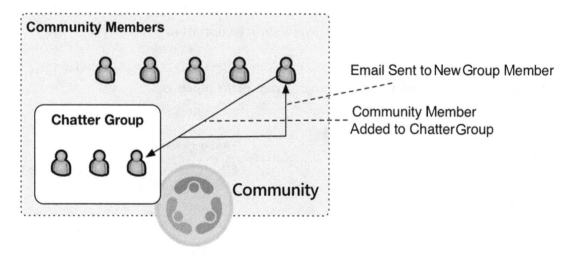

Figure 11-5. *A basic community process that can be automated*

The first step is to determine whether the email should be community-specific or generic across all communities within the org. Figure 11-6 shows the setup for one community, and Figure 11-7 shows how a more generic workflow rule should be structured. The difference is the Network field; either it needs to contain a specific record ID or needs to be simply be populated.

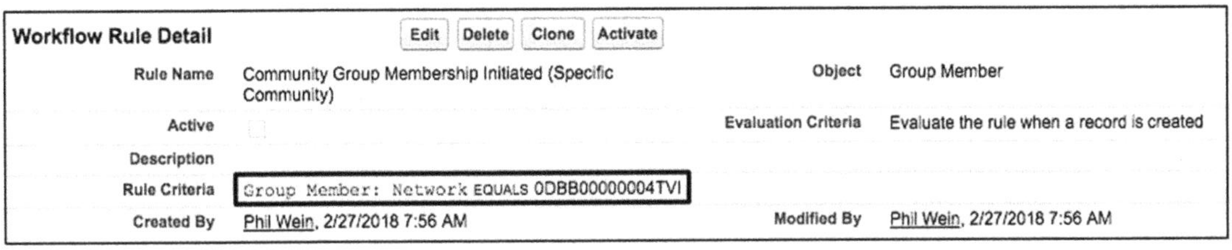

Figure 11-6. *Here the rule looks at a specific network (community)*

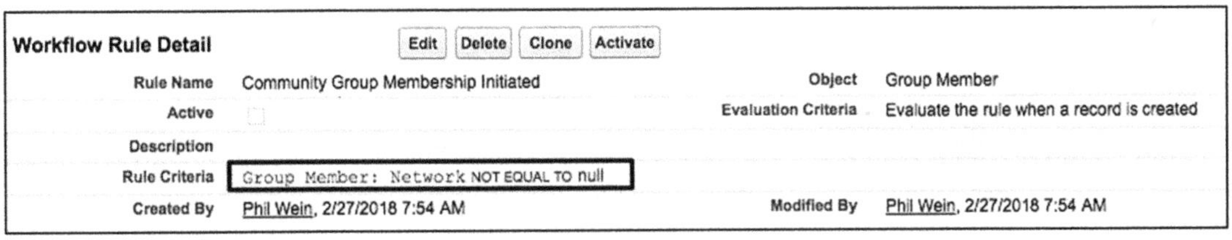

Figure 11-7. *Here the rule looks for any value in the network field*

In this scenario, the workflow rule will be evaluated upon creation only (i.e., not upon the update of an existing record) and will use the network (community) field for the corresponding criteria. In Figure 11-6, the workflow rule is "scoped" to a single community; in Figure 11-7, all communities are impacted.

For the related actions, a variety of activities could be performed. In this case, I created a new email alert that sends an email to the community member who just joined the applicable Chatter group.

Note In the example shown in Figures 11-6 and 11-7, a Salesforce record ID is "hard-coded." It is generally discouraged to include a Salesforce record ID as criteria or in a formula, as it means that the criteria may no longer be valid in a different org (in which the network ID could vary). Here we do not have a choice without further customization since fields cannot be modified or added to the Group Member object.

Process Builder

Process Builder is the newest of the process automation tools on the platform, and it was met with widespread acclaim among administrators and business analysts. I would propose that the reasoning behind this fan following is threefold.

- An intuitive, visual interface (see Figure 11-8)

- Significantly expanded capabilities beyond those of Workflow (see Figure 11-9)

- Power without requiring any knowledge or use of code

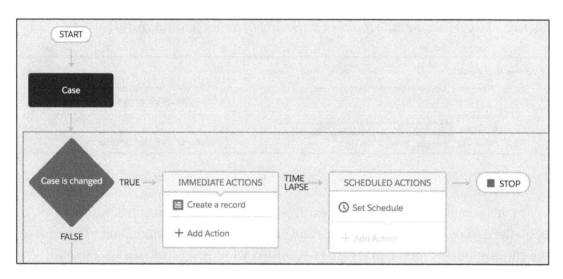

Figure 11-8. *Process Builder's user interface*

Action	Available in Workflow?	Available in Process Builder?
Apex	No	Yes
Create a Record	Partial	Yes
Email Alerts	Yes	Yes
Flows	No	Yes
Post to Chatter	No	Yes
Quick Actions	No	Yes
Submit for Approval	No	Yes
Update Records	Partial	Yes
Call a Process	No	Yes
Outbound Messaging	Yes	No

Figure 11-9. *A side-by-side comparison of Workflow versus Process Builder functionality*

At this time, there are no community-specific aspects built into Process Builder, but it's fairly straightforward to create a process from the tool that is specific to a community. I will look at a few automation scenarios for communities that can benefit from the power of Process Builder.

New Community Member Actions

The addition of a new community member is a big deal, as they are the lifeblood of a community. Many times, it's important to internal employees to know who these new members are, but they might not necessarily want to visit the community or navigate to a report to see the activity each time. With a public Chatter group in the internal org, posts can be included to let a broad audience know about these community newcomers.

The first step is to create a Chatter group in an internal org to which the new member notifications will be posted; see Figure 11-10 for an example group.

Figure 11-10. *Internal Chatter group to be used in the Process Builder example*

Next, I will create the process and include basic setup information. See Figure 11-11.

New Process

Process Name *	API Name * ⓘ
New Member Alert for Employees	New_Member_Alert_for_Employees

Description

This group will inform internal employees of new community members.

The process starts when *

A record changes ▼

Figure 11-11. *Basic information for new member alert*

Next, I will identify the object that will be initially evaluated to run the process. This object will be Network Member, which exists for all community members within an org; see Figure 11-12 for object setup details.

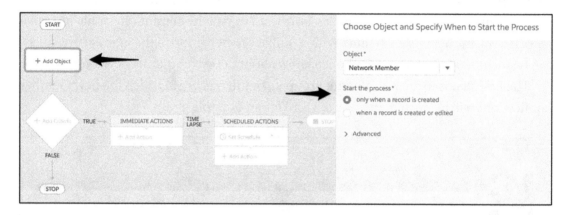

Figure 11-12. *Network Member will be the object to be used in the process*

Once the object is identified, I establish the criteria to determine whether an action will fire. In this case, I considered the following for the criteria:

- The community is live (NetworkMember.Network.Status = "Published").

- The network member is active (NetworkMember.Member.IsActive = "True").

Figure 11-13 shows the necessary criteria as configured.

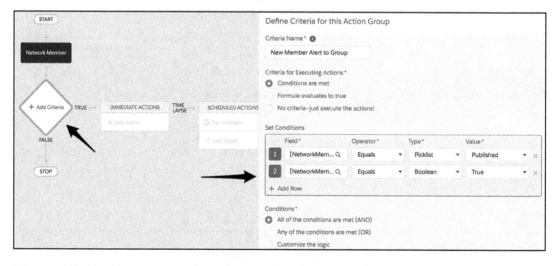

Figure 11-13. *Process criteria to be used in the example*

Once the criteria are set, I may now add an action. In this case, I select the action type Post to Chatter, select Chatter Group (as opposed to a user), and then identify the group and craft my message. See Figure 11-14.

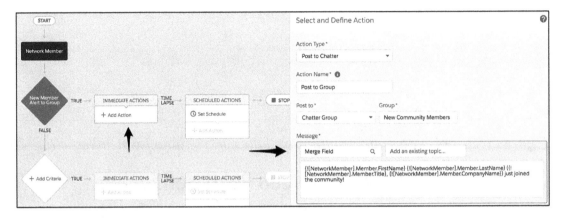

Figure 11-14. *Post to Chatter action within Process Builder*

Once I activate the process, I'm ready to see it in action! First, I navigate to a contact and enable the customer user. See Figure 11-15.

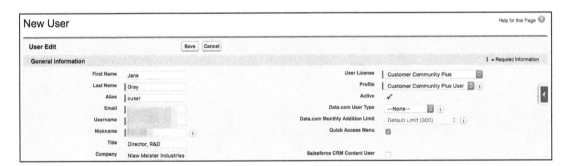

Figure 11-15. *Creation of a new community user to trigger the process*

And...it works! Take a look at Figure 11-16.

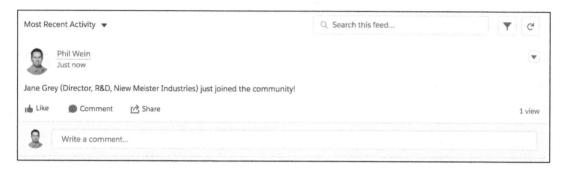

Figure 11-16. *A Chatter post resulting from the new community member*

Community Member Reputation Point Notification

Let's continue down the path of driving a flow based on a network or community member. Here I will show how to create a process that automatically updates the user's status as a special "gold" member based on obtaining a certain number of points, but it also notifies them of this change.

I start with Figure 11-17, where the object is identified (Network Member) and the process kickoff is defined (record created or edited).

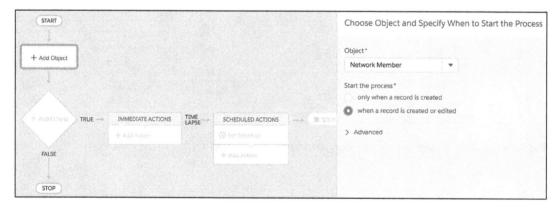

Figure 11-17. *Again, Network Member is used as the object*

Next, I configure simple criteria to look at when the user exceeds 50,000 Chatter reputation points. The field in the conditions box is NetworkMember.ReputationPoints. See Figure 11-18.

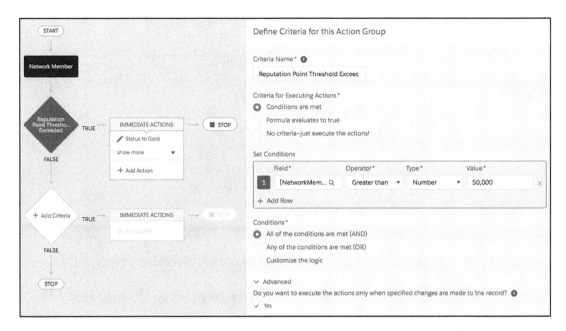

Figure 11-18. *Criteria added: more than 50,000 community members*

Next, I establish the record update action that, I update a custom field on the contact record that is related to the network member. Figure 11-19 shows how to select that record (NetworkMember.User.Contact).

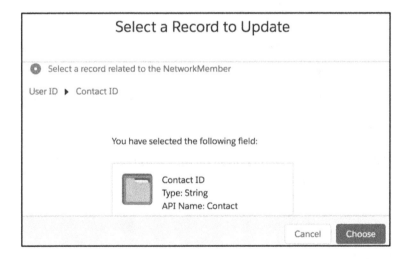

Figure 11-19. *Select the contact record related to the community user record*

In Figure 11-20, I show the corresponding update record action.

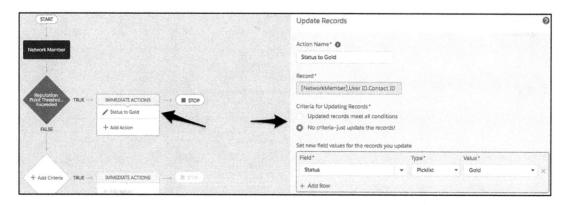

Figure 11-20.   *Update the record action on the network member object*

Once that is done, I add an email action to alert the member, as shown in Figure 11-21.

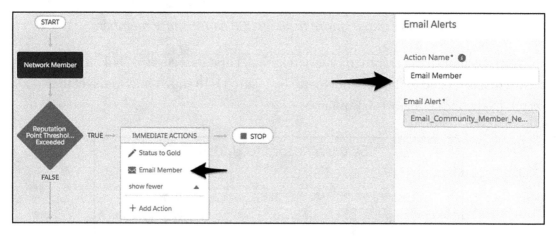

Figure 11-21.   *Email an alert to notify the community member*

After activation, it's time to try this. Once Jane hit her 50,000 points, I pulled up her contact record. See Figure 11-22 for the result. Spoiler alert…it worked!

Figure 11-22. *The community member's status was updated to "gold"*

Other Examples/General Approach

In general, the suggested approach here is to focus on a change that happens in or as a result of the community and then drive the automated actions from that. The following are a few more ways to leverage Process Builder within communities.

Case Notification Automation

Follow these steps:

1. Add a new picklist value for the Case Origin field that is specific to the community.

2. Create a global action for the Case object and prepopulate the case origin with the Case Origin value that was created for the community.

3. Create a process that looks at the Case object and, specifically, the Case Origin field value for the new value that was added. Configure the desired action.

4. Drop the global action into the community (this can be done directly from the navigation menu).

5. Success! A case created with the custom action in this community will automatically kick off the process.

Custom Object Automation

Follow these steps:

1. Create a field on the custom object called NetworkID that takes in the Salesforce record ID of the related community in which the record was created.

2. Ensure that the NetworkID field is set properly through configuration or code whenever a record is created in that community.

3. Create a process that looks at the custom object and, specifically, the NetworkID field for a specific value. Associate some actions with the process.

4. Success! A record of the specific object that is created and/or modified and meets the criteria will trigger the process actions.

Flow

Flow, also known as *visual workflow*, is by far the most powerful of the available tools to automate business processes on the Salesforce platform. And, as of the Winter '18 release, it is available in Lightning communities without the use of code.

So, what makes Flow so useful? Sure, there are aspects like dynamic picklists based on record values, looping capabilities, and decision points. In my opinion, more than anything else, it's the Flow screens that set this tool apart. At least as of Summer '18, Process Builder has no concept of screens or screen interaction; with Process Builder, it's all about the data. However, with Flow, an administrator or developer can construct a multiscreen, automated process flow that handles user interaction, user interface details, and all the back-end logic.

In the Winter '18 release, the Lightning Flow component was introduced to both Lightning Experience and Lightning communities. Spring '18 followed soon after with the capability of embedding a Lightning component into a flow. By combining these major enhancements, admins can deliver a powerful flow within a Lightning community and, if the custom component already exists, do so without code. I would like to share a few example of flows I've built for communities that highlight the value of Lightning Flow.

Warranty Status Check

Many organizations leverage Salesforce as the system of interaction for customer support related to a particular product. One scenario that Flow handles beautifully is user interaction to drive a simple query, followed by displaying the resulting information. A warranty status check scenario is great to highlight how this works.

Here's the scenario: An organization tracks purchase info by serial number but doesn't offer a full order history for all customers. As a result, customers call in quite a bit to find out whether their product is covered. The organization wants to deflect some of these calls and let customers find out about coverage themselves. The organization uses all standard objects, including Product and Asset. Figure 11-23 shows the flow itself as a reference.

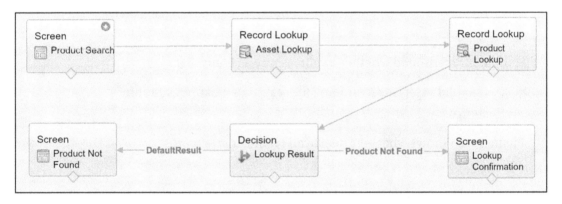

Figure 11-23. *Warranty status check flow*

The first step is allowing a user to provide a serial number to look up an asset. See Figure 11-24.

> **Check Your Warranty Status**
>
> Please enter the serial number of your product in the field below. This will be a 10-12 character string of letters and numbers.
>
> *Product S/N
>
> [   ]
>
> [Next]

Figure 11-24. *Initial screen, where customers enter a serial number*

The user will then enter a serial number. See Figure 11-25.

Figure 11-25. *The serial number will be queried to see whether the warranty is still valid*

Once the data is submitted, a few things occur:

1. An asset lookup occurs to determine whether there is any record of the asset itself.

2. A product lookup occurs based on the product referenced on the asset to grab additional info about the product (e.g., product image).

3. It is determined whether a valid asset was identified.

4. If a valid asset was identified, the warranty lookup results are shown.

Figure 11-26 shows what gets displayed on the final screen.

Figure 11-26. Warranty status check results

What if the product is not found? Then a different screen is shown, as displayed in Figure 11-27.

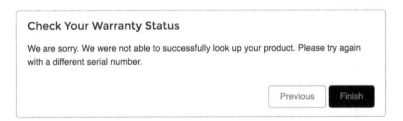

Figure 11-27. Information shown if an asset is not found

Community Engagement Wizard

The process of "activating" a new community member is key for adoption and long-term success. It's great to have a bunch of people initially access a community, but the real key is whether they continue to come back and get value out of it on an ongoing basis.

To help with this, I created a Community Engagement flow to assist new users after first joining a community. They might want to know what they should do, where they should explore, or who they should chat with. This flow covers those bases by providing a guided wizard for onboarding. First, take a look at the overall Flow component in Figure 11-28.

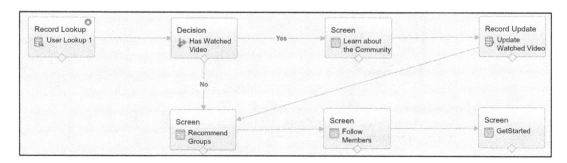

Figure 11-28. *Community engagement wizard flow*

Note   It's important to understand that this example is fundamentally different from the first (warranty status check) because I am using Lightning components embedded in my flow. I am not going to dive into Lightning component development in this book, so it is assumed that you could have these components built or would have one or more custom components to work with already to make this flow a reality.

On the first screen, I welcome users and help introduce them to the community and the company by displaying a related video. This is done via a Lightning component that shows a configured video from YouTube or Vimeo in the middle of the Flow screen. Members can communicate that they don't want to see the video again next time but can leave the box unchecked, if desired; see Figure 11-29.

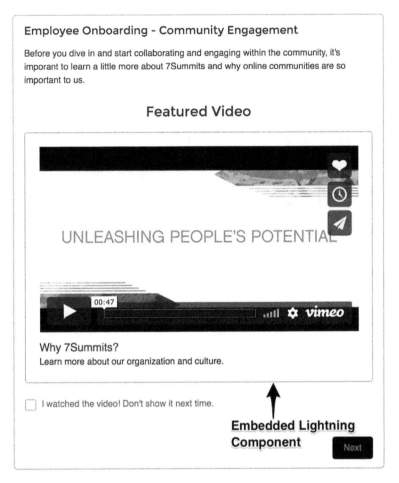

Figure 11-29. *First screen of the community engagement wizard flow*

On the next screen, another Lightning component is used, this time to introduce the new member to various Chatter groups in the community. With just a click, the new member can join a group, which will immediately result in that individual receiving a regular email digest from the group (and increasing the likelihood of a successful activation). See Figure 11-30.

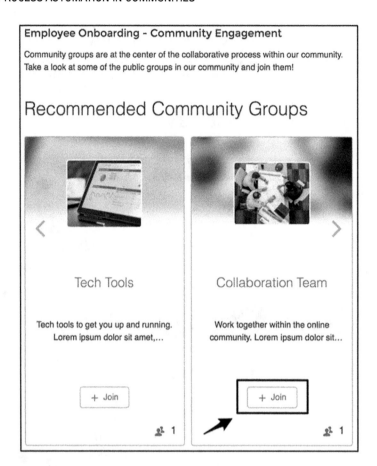

Figure 11-30. *The second screen of the community engagement wizard allows users to join existing Chatter groups*

Next, I move the member to look at other members of the community who are active and seen as influencers. With one click, members can follow those individuals. See Figure 11-31.

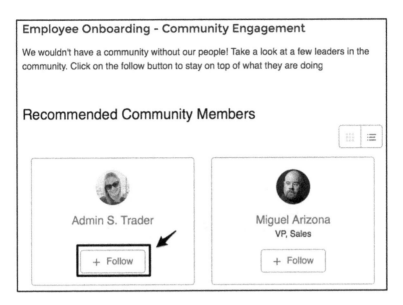

Figure 11-31. *The third screen of the onboarding wizard suggests popular community members to follow*

Once that's done, the member is equipped and ready to hit the ground running! See Figure 11-32.

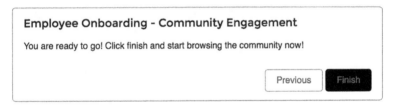

Figure 11-32. *Final screen of the community engagement wizard flow*

Placement of Lightning Flows in Communities

Building a flow is the first step, but an administrator will still need to place the flow somewhere within a community. I'll walk through this process and show how easy it is to enable a community with the Flow component.

Everything starts in Community Builder. An admin will take the Flow Lightning component and drop it where they want it on the page. See Figure 11-33.

Figure 11-33. *Drop the Flow component onto a Lightning page*

Once the Flow component is dropped onto the page, a few options become visible; see Figure 11-34.

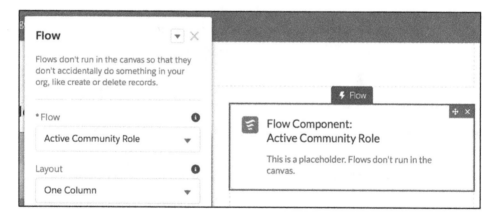

Figure 11-34. *Once placed, the property editor becomes available*

Once the component is in place, a flow needs to be selected. In this case, the Employee Onboarding - Community Engagement flow is the desired choice. Figure 11-35 shows the component once a flow has been selected.

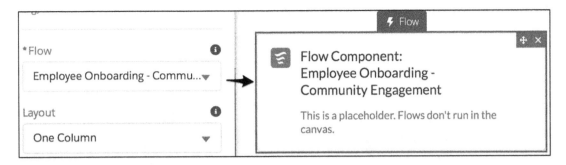

Figure 11-35. *Select the appropriate flow from the property editor*

When a component is selected, optional input values may appear in the property editor. This all depends on how the flow itself is built. See Figure 11-36; the selected component has an optional input called CurrentMembershipStatus.

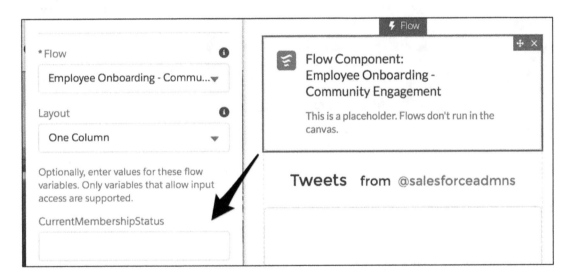

Figure 11-36. *Selecting a flow potentially opens up new configuration settings*

Note   The one-column and two-column layouts do have some application, lending themselves to narrow and wide page sections, respectively. However, administrators and developers should know that there is no control over which fields display in which column when using the two-column layout, sometimes causing less-than-desirable UX. Always test first.

Once the flow is in place, it's time to publish the community and see the results. Figure 11-37 shows how everything looks with a Lightning flow positioned, configured, and published in a Lightning community.

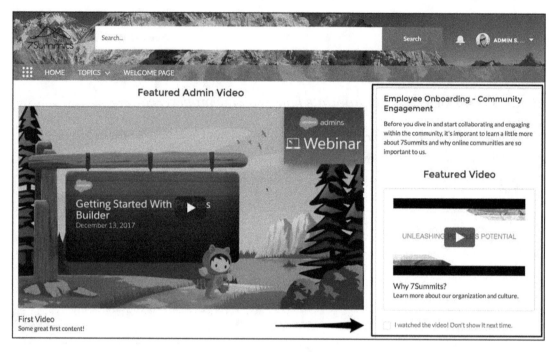

Figure 11-37. *The community engagement wizard in action*

Paused Flows

As of the Summer '18 release, an additional flow-related component called Paused Flows is available in Lightning communities. This component will display flows that are paused by community members. Members can pause, view, and resume flows via this component, while service agents can resume or delete the flows, as well. See Figure 11-38.

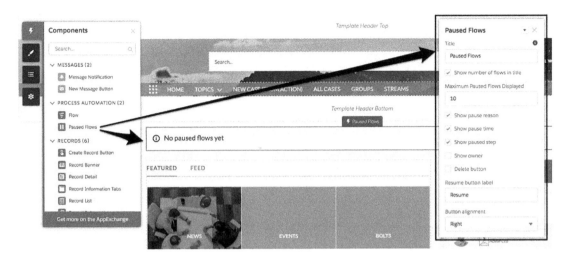

Figure 11-38. *The Paused Flows component*

Recap

In this chapter, I covered the world of business process automation on the Salesforce platform and explored the relevance to communities. I walked through Workflow, Process Builder, and Flow, providing use cases that could appropriately be met by each and then providing a lower level of detail to explain how the automation can be developed (without code). This area of the platform is extremely exciting; I would expect to see even more great capabilities for communities down the road!

CHAPTER 12

Audience Targeting and Personalization

Regardless of whether a community's audience is primarily made up of customers, partners, or employees, its members want to feel like they are known. Often, they desire a personalized experience that is tailored to them, cringing at the idea of a one-size-fits-all site (or even page) that fails to take their purpose and needs into consideration. Enter audience targeting functionality for communities from Salesforce.

In the past, any notion of a personalized experience in a Salesforce community had to be custom; there was just no way around that. Sure, some of the data would be dynamic, but the actual look and feel itself could not vary unless it was buried within Visualforce and Apex, far from the reach of nontechnical resources.

However, all that changed when page variations and audiences were first introduced to Lightning communities. Now, an array of weapons is available to declaratively manage unique experiences for specific community users, empowering administrators, business analysts, and community managers to get more involved and help drive this personalization. In this chapter, I'll cover the following audience targeting topics:

- Audience definition and management

- Branding sets

- Page variations

- Component audiences

© Philip Weinmeister 2018
P. Weinmeister, *Practical Guide to Salesforce Communities*, https://doi.org/10.1007/978-1-4842-3609-3_12

Overview

Before I dive into specific elements of audience targeting, I think it's important to ensure that the concept of personalization is clear. The premise for this chapter lies in the notion that users want to have unique, personalized experiences and the organization that owns the community wants to manage it without enduring an extreme burden in doing so (i.e., they want to avoid a time-consuming change that requires extremely technical resources). At the end of the day, it's as simple as what is shown in Figure 12-1; what one user sees may differ from what another sees.

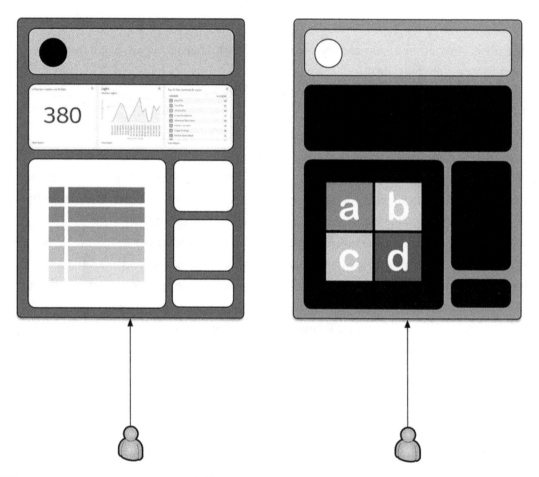

Figure 12-1. *Two users, two different experiences*

Everyone understands the basic concept of unique experiences; one can simply navigate to two different websites. However, there is much more to consider. First, the multiple experiences I am talking about within Community Cloud occur within the same site and sometimes even the page or same component. Additionally, the maintenance/management piece makes this scenario typically very tricky. With Salesforce communities, administrators can set up a community to provide personalization without using code or making frequent changes to keep everything functioning properly.

Figure 12-2 goes a bit deeper. In this example, I show an example of how a community page is represented to two unique audiences (differentiated by authentication) differently. The page contains additional content and is branded for the customer, while the guest version has a subset of the page content and is shown generically.

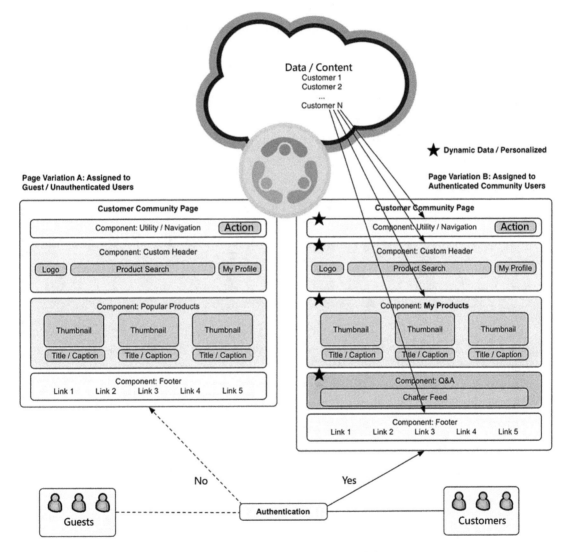

Figure 12-2. *Different audience-based experiences of the same page*

Audiences

Audience targeting within online communities is essentially a definition of *who* and *what*, as applied to a visual and functional experience. The first area to examine when one is looking at audience targeting is the *who*, or the audiences themselves. Fortunately for community administrators, Salesforce has created a logical system that allows for central management of audiences and application of experiences to those audiences.

Note   Audiences for audience targeting within Salesforce communities are completely separate from and not related to community "recommendation audiences" in any way.

The first priority when tackling audiences is to clearly understand the concept. At its most basic level, a community audience is simply the identification of a group of individuals that may be accessing the community. Figure 12-3 shows a simple example of two different audiences.

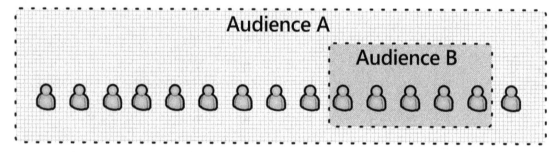

Figure 12-3.   *Audiences can overlap. In this case, Audience B is a subset of Audience A*

After seeing Figure 12-2, the critical question must be asked: how is each audience constructed/defined? Within Salesforce communities, as of Summer '18, audiences can be defined by using one or more of the following as criteria:

- Profile
- Location
- Domain

- User (fields; includes related objects)

- Record type (this is considered advanced)

Profile

One or more profiles can be assigned to an audience. See Figure 12-4 for a view of an audience with two selected profiles; note the drop-down list from which additional profiles can be selected.

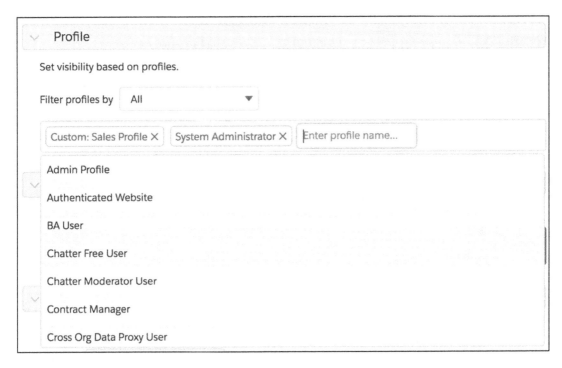

Figure 12-4. *Profiles can be added to an audience*

To expedite the profile search, profiles can be filtered; see Figure 12-5.

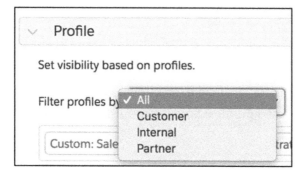

Figure 12-5. *Group profiles by type to find the desired profile faster*

Location

Locations can be added to an audience, as well. A location is a user's physical location, determined by his or her IP address. An administrator can start to type in a city, state/subdivision, or country and select from a displayed list of results. See Figure 12-6 for example of the search.

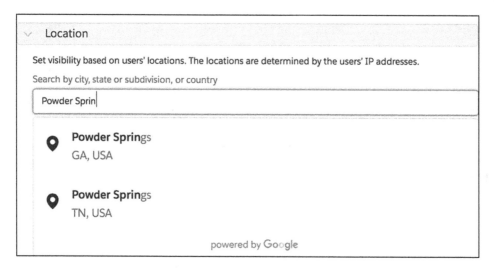

Figure 12-6. *Type-ahead feature to find city, state/subdivision, or country as a location within an audience*

Once all locations are selected, the list will be displayed below the search (and to the right, as well, as part of the overall summary). See Figure 12-7.

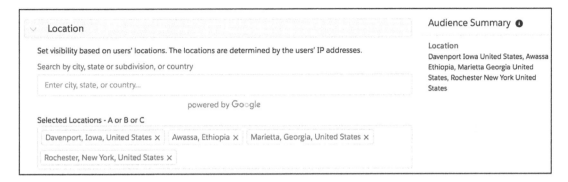

Figure 12-7. *Selected audience locations*

Domain

While not the most commonly applied criteria type, a domain can be valuable as a means to define an audience. Through the standard Salesforce setup, organizations can establish custom domains. Let's say an organization (WeinCo Industries) sets up the following domains for its partners:

- partner1.weinco-industries.com

- partner2.weinco-industries.com

- partner3.weinco-industries.com

These domains can then be used as part of the overall audience criteria definition to target users based on the domain they are accessing.

User Object

Of course, profile and location have clear applications when it comes to audience targeting. However, the power and flexibility of the User object as audience criteria must not be ignored. While the scope of profile and location is extremely straightforward (and limited), the User object opens up limitless options for audience definition. Community administrators can leverage any text or picklist field of the following as part of the User object:

- User object

- Contact

- Account

- Profile

- Manager

- Profile

- Role

- Many more standard lookups through the previous objects

- Other custom lookups

Note   The Contact and Account objects are identified via a lookup on a community member's user record (User.Contact.Account).

One subtle detail that requires the attention of every community builder is that custom fields can be used. That means an administrator can create a custom picklist and use that to define an audience. The administrator could even allow a user to update the field him or herself! Translation: with this functionality, a community could be configured to allow a user to change his or own experience by giving a user access to a custom field that impacts the experience.

Figure 12-8 shows the view when creating User object criteria for an audience.

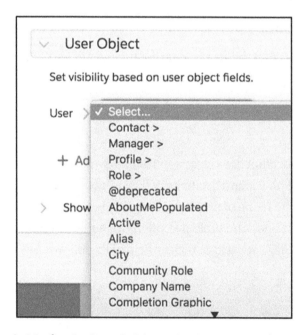

Figure 12-8.   *User fields (including fields on lookup objects) can be added to an audience*

See Figure 12-9 for an audience with multiple criteria related to the User object, two based on object lookups.

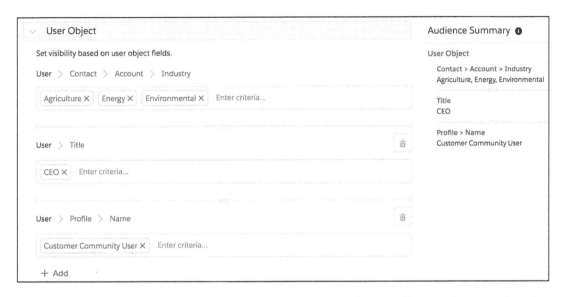

Figure 12-9. *This audience includes multiple fields from different objects related to (and including) the User object*

Record Type

A final criteria type that can be used to determine an audience is record type. An administrator can define an object-specific record type to drive visibility for the audience. See Figure 12-10 for a view of the configuration process for the Email Send object.

RECORD TYPE
Set visibility based on record types.

Object   Email Send   ▼

Enter record type...

Queued Send Definition

Send Definition

Trackable Send Definition

Figure 12-10. *Adding a record type to an audience*

Why are record types considered advanced? They are inherently different from other audience criteria. Other audience criteria simply defines the *who*; the record type inclusion also contributes to the *what*. In the example in Figure 12-11, two different audiences each have a record type. This audience may impact the look, feel, and content of the page, just like all other audiences. However, because of record type, the page layout is impacted, as well.

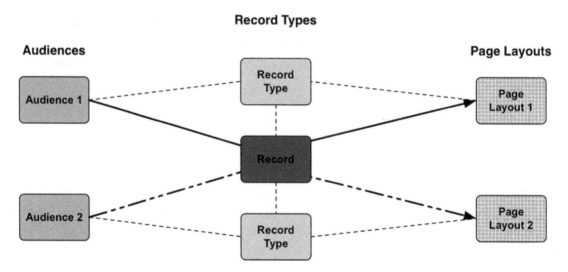

Figure 12-11. *Record types are advanced audience criteria, as they can impact the experience beyond what is possible with other criteria types*

The end result is that an admin can control which fields display for particular users by leveraging audiences with record types (of course, assuming that unique page layouts are properly configured).

Audience Criteria Logic

To make sure the "filter logic" (to use a common declarative phrase on the Salesforce platform) is clear, I want to break down an audience and explain exactly how a user is applied to it. The logic is OR within a specific criterion and AND between criteria. In other words, it looks like this:

- Criteria 1 = (Criteria 1A **OR** Criteria 1B) **AND**

- Criteria 2 = (Criteria 2A **OR** Criteria 2B) **AND**

I will take two hypothetical audiences and four users to bring this concept to life.

- Audience 1

    - User ➤ Title = SVP, EVP, AVP (SVP, EVP, AVP are unique selections)

    - User ➤ Department = Sales, Support (Sales and Support are unique selections)

- Audience 2

    - User ➤ Title = SVP, EVP (SVP and EVP are unique selections)

I'll consider a few users and convey the whether a user is part of the audience or not:

- User 1

    - Title = VP

    - Department = Sales

    - Result: Not in either audience

- User 2

    - Title = SVP

    - Department = Marketing

    - Result: Audience 2

- User 3
  - Title = AVP
  - Department = Marketing
  - Result: Audience 1
- User 4
  - Title = SVP
  - Department = Sales
  - Result: Audience 1 and Audience 2*

Note   *User 4 in the previous example is part of Audience 1 and Audience 2. Which audience applies if each audience is associated with different elements (e.g., page variations)? The audience with the most criteria does; in this case, that would be Audience 1. If similar criteria exist, the criteria types themselves are assessed in this order of priority: profile, record type, and location (going from most specific to most general).

Bringing It Together

Once audience criteria have been established, a picture that can vary dramatically from Figure 12-2 comes into focus. Figure 12-12 shows a couple examples of how audiences could be constructed.

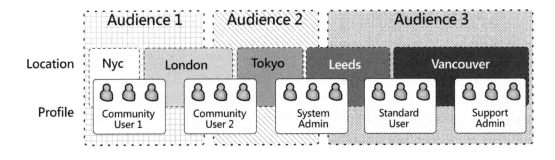

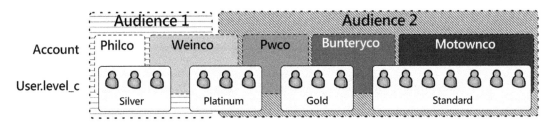

Figure 12-12. *Examples of possible audiences*

When I add in record types, it adds another layer of detail; see Figure 12-13. In this case, I will take a closer look at one of these users.

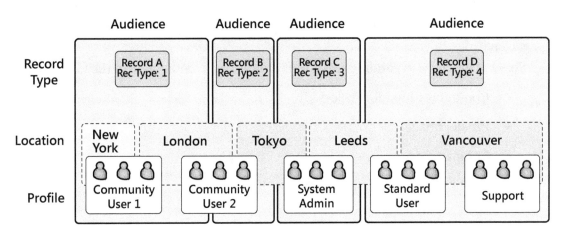

Figure 12-13. *Audiences with record types, locations, and profiles*

Audience Targeting Types

Now that I've walked through the *who*, it's time to discuss the *what*. Audiences are pretty interesting, but, by themselves, they are not terribly useful. The *assignment* of audiences to a particular experience to drive personalization is the real power of audience targeting within Salesforce communities. As of the Spring '18 release, audiences can be associated with three types of targeting entities.

- Branding sets

- Components

- Page variations

I will walk through each in detail, provide an explanation of how each works, and provide an example of how it can be appropriately applied.

Branding Sets

With branding sets, community administrators and builders can tailor unique branding experiences to different audiences. Partner communities, in particular, are a great fit for this powerful feature because it allows an organization to present a unique experience for each partner.

So, what exactly is a branding set? A branding set is a combination of the following:

- Community branding colors

- Header image

- Company logo

Figure 12-14 shows an example of multiple branding sets.

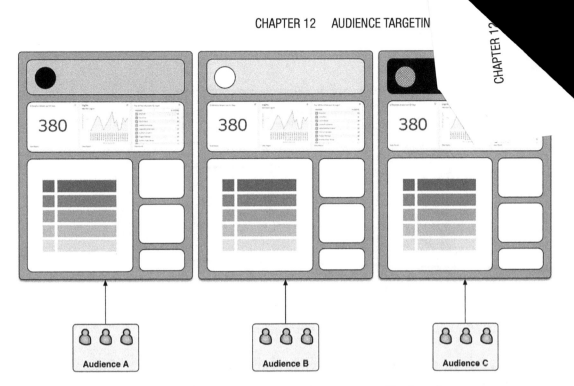

Figure 12-14. *With branding sets, an organization can display the same content and layout but a different header to multiple audiences*

To create a branding set, a community administrator clicks the Theme tab on the left, then the downward arrow at the top right, and finally Manage Branding Sets. See Figure 12-15.

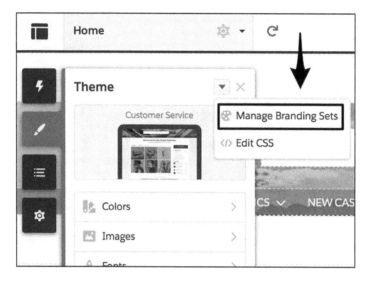

Figure 12-15. *Navigation to Manage Branding Sets*

This will cause the branding set menu to be displayed. Without any branding sets having been created, the administrator will only see the current branding settings displayed as the first branding set. To create a new branding set, the administrator will need to click New Branding Set at the top right; see Figure 12-16.

Figure 12-16. *Creating a new branding set*

In this scenario, I'll create two additional branding sets, one for Partner A and one for Partner B. See Figure 12-17.

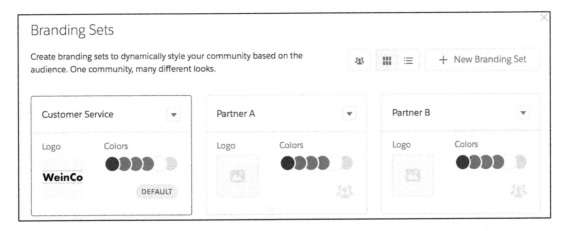

Figure 12-17. *Two additional branding sets, one for Partner A and one for Partner B (once completed, the logos and colors will differ for each)*

To edit a branding set, an administrator clicks the arrow at the top right of the applicable branding set and selects Edit; see Figure 12-18.

Figure 12-18. *Editing a branding set*

Once selected, an administrator can change the branding settings in the same way that the "original" branding was configured. See Figure 12-19.

Figure 12-19. *Making changes to a branding set*

In Figure 12-20, the branding set is configured for Partner A with a company logo and a header image. Figure 12-21 shows how this branding set and two others appear on a mobile device.

Figure 12-20. *The new Partner A branding set*

Figure 12-21. *Three branding sets for the same community (mobile view): WeinCo, WeinCo Partner A, WeinCo Partner B. Note the header and logo*

To create or apply an audience, an administrator can click the arrow to the right of Status and then select from the Audience section at the bottom. The options will vary depending on the context (e.g., Edit Audience will appear if an audience has already been assigned). See Figure 12-22.

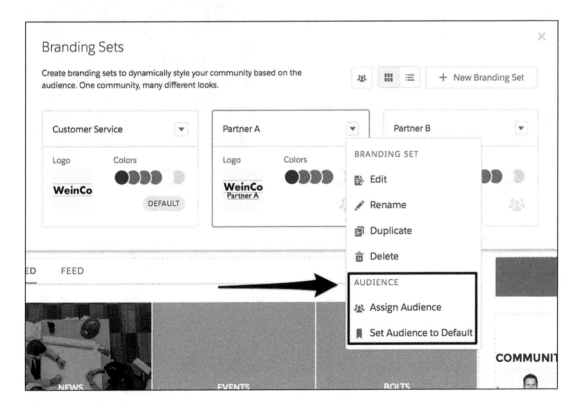

Figure 12-22. *Applying an audience to a branding set*

Page Variations

Page variations are the next step in audience targeting and allow community builders and administrators to create different experiences through the same page for different users. A page variation enables two different users to navigate to the same page and have a personalized view. See Figure 12-23.

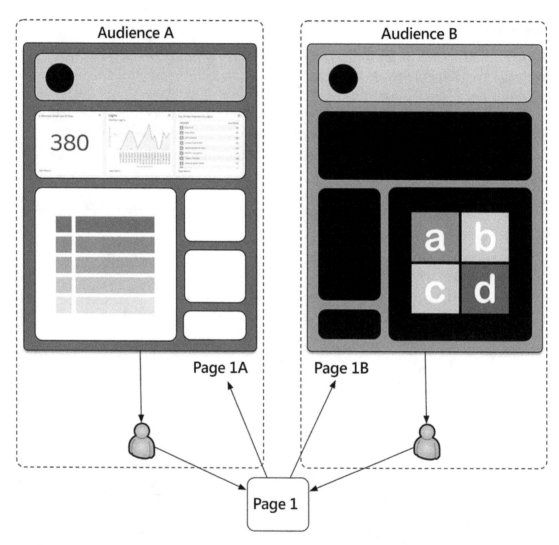

Figure 12-23. *Two variations of the same community page*

Some scenarios for page variations include the following:

- Showing completely different content to different audiences on the same common page (e.g., the Home page)

- Displaying similar content, but with a different layout, to different audiences

---

Note If the desired variation is at the component level (e.g., show/hide one specific component), component audiences should be considered. I'll cover that next.

To create a page variation, an administrator must navigate to the page setup screen first. From there, New Page Variation can be selected. See Figure 12-24.

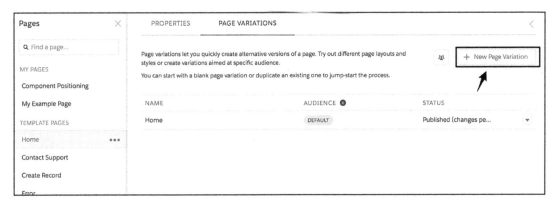

Figure 12-24. *Creating a new page variation*

When a new page is created, the administrator has the option to create a new page from scratch or to select an existing page (see Figure 12-25). To learn more about creating and exporting a page for reuse, check out Chapter 6. Here, I will go ahead and create a new page.

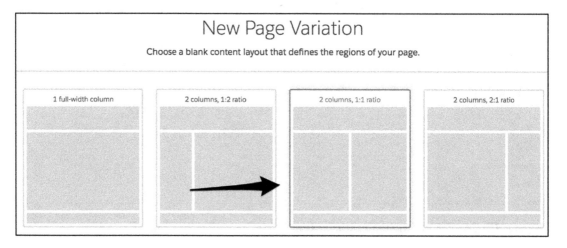

Figure 12-25. *A new page variation can be created from an existing page or made from a new blank page*

Next, the layout is selected; see Figure 12-26.

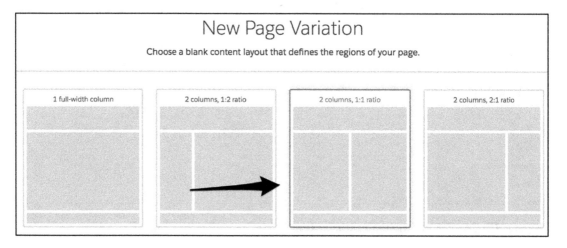

Figure 12-26. *The layout of a page variation can differ from the original page's layout*

Finally, a name is selected, and the page variation is all set. The administrator is pushed right to the new page, from which he or she can place and configure components, as desired. See Figure 12-27 and Figure 12-28 for an example of Home page variations.

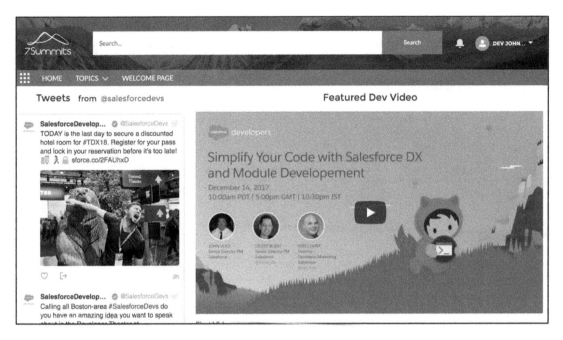

Figure 12-27. *Variation A*

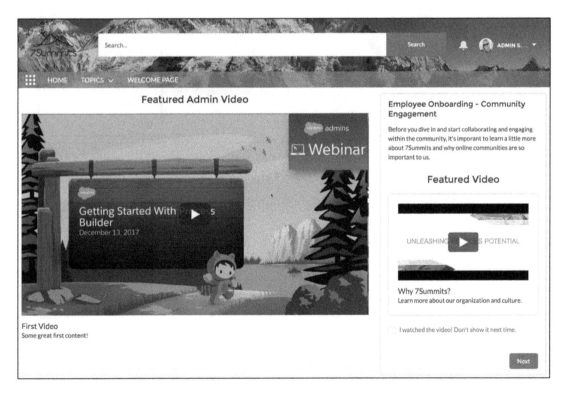

Figure 12-28. *Variation B*

To create or apply an audience, an administrator can click the arrow to the right of Status and then select from the Audience section at the bottom. The options will vary depending on the context (e.g., Assign Audience will appear if no audience has been assigned). See Figure 12-29.

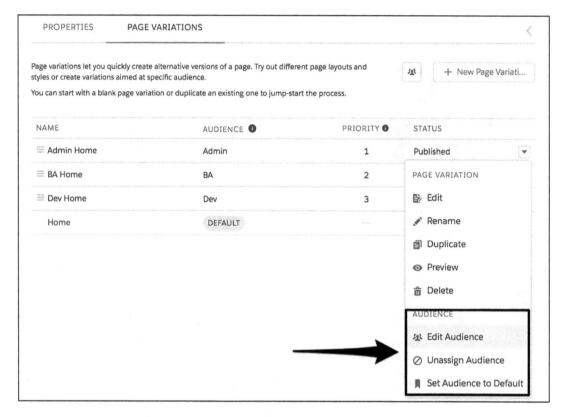

Figure 12-29. *Editing an audience of a page variation*

Page variation application can be fairly straightforward. See Figure 12-30.

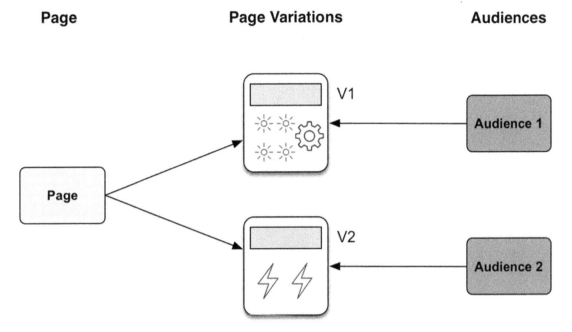

Figure 12-30. *Here a single page is shown in two different ways to Audience 1 and Audience 2*

The complexity increases when record types are brought into the picture. Take a look at Figure 12-31.

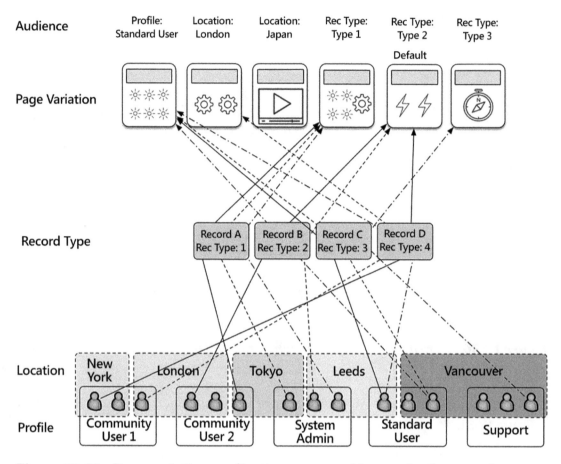

Figure 12-31. *Page variation application can get a bit complex because the number of variations, audiences, and audience criteria all grow*

Component Audiences

The last piece of audience targeting as of Spring '18 is Component Audiences. With this new capability, an individual component can be displayed to a specific audience. This allows an administrator to avoid managing multiple page variations (which adds extra overhead), instead of allowing the management of the content at the component level. At a high level, there are a couple different approaches to this functionality.

- Show or hide a component for specific audiences

- Configure a nondynamic component uniquely per audience to drive dynamic-like experiences (i.e., show a component to multiple audiences but configure it differently)

Configuring component audiences are really all about the audience; the component aspect really doesn't change. An admin would place and configure the component as would be done for a non-audience-specific component, with a couple exceptions.

- The component for an audience needs to be configured for that specific audience.

- If the component will be shown to multiple audiences, the component needs to be placed and configured multiple times.

See Figure 12-32. Here, I've placed a custom 7S Banner component and configured it for three different audiences. Note that, as an admin, I see the component three times since, technically, three components are present on the page.

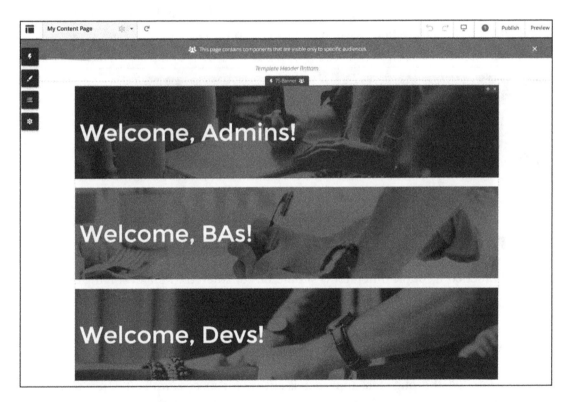

Figure 12-32. *Three versions of one audience-specific component*

When an audience member navigates to the page shown in Figure 12-31, the member will only see the component as configured for their specific audience. See Figure 12-33.

Figure 12-33. *Same page (not a page variation), but two users are not seeing the same thing; this is a result of component audiences*

To create or apply an audience to a component, an administrator can click the arrow at the top right of the property editor and then select from the Audience section at the bottom. The options will vary, depending on the context (e.g., Assign Audience will appear if no audience has been assigned). See Figure 12-34.

Figure 12-34. *Adding an audience to a component*

Other Considerations

As a best practice, a couple other items should be considered when leveraging audience targeting for Salesforce communities.

Testing

Having a detailed, thorough test approach is critical for success with audience targeting. Since the nature of this capability requires specific definition of the audience, verifying expected functionality should not (and cannot) be properly executed by one logged-in user, even a system administrator. At a minimum, the following users should be created for effective testing:

- Users who correspond to each of the defined audiences

- Users who correspond to more than one audience (to verify priority)

- Users who do not correspond to any of the defined audiences (i.e., these users would be part of a default audience)

Additionally, consider audiences that include location-based criteria. Either an IP emulator will be needed or the location of users conducting tests will need to match the defined criteria, based on IP address.

Suitability/Application

Audience targeting does not address all UX personalization scenarios that can be envisioned within a Salesforce community. Simply put, it is the wrong solution in some cases. I will capture those conditions next, along with a possible alternative approach:

- *Significant volume of audiences*: At a point, audiences will become unwieldy and hard to manage. I won't personally define a cutoff point (the threshold for each organization may differ), but audience targeting works best with a reasonable number of audiences.

- *Frequently changing audience criteria*: The current UI and corresponding process to manage an audience makes this scenario less than ideal. Audience criteria should be relatively static.

- *Hybrid customization and configuration*: As of the Summer '18 release, a custom theme has limited options for being used with audience tools, specifically branding sets.

- *Extreme dynamic branding*: As of the Summer '18 release, branding sets have a fairly limited scope. While I wouldn't be shocked to see dynamic themes come out at some point, they are not available at this point.

So, what are the alternatives?

- *Dynamic custom components*: This is the best solution for creating personalized experiences when criteria is changing or audience volume is high. Build out the front end to handle back-end criteria/logic to show different content or branding on the fly.

- *Dynamic theme components*: This is the same idea as the last bullet point but specifically applied to custom theme components.

- *Separate communities:* This doesn't solve a scenario with a large number of audiences, but it allows for extreme differences. A decision to consider separate communities, however, is much larger than just a personalization topic. This typically wouldn't be the first recommended option, although it is definitely an option.

Recap

Audience targeting is a key area of communities, and it's sure to expand further in future releases. In this chapter, I provided an overview of audiences, both conceptually and practically, and then explored the targeting types that can be used with audiences.

- Branding sets
- Page variations
- Components

With a solid understanding of how audiences work and the tools to configure them, community administrators can create dynamic, personalized experiences within a community.

CHAPTER 13

Lightning Bolt for Communities

One of the most significant (and most misunderstood) features to come out of Community Cloud in the past few years is the Lightning Bolt. With the introduction of Lightning Bolts, declarative app builders and programmatic developers alike have been, once again, empowered immensely on the Salesforce platform. In this chapter, I will clearly explain what Lightning Bolts are and demonstrate how to build and distribute them.

At least through the Spring '18 Salesforce release that hit orgs in early 2018, Lightning Bolts have equated to community templates; the terms are essentially interchangeable. As with a template, a bolt provides the means to define, deliver, and implement a specific starting point for a community that differs from one of the other, currently existing templates. See Figure 13-1 for a visual of this concept.

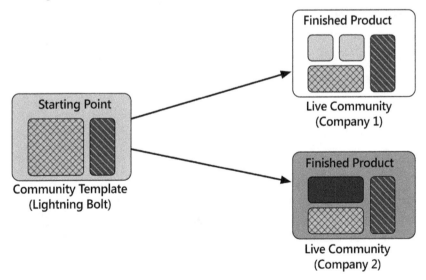

Figure 13-1. *A Lightning Bolt serves as a starting point for a variety of different communities that have some overlapping requirements or use cases*

© Philip Weinmeister 2018
P. Weinmeister, *Practical Guide to Salesforce Communities*, https://doi.org/10.1007/978-1-4842-3609-3_13

While this may evolve over time, a bolt currently has no specific scope; it could be a fairly simple, straightforward community use case or could entail a highly complex solution. Figure 13-2 shows a basic example of two templates. Template A has two pages, while Template B has three. The components on page 2 in both communities are laid out similarly, but the other pages are unique to each template.

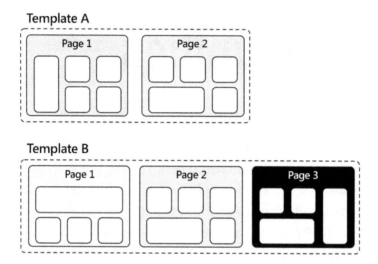

Figure 13-2. *Two different bolts, or templates, could include a different number of Lightning pages*

The pages and components in Figure 13-2 are for clarification but don't fully capture the complete contents of a bolt. A bolt contains a variety of community content and metadata to allow for a complete solution for the recipient on the installing end. See Figure 13-3 for a list of items that are included.

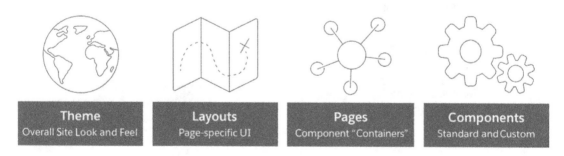

Figure 13-3. *Bolt elements range from communitywide to component-specific*

To get more specific, here are the likely candidates for inclusion in a bolt:

- Custom theme (including configuration)

- Custom Lightning pages

- Custom content layouts (including application to certain pages)

- Additional standard components (e.g., Survey, Tile Menu, etc.)

- Custom components (e.g., geolocation app, Twitter feed, etc.)

The best way I can describe a Lightning Bolt is as a means to deliver a templated, packaged communities solution that includes a branding and marketing layer for a complete picture of the business challenges being addressed. Although system integrators (SIs) in the communities space are primed to deliver bolts, anyone with appropriate access can create one. The Salesforce AppExchange even has a new Bolt Solutions section; see Figure 13-4.

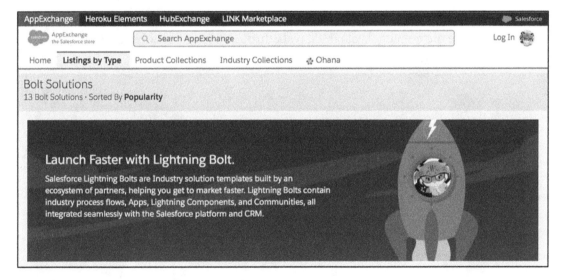

Figure 13-4. *Bolt Solutions page within the Salesforce AppExchange*

From a Salesforce perspective, bolts are ideal ways to deliver foundations for specific horizontal or vertical solutions. Horizontally, broad solutions such as the following are prime candidates:

- Employee communities

- Partner communities

Additionally, a large number of vertical use cases lend themselves well to the bolt framework. Look for some of the following industries to have a series of bolts over the next few years:

- Healthcare and life sciences

- Manufacturing

- Retail

- Financial services

Building a Bolt

At a high level, the concept of building a bolt is pretty simple. An organization starts with, ironically, a bolt. It then builds a community through adding, removing, and modifying the initial bolt contents. Finally, the ultimate end state of the community is captured, becoming a new bolt. Figure 13-5 provides a basic overview of the process.

To make sure the concept is clear, I'll walk through a more detailed theoretical example of the process. It's time to build a bolt!

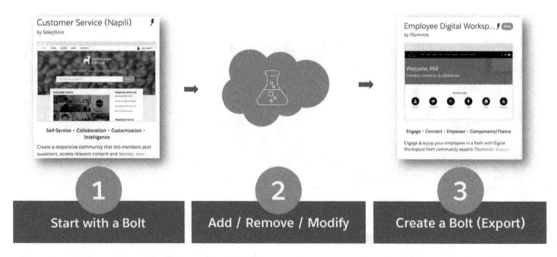

Figure 13-5. *High-level overview of the bolt-building process*

Step 1

Creating a community from an available bolt is the starting point. In this case, the community has the following details:

- Page 1
  - Component 1
  - Component 2
- Page 2
  - Component 1
  - Component 3
- Page 3
  - Component 1
  - Component 4

Figure 13-6 shows this starting point.

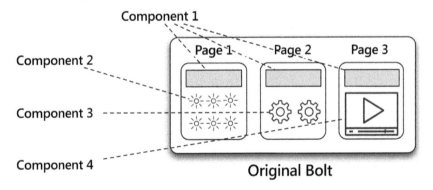

Figure 13-6. *Bolt building, step 1*

Step 2

In this step, the change process is initiated (see Figure 13-7). The following changes are made:

- The page 1 layout is changed.

- Page 2 is removed.

- The component 1 configuration is changed.

- Component 4 is removed.

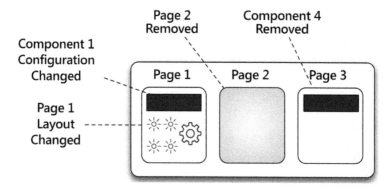

Figure 13-7. *Bolt building, step 2*

Step 3

Here, some additional components come into play (see Figure 13-8).

- Page 4 is added.

- Component 5 is added to page 4.

- Component 6 is added to page 3.

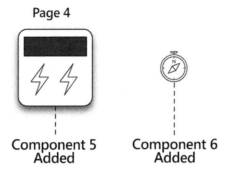

Figure 13-8. Bolt building, step 3

Step 4

Now that the new community is ready to go, it can be exported as a bolt. See Figure 13-9.

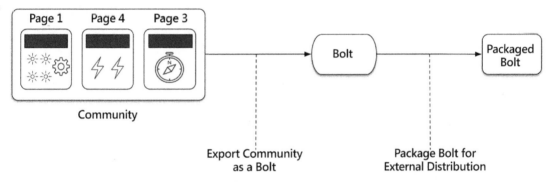

Figure 13-9. Bolt building, step 4

Bolt Creation in Community Builder

While the conceptual understanding of bolt creation is important, administrators and community builders will also need to understand the specifics of how a bolt is actually constructed within Community Builder. Once a community has been updated and is ready to be "stamped" as a bolt, the community administrator will navigate to the Settings tab on the left and then click Developer. See Figure 13-10.

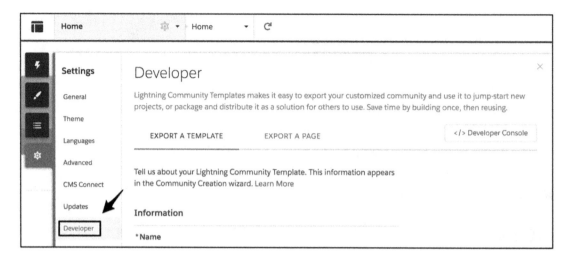

Figure 13-10. *Developer page on the Community Builder Settings tab*

Once on the Developer page, Export a Template will be selected. This is where the branding and marketing layer is created for the bolt. The following will be needed:

- Name

- Category

- One to three images (recommended dimensions: 1260px × 820px)

- One to four features (including a feature title and feature description)

Figure 13-11 shows the creation screen with the required fields populated.

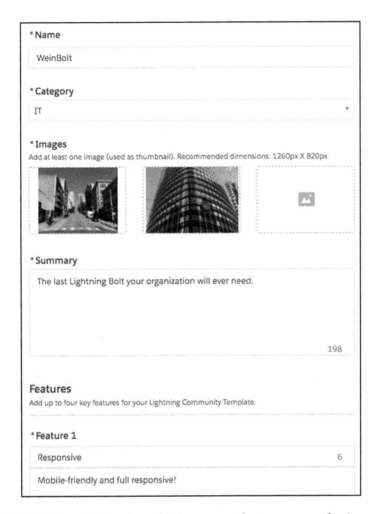

Figure 13-11. *Bolt description/marketing page that appears during creation*

Click Export, and the bolt creation is finalized. See Figure 13-12, Figure 13-13, and Figure 13-14.

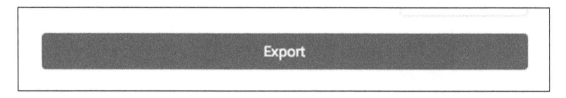

Figure 13-12. *Click the Export button to kick off the final bolt creation step*

Figure 13-13. *Wait for it...*

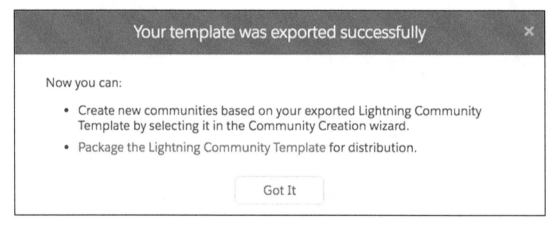

Figure 13-14. *Success! The template was exported successfully*

Bolt Installation

Are you curious what it looks like to walk through new community creation using the bolt from Figure 13-11? Figure 13-15, Figure 13-16, Figure 13-17, Figure 13-18, and Figure 13-19 show the corresponding views from the bolt installation process.

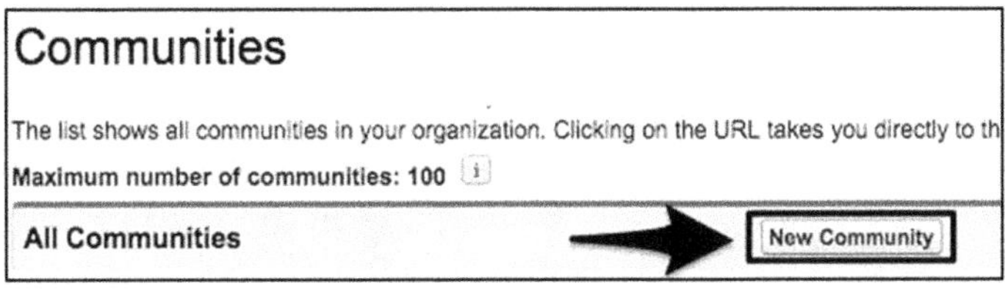

Communities

The list shows all communities in your organization. Clicking on the URL takes you directly to th

Maximum number of communities: 100 ⓘ

All Communities ──────────▶ [New Community]

Figure 13-15. *Click New Community*

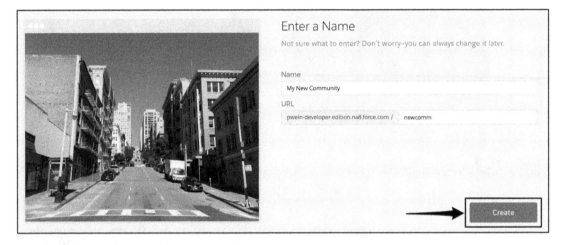

Figure 13-16. *Provide a name and URL. Click Create*

Figure 13-17. *Select the desired Lightning Bolt*

Figure 13-18. *Click Get Started*

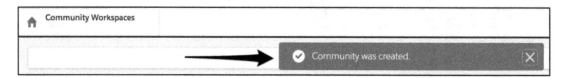

Figure 13-19. *Success! A new community has been created from a bolt*

End-to-End Overview

Success! A bolt has been created from scratch, and now it is ready for use (or further configuration/customization), if desired. For actual distribution of the exported bolt to be installed in customer orgs, it's important to understand a few additional steps: building and installing a corresponding package. The package will be the means to bundle up the created bolt and ship it off to another Salesforce org for use.

See Figure 13-20 for an overview.

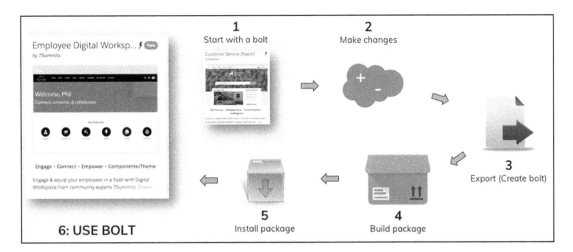

Figure 13-20. *The bolt creation, packaging, and export process*

Lightning Bolt for Salesforce

It is important to know that Lightning Bolts are expanding to other areas of the platform. As of the Summer '18 release, a feature called Lightning Bolt Solutions (or Lightning Bolt for Salesforce) is now available. The "for Salesforce" part basically means that apps and flows can be bundled with (or without) a community template to become a Lightning Bolt solution. See Figure 13-21, Figure 13-22, Figure 13-23, and Figure 13-24 for a walk-through of the process.

Figure 13-21. *Navigate to Lightning Bolt Solutions in the setup menu*

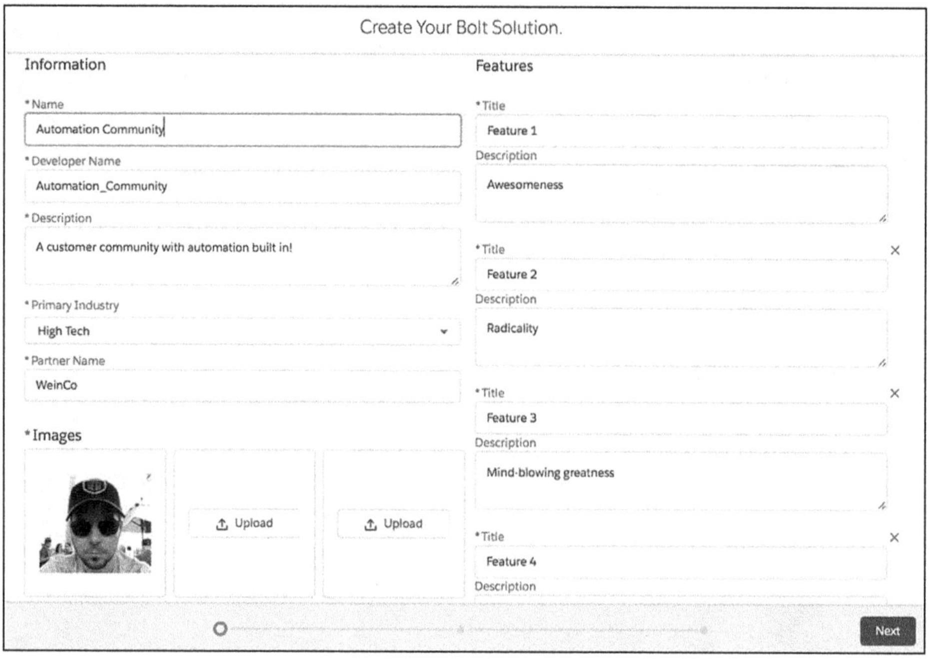

Figure 13-22. *Provide details about the solution*

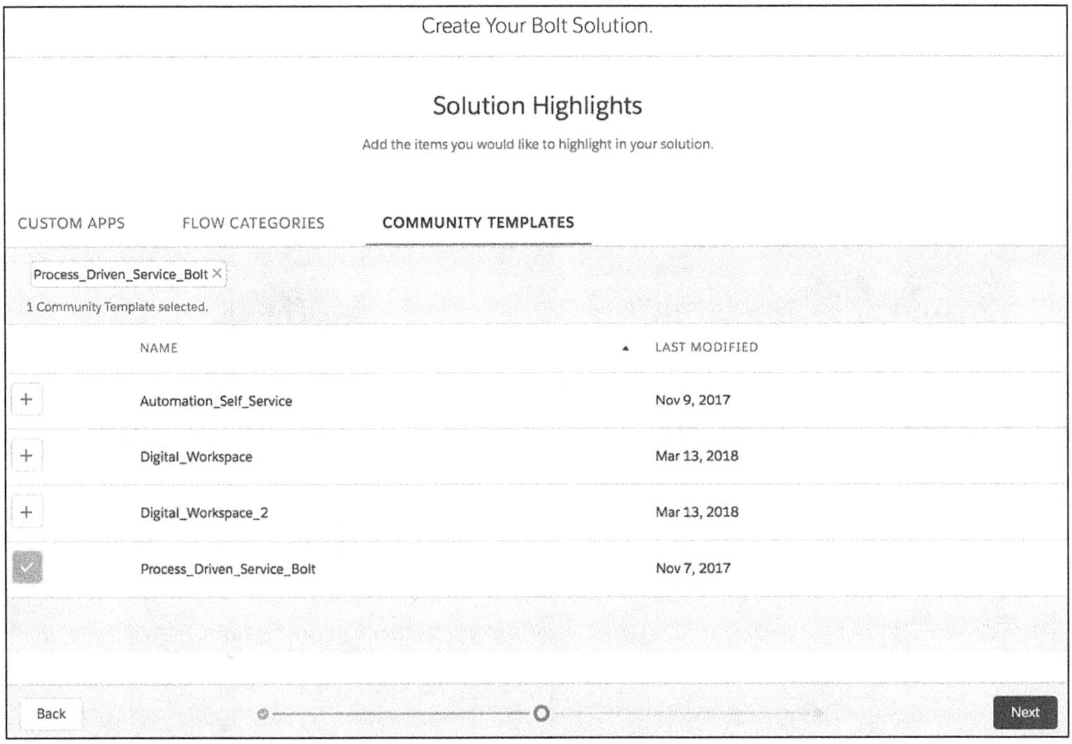

Create Your Bolt Solution.

Solution Highlights

Add the items you would like to highlight in your solution.

CUSTOM APPS   FLOW CATEGORIES   **COMMUNITY TEMPLATES**

Process_Driven_Service_Bolt ✕

1 Community Template selected.

	NAME	LAST MODIFIED ▲
+	Automation_Self_Service	Nov 9, 2017
+	Digital_Workspace	Mar 13, 2018
+	Digital_Workspace_2	Mar 13, 2018
✓	Process_Driven_Service_Bolt	Nov 7, 2017

Back   Next

Figure 13-23. Add the solution highlights (apps, flows, or community templates)

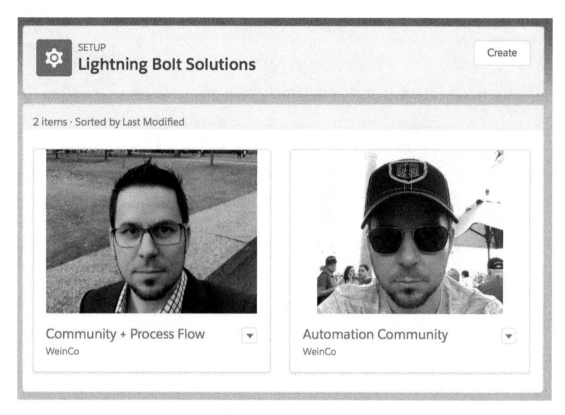

Figure 13-24.   Library of completed Lightning Bolt solutions

Recap

This chapter will arm any community administrator/builder with a solid foundation to become a bolt builder. In this chapter, I detailed the following:

- Definition of Lightning Bolts (community templates)

- Purposes and suitable use cases for bolts

- Bolt creation process

- Bolt packaging and installation process

- Lightning Bolt for Salesforce

CHAPTER 14

The Best of the Rest: Additional Communities Topics

The breadth of Community Cloud is a microcosm of the Salesforce platform. As new features and capabilities are introduced with each release, it has become increasingly difficult to maintain comprehensive expertise on Salesforce overall, let alone this single "cloud." As such, there is a significant amount of information that can be covered within the realm of Salesforce communities, and individual chapters could be written about a number of additional topics. To balance the need for breadth across common community areas and the unwieldy and awkward nature of a 600-page book, I've identified a number of specific topics that I'll be covering in brief throughout this chapter. My goal is to provide a practical starting point or common reference from which readers can explore additional detail via Salesforce Help & Training and other resources. Specifically, I'll cover the following in this chapter:

- Analytics

- Moderation

- Deployment

- Salesforce app (Salesforce1)

- Search

- Messages

- Notifications

- Chatter streams

P. Weinmeister, *Practical Guide to Salesforce Communities*, https://doi.org/10.1007/978-1-4842-3609-3_14

- Additional items (Guided Setup, Marketing Cloud, Quip, Einstein, CMS Connect)

Analytics

The appropriate starting point for any discussion regarding analytics in a Salesforce community is the Community Management Package for Communities app from Salesforce. The full name includes the release name, and two versions exist (depending on whether Chatter is enabled).

- [Release] Salesforce Community Management Package for Communities without Chatter (e.g., Spring '18 Salesforce Community Management Package for Communities with Chatter)

- [Release] Salesforce Community Management Package for Communities with Chatter (e.g., Spring '18 Salesforce Community Management Package for Communities without Chatter)

Figure 14-1 shows the Winter '18 version of the app.

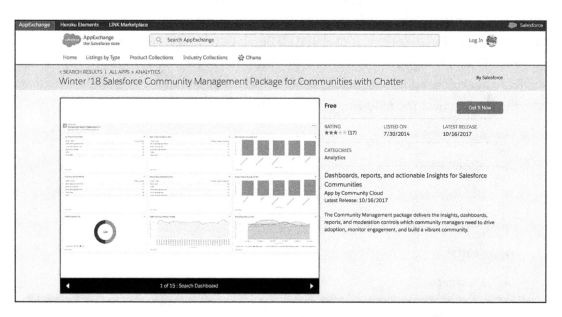

Figure 14-1. *Community Management Package on AppExchange*

This app has some serious meat to it. As of the Winter '18 version, the package contains the following:

- 61 custom report types

- 26 dashboards

- 396 reports

Once installed, an administrator of the community can navigate to Workspaces ➤ Dashboards and view a suite of valuable dashboards that bring the community to life. See Figure 14-2.

Figure 14-2. *Content (files) dashboard for communities*

Moderation

Moderation is a critical consideration for a community. While the nature of some communities simply won't need or benefit from much moderation, others will require it to be successful. Why? Because community members are people! While members of most communities will honor the general guidelines and rules of engagement, there are those who may push the boundaries a bit. Unfortunately, there are also those who are simply destructive and are bent on stirring up havoc within a community.

Salesforce has provided a number of tools to help with moderation. To access these, an administrator can navigate to Workspaces ➤ Moderation. See Figure 14-3 for a view of the workspaces section with Moderation.

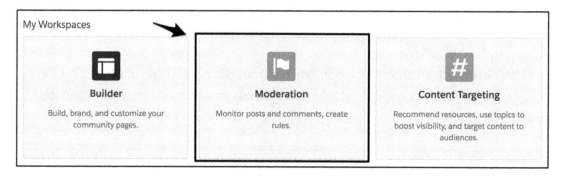

Figure 14-3. *Moderation in My Workspaces*

Moderation is a multistep process in Salesforce communities:

- *Establish criteria*: Set up content criteria and/or member criteria for use in moderation rules. For example, content criteria might involve a keyword list for inappropriate words.

- *Create rules*: Create content and/or rate rules to enable automated handling of activities that satisfy the defined criteria. For example, a rule could be created to place a post containing an inappropriate word into Review status for moderator review and action.

- *Activate rules*: Turn on the rules.

- *Review/manage*: Stay on top of flagged discussions, files, messages, and members by using the provided analytics and dashboards.

- *Take action*: Unless an action is fully automated, a decision will need to be made on flagged items, and that decision may require some action.

Figure 14-4 shows an example of a rule that uses content criteria and automatically blocks profane words within a community.

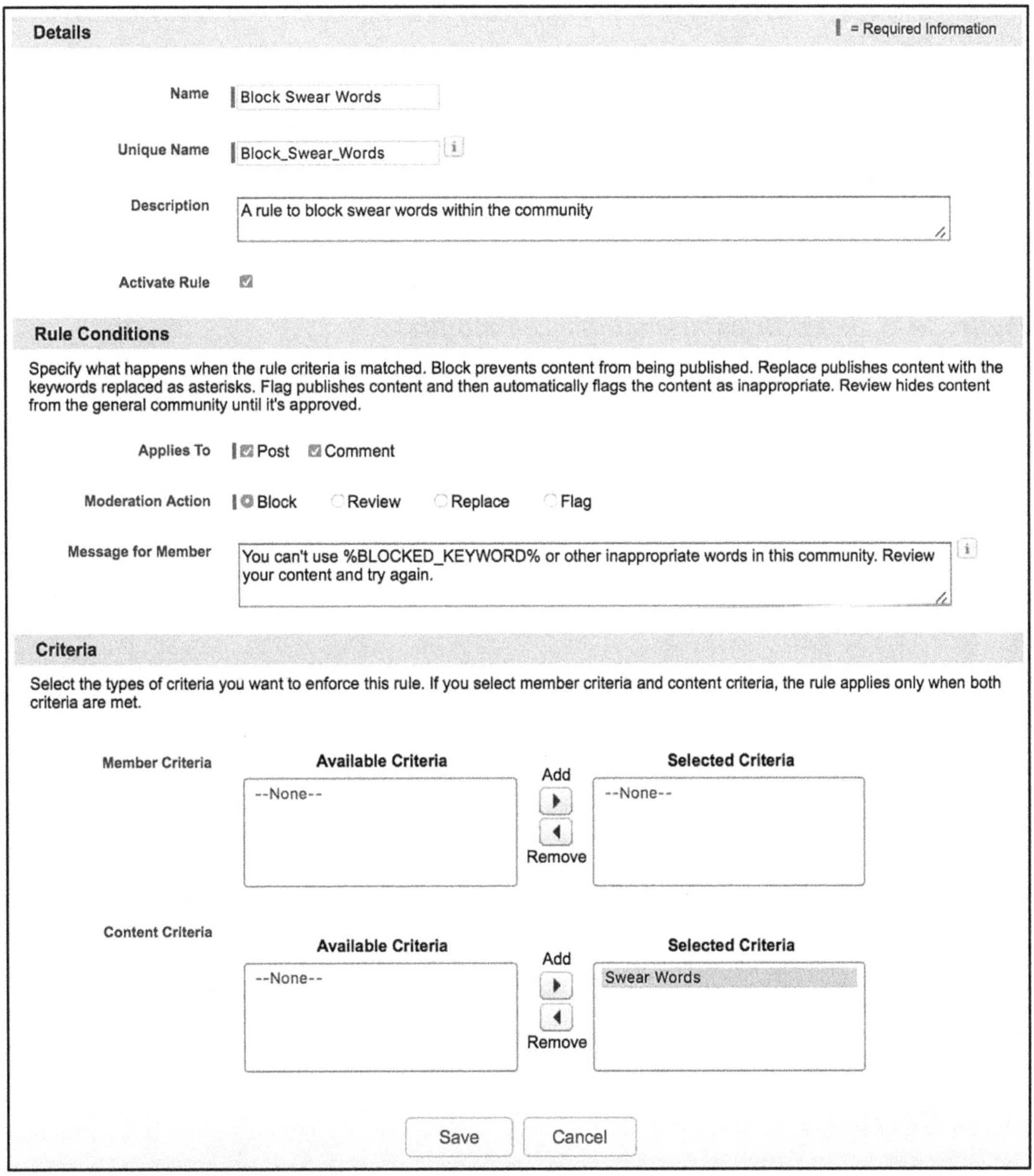

Figure 14-4. *A community moderation rule that blocks any text strings found in the defined content criteria ("swear words")*

Note that, in the preferences section within the Administration workspace, file types and sizes can be moderated, as well. See Figure 14-5 and Figure 14-6 for the settings and the corresponding result.

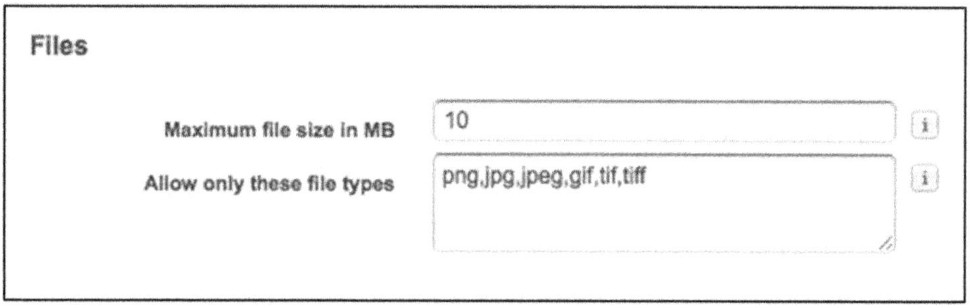

Files

Maximum file size in MB	10
Allow only these file types	png,jpg,jpeg,gif,tif,tiff

Figure 14-5. *File restrictions within a community*

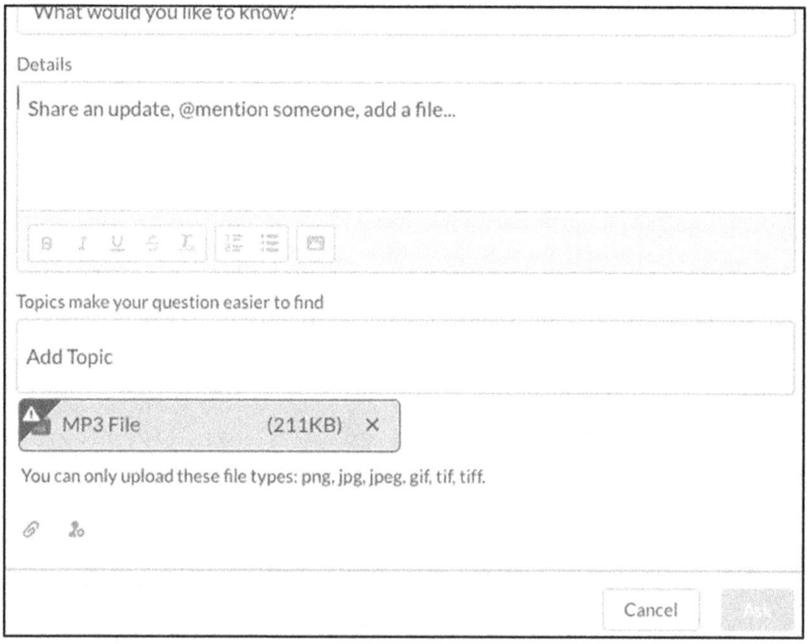

What would you like to know?

Details

Share an update, @mention someone, add a file...

Topics make your question easier to find

Add Topic

MP3 File   (211KB) ×

You can only upload these file types: png, jpg, jpeg, gif, tif, tiff.

Cancel

Figure 14-6. *Result of a file type restriction*

Deployment

Deployment is a critical topic when it comes to Salesforce communities. While deployment of "standard" platform elements and entities, such as objects, fields, workflow rules, Apex classes, and so on, has become a fairly well-known and mature process, communities have required different processes and have not always fit into standard deployments. In this section, I won't be giving a simple formula for all deployment scenarios; instead, I'll cover the available options and call out some key considerations.

Site.com Export

For Lightning communities only, Site.com allows a method for full site export and import. To do this, a community administrator will need to navigate to Site.com by going to Community Workspaces ➤ Administration ➤ Pages ➤ Site.com Studio. From there, the Settings cog will reveal the Export Site option. See Figure 14-7.

Figure 14-7. *Exporting a Lightning community via Site.com*

In the target org, a target community must exist. Following the same path to the Site. com Settings cog, an administrator will select Overwrite Site and select the exported file to import the file and update the community. See Figure 14-8.

Figure 14-8. *Overwriting a site requires the import of the site file that was previously exported from the source community*

Overall, the Site.com export/overwrite process is simple and straightforward. This is a great option for deploying Lightning communities. Figure 14-9 provides an overview of the entire process.

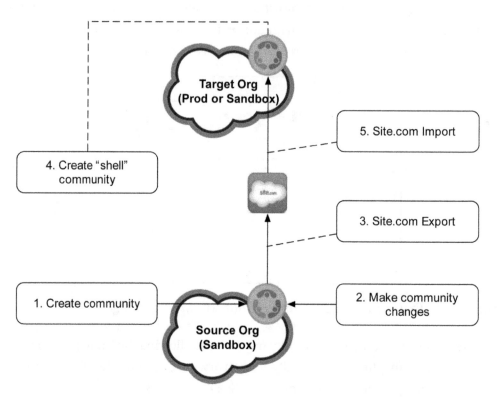

Figure 14-9. *Overview of the Site.com export/overwrite process*

Change Sets

Change Sets are established platform elements in the Salesforce ecosystem and allow the inclusion of communities for the purpose of deployment. The following are a couple key items to know about Change Sets, as they relate to communities:

- Change Sets require that a community with the same name as the source community exists in the target org.

- Change Sets work for both Lightning and Tabs + Visualforce communities.

As Change Sets are well known on the platform, I won't go into extreme detail on the process. However, I will call out the main "gotcha," which is that communities are represented as "networks" within Change Sets. See Figure 14-10.

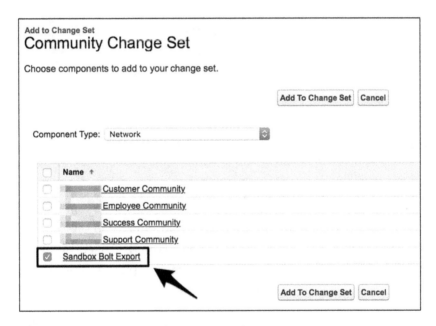

Figure 14-10. *Select a network (community) within a Change Set*

Overall, the Change Set process looks like the diagram shown in Figure 14-11.

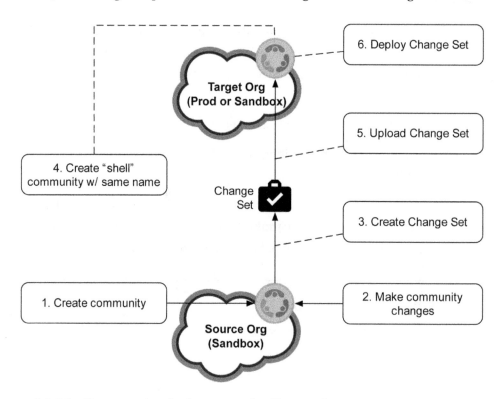

Figure 14-11. *Community deployment via Change Set*

IDEs and the Metadata API

Integrated development environments (IDEs) provide a means to save org contents to the cloud or a local server. An IDE (such as the Force.com IDE, used with Eclipse) uses the Salesforce Metadata API to extract and save a network (i.e., community) and all related content and then deploy it to a different org (see Figure 14-12).

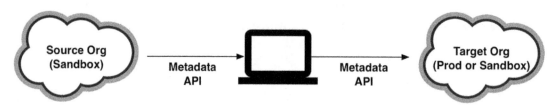

Figure 14-12. *Overview of leveraging an IDE to deploy a community from a source org to a target org*

Once contents are locally saved, an administrator can deploy the selected contents to a particular target org. See Figure 14-13 for the Eclipse menu option that allows this action.

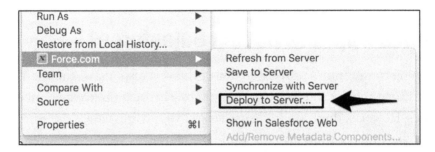

Figure 14-13. *Deploy to Server (within Eclipse) allows for specific contents, including a network, to be moved from one org to another*

Packaged Lightning Bolt

Custom Lightning Bolts, covered in Chapter 13, are fairly new and continue to evolve at the time of this book's publication. I wouldn't say that the process for bolt deployment is mature, so I am not going to say too much about a suggested approach. However, Lightning Bolt technology does provide a means to export a community in its current state. The export can then be either packaged (and then installed) or migrated via the Metadata API. The concept of the Lightning Bolt framework is that it allows the output of a community starting point (i.e., a template). Ultimately, though, a bolt captures everything about a community at the point an export is created, and it could absolutely be used to "move" a community from one org to another.

Again, I don't recommend this as a standard deployment approach, but there is value in understanding how Lightning Bolt technology can potentially facilitate community deployment.

Manual Replication

With all of the other deployment tools available, manual replication is not generally recommended as an approach; however, it is an option. The only advantage to this approach is that it does put all the control in the hands of the individual or individuals doing the deployment, down to each aspect of the community. In other words, if an individual wants to make sure that everything is moved properly and set up in the same way as it was in the source org, this might provide a level of comfort. It does not increase the likelihood of success, though. Rather, it introduces many potential opportunities for manual mistakes.

Salesforce App (Previously Salesforce1)

Since Lightning communities provide an out-of-the-box responsive, mobile-friendly UX, the Salesforce app doesn't play a prominent role in the mobile experience for communities. However, there are some use cases I've run into where the app has come into play. I'd like to share a few tips that could be relevant.

- *Usage in a LEX-based employee community*: There are times when it makes sense to build a LEX-based employee community/portal versus one leveraging Lightning communities (e.g., an HR help desk because of the nature of case visibility). In these situations, the app will potentially apply. See Figure 14-14.

- *Security/network limitations*: I have encountered a situation where employees are not able to access the community on a mobile browser on their phone, for security-related reasons. In that situation, the Salesforce app provides a means to access some elements of the community that are not prohibited by security configurations.

- *Flexible Lightning approach*: The Salesforce app provides a great use case for building Lightning components in a flexible way to be used via different mediums. Any component that includes `implements=` `"force:appHostable"` in the `aura:component` tag can be surfaced as a Lightning component tab in the app.

- *Modifying the tab menu*: In setting up the Salesforce app to work for a user of a Lightning community, I found myself struggling to figure out how to actually manage the app tab menu. The answer was not obvious; you have make the Tabs menu within Administration visible and then set up the tabs there. See Figure 14-15 and Figure 14-16 for the result of a custom tab set for a community within the app.

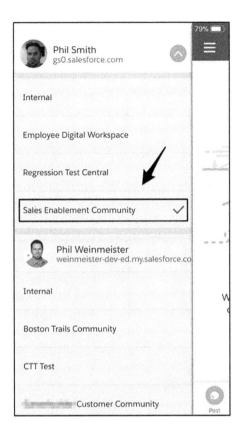

Figure 14-14. *Selection of a community from within the Salesforce app*

Figure 14-15. *Configured tabs in the Salesforce app*

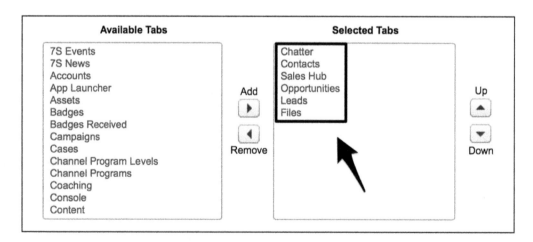

Figure 14-16. *Corresponding tab settings from community administration to display what is shown in Figure 14-15*

Search

I covered some of the component-specific aspects of search in earlier chapters but thought it was important to call out a few additional items here. At least as of Spring '18, out-of-the-box search within communities has yet to blow anyone away; Figure 14-17 shows an example of some search results on the standard results page available within communities. The fact that a community admin can prevent an accessible object from showing up in the search results is a welcome feature, but no one would call native search capabilities "advanced." I point this out to set proper expectations for a community implementation and to show that the options are limited.

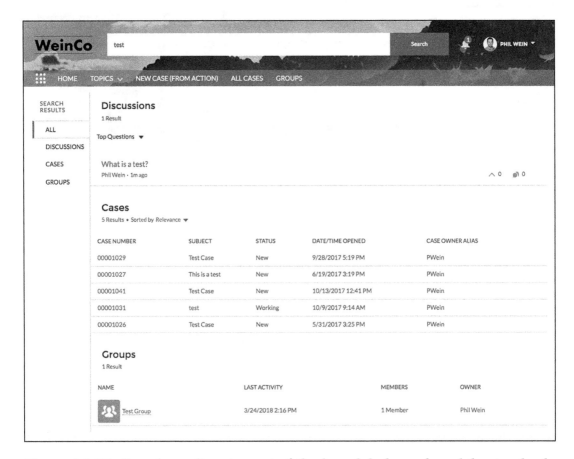

Figure 14-17. *Search results using out-of-the-box global search and the standard search results component*

If the native search features don't satisfy the needs of a particular organization, a couple options are available. First, there's the custom development approach. Custom search functionality can absolutely be provided, either through Visualforce or through Lightning. Additionally, admins may want to consider third-party options. AppExchange has a few community-enabled search apps that can be installed and configured to override the standard search experience.

Messages

Direct messages through Chatter have been available for some time, but direct messaging in a Lightning community has not. There does now exist the capability to directly (and privately) message other users within the community. See Figure 14-18.

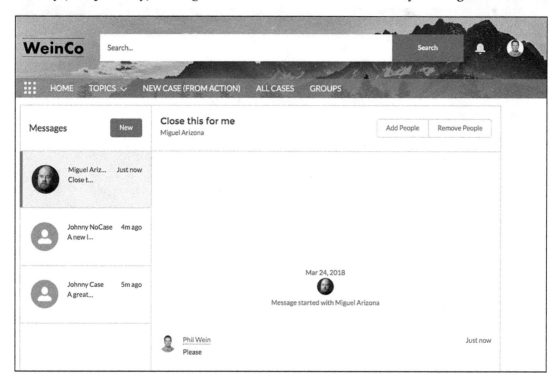

Figure 14-18.   *Direct message home page within a Lightning community*

Although the messages page can't be directly added to the navigation menu without specifying a message ID (at least through Spring '18), there is a messages home page that can be referenced. The relative URL is /s/messages/Home and will default to the first message when the page is loaded.

Notifications

The need to surface notifications and allow community users to easily manage them was a feature gap for a while, but that gap was filled in 2017. Now, a setting exists that can show or hide notifications within the standard header. See Figure 14-19.

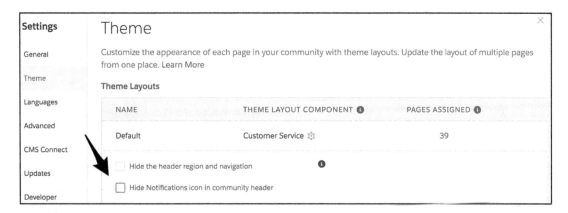

Figure 14-19. *A setting on the Theme page allows the notification icon to be shown or hidden*

If the notification icon is enabled, users will be able to review any event that triggers a notification. See Figure 14-20 for a view of the Notifications menu with content.

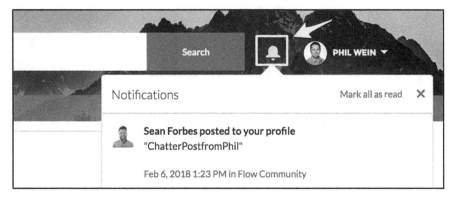

Figure 14-20. *Notifications menu with an example notification displayed*

Chatter Streams

Chatter streams are a relatively new feature that might be useful for some organizations. Chatter streams basically allow a user to create a custom feed that provides these two functions:

- Cuts through the noise that is found in the main community feed

- Allows for an aggregation of individual feeds to allow a user to hand-select feeds from multiple entities/records

To enable streams, an administrator can simply add the Stream List page to the navigation menu. Once that's set up, a user can create a stream by clicking the New button. See Figure 14-21.

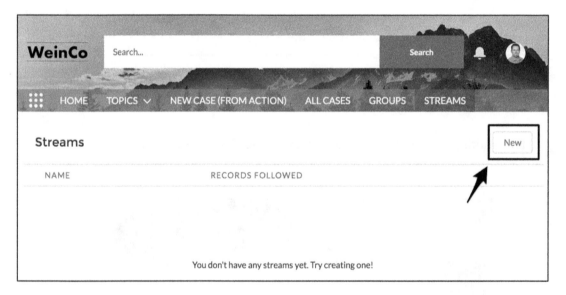

Figure 14-21. *Clicking New on the Streams home page allows a community member to create a new stream*

To assemble the stream, identify the objects and the corresponding records whose feeds will make up the fully aggregated feed. See Figure 14-22.

Figure 14-22. *Different records can be selected when creating a stream*

Once the brief setup is done, the feed will start to show the tailored content selected by the end user. See Figure 14-23 for an example of a live Chatter stream.

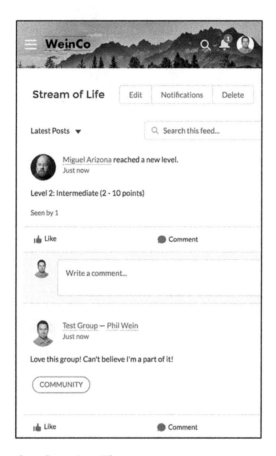

Figure 14-23. *A completed, active Chatter stream*

Other Capabilities

Community builders will continue to find powerful new communities capabilities with each Salesforce release. In this section, I will call out additional capabilities that will warrant more research and consideration for many organizations.

Guided Setup

Guided Setup is an additional workspace that corresponds to partner communities, walking administrators through a series of steps to help set up the community quickly and thoroughly. Figure 14-24 shows a view of the Guided Setup landing page.

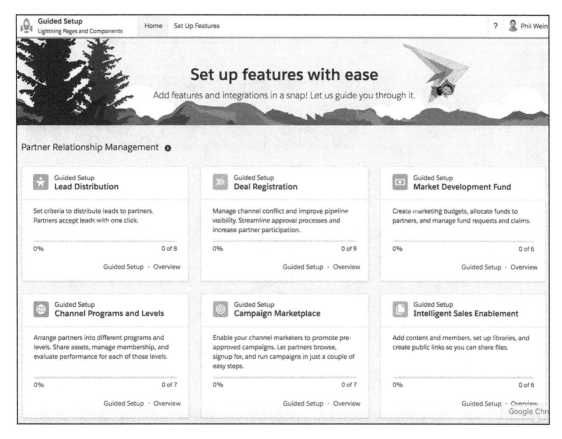

Figure 14-24. *Guided setup landing page*

Marketing Cloud

For organizations leveraging Marketing Cloud, Community Cloud now offers built-in tools for direct integration with a community.

- Distributed marketing allows for the creation of personalized partner campaigns.

- Journey Builder for communities enables the configuration of marketing journeys for community members.

Quip

Incorporate record-specific activity from Quip into a Lightning community with standard Quip components. Figure 14-25 shows the Quip Lightning component being dropped onto a Case Detail page.

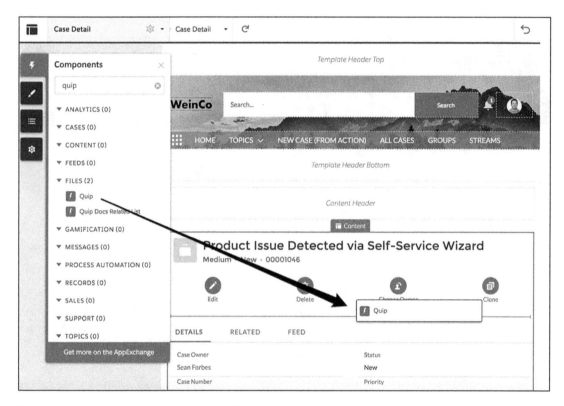

Figure 14-25. *Dragging the standard Quip component onto a Case Detail page*

Einstein for Communities

Einstein functionality, once fully released, will provide an enhanced engine for recommending responses to questions submitted within a Salesforce community. This will have significant value for self-service scenarios by increasing the probability that those following the question will truly find the information that they are looking for. Stay tuned to this space.

CMS Connect

CMS Connect is a major addition to the communities platform. It has evolved rapidly and will likely continue to see significant investment for some time. CMS Connect allows organizations to connect to HTML, JSON, CSS, and JavaScript from third-party content management systems to provide consistent branding and UX across multiple sites. As of Spring '18, the following providers are supported: Adobe Experience Manager, Drupal, Sitecore, WordPress, and SDL.

Figure 14-26 shows the New CMS Connection page, while Figure 14-27 shows the standard CMS Connect (HTML) component available within Community Builder.

Figure 14-26. *New CMS Connection page*

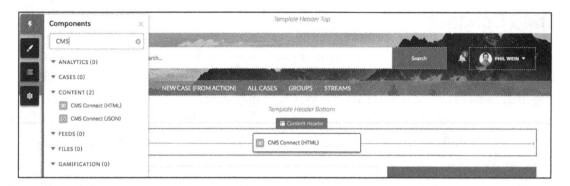

Figure 14-27.   *The standard CMS Connect (HTML) component*

Recap

In this chapter, I reviewed a number of Community Cloud capabilities that round out the majority of the full communities feature set available on the Salesforce platform. Topics covered included analytics, moderation, deployment, search, and more. The information in this chapter was intended to provide a starting point for understanding these areas.

CHAPTER 15

Next Steps: Keep Learning

I hope this book brings significant value to the growing number of individuals looking to become "community trailblazers." That being said, this book is only one of many resources available on the path to becoming an expert on Salesforce communities. In this final chapter, I'll suggest some supplementary options for forging ahead.

Trailhead

How could any breadth of educational Salesforce material be considered complete without Trailhead? Trailhead is an online learning management application that is self-paced and free and has helped thousands of individuals improve their understanding of and capabilities on the Salesforce platform. While communities don't have the same number of modules as some more mature areas of the platform, lots of educational goodies exist to help learn Community Cloud.

I've selected a series of communities topics for you by creating a *trailmix*. Trailmixes are community-sourced groupings of related Trailhead modules and projects. The first trailmix is "Community Cloud," and it provides a broad overview of Salesforce communities. This trailmix can be found at `http://bit.ly/trailmix-community-cloud`. My other trailmix is "Process Automation + Communities," covering communities, Flow, and Process Builder. It can be found at `http://bit.ly/trailmix-process-communities`.

Additionally, the full list of all my trailmixes is at `http://bit.ly/mytrailmix`.

© Philip Weinmeister 2018
P. Weinmeister, *Practical Guide to Salesforce Communities*, https://doi.org/10.1007/978-1-4842-3609-3_15

WeinBlog

Want to learn about all the latest and greatest Community Cloud features with every new release? My blog covers key features and functions, providing both my perspective and Salesforce's for each item. My blog URL is `http://bit.ly/weinforce`. Figure 15-1 shows a snapshot of my blog's home page.

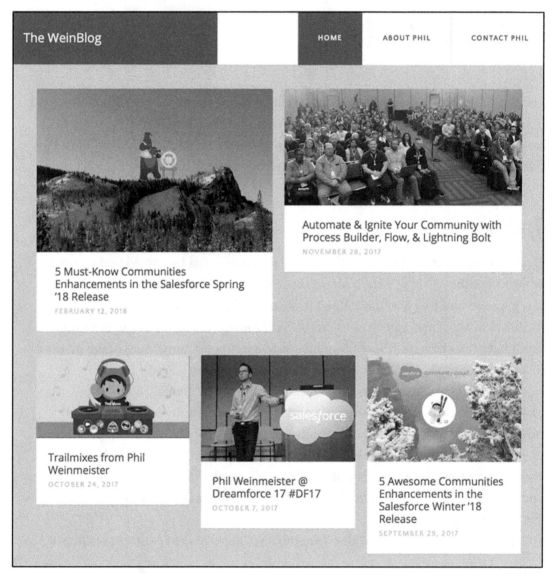

Figure 15-1. *The WeinBlog*

It's possible that I will release a subsequent version of this book down the road. However, until that happens (if it does), I will post relevant Community Cloud updates to my blog as they come up, so visit often!

Release Notes

While the volume of information can be overwhelming, getting to know the release notes three times a year is critical for those who want to stay ahead of the curve. The official release notes URL is `https://releasenotes.docs.salesforce.com`, and the notes are typically updated a few months before each release. Figure 15-2 shows the Communities section from Summer '18.

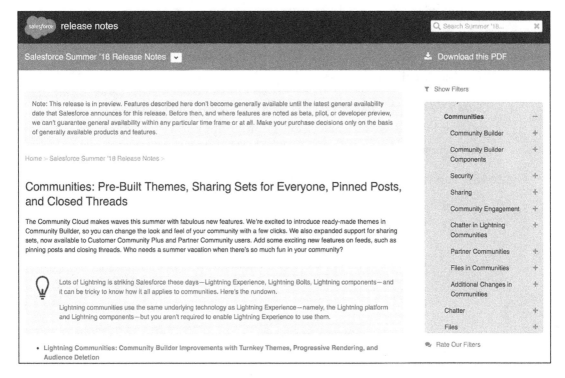

Figure 15-2. *Official release notes from Salesforce*

Twitter

Admittedly, there is a lot of noise in the world of social media, and Twitter is no exception. Following the right accounts will bring a steady flow of useful communities information. Here are some recommended accounts to follow:

- *Community Cloud*: @CommunityCloud is the official Twitter account of the Salesforce Community Cloud team. It highlights product updates, event info, and more.

- *Arnab Bose*: @ArBose heads up the process automation arm at Salesforce and is quite active with showing examples of how customers and partners are leveraging process automation with communities.

- *Anna Rosenman*: @anna_rosenman is the VP of product marketing for Community Cloud and provides steady updates on Community Cloud activity in the ecosystem.

- *Yours Truly*: @PhilWeinmeister (that's me!) shares tips, tricks, updates, and insights on Salesforce communities and a variety of other Salesforce topics.

Figure 15-3 shows my Twitter home page.

Figure 15-3. @PhilWeinmeister on Twitter

Dreamforce, TrailheaDX, and World Tours

For those who want to immerse themselves in the world of Salesforce for a day or an entire week, a few great options are out there. Dreamforce, TrailheaDX, and even World Tours offer Community Cloud goodness. Personally, I recommend going to at least one of the two big events (Dreamforce and TrailheaDX) and seeking out all the Community Cloud sessions that are available. The following are the relevant event pages:

- *General Salesforce events*: https://www.salesforce.com/events

- *TrailheaDX*: https://developer.salesforce.com/trailheadx

- *Dreamforce*: https://www.salesforce.com/dreamforce

For those who are lucky, an experience like the one I captured in Figure 15-4 will be waiting.

Figure 15-4. *Two Community Cloud product managers running a live demo at Dreamforce*

Salesforce Training and Certification

There is an "official" route to learning communities that is delivered through Salesforce training. As of 2018, two classes exist.

- *CRT-271*: Certification Preparation for Community Cloud Consultants (`https://help.salesforce.com/HTTrainingCourse Detail?id=a230M000000Q5Y5`)

- *ADM-271*: Get Started with Communities (`https://help. salesforce.com/HTTrainingCourseDetail?id=a2330000000Q0CN`)

As implied in the title of the first course, there is a prestigious honor for those considered experts on the platform: a shiny certification from Salesforce. The one communities-related certification is Salesforce Certified Community Cloud Consultant (Certified Administrator is a required prerequisite). The CRT-271 course is obviously great prep for the communities certification, but there's also an official study guide that is available. This certification is a must for anyone who works with Salesforce communities on a regular basis.

Pluralsight

I'm excited to announce that I have joined a star-studded lineup of Salesforce authors on Pluralsight, a video-based technology learning service. Pluralsight has an entire category of Salesforce-specific courses on topics such as Apex, Lightning components, Visualforce, data models/architecture, and more. Look for my "play-by-play" focused on audience targeting within Salesforce communities, coming out in 2018. It will be titled *Crafting Audience Experience with Salesforce Communities* and will available at `https://www.pluralsight.com`.

Recap

The world of Salesforce is expanding by the day, and the amount of information available on Salesforce Community Cloud is following suit. I am honored to be part of this ecosystem, and I hope this chapter (and entire book) provides valuable information and guidance on your personal career journey.

Index

A

Administration
- branding, 158, 161, 169
- emails, 168, 178
- login & registration, 160, 178
- members, 150, 152, 155, 166, 168
- pages, 148, 150–151, 155, 158–163, 165–167, 170–171
- preferences, 150, 178
- reputation levels, 152, 172–174
- reputation points, 152, 172–174
- rich publisher apps, 175–177
- tabs, 143, 157–158

Analytics, 66, 90–92, 306–308

Article management, 224–225, 229

Articles, 201–202, 204, 214
- types, 219–220, 223–224, 229
- visibility, 222–223

Assignment, 224, 226, 229

Audiences
- domain, 262, 265
- location, 262, 264–265, 271, 287
- profiles, 262–263, 265, 271
- record type, 263, 267, 269, 271, 283
- user criteria, 265–266

Authentication
- private, 180
- public, 180

Automation, 231

B

Blog, 330–331

Bolt creation, 295–296, 298

Bolt store, 291

Branding sets, 259, 272, 274–277, 287–288

Build Your Own, 43, 57

C

Certification, 334–335

Chatter streams, 322, 324

Cloud, 1–2, 6–7

CMS Connect, 327–328

Community, 1, 3–9, 201

Community builders, 61, 295–296, 298

Community creation, 293, 295–297, 300

Component audiences, 259, 284, 286

Components, 62–63, 65–68, 77, 79–81, 84–85, 92, 95–96, 104–105, 108

Customer Service, 43

D

Data, 3–6
- categories, 219–221, 223, 229
- data sources, 17–18
- model, 202–203

Deployment, 310–316

Display, 227

© Philip Weinmeister 2018
P. Weinmeister, *Practical Guide to Salesforce Communities*, https://doi.org/10.1007/978-1-4842-3609-3

Distribution, 289, 300
Dreamforce, 333–334

E

Einstein, 326
Export, 295–298, 300–301
External users, 185, 188, 191

F

Fields, 179, 182, 184, 186, 195, 199
Flow, 50, 54–55
    configuration, 255
    engagement, 249–254, 256
    paused flows, 256–257
    placement, 253–256
    status check, 247–249

G, H

Guided Setup, 325

I, J, K

Ideas, 53, 55
Installation, bolt, 290, 298–300
Interactions, 3–6
Internal Salesforce, 201, 213

L

Languages, 81, 87–90
Licenses, 187–189, 196
    access, 21, 23–27, 30
    external, 24–26
    internal, 23–25, 27
    permissions, 21, 24

Licensing, 217–219, 223
Lightning, 41–58, 60
Lightning Bolt for Salesforce, 301–302, 304
Lightning components
    custom, 119, 124, 129, 141–142
    standard, 117, 120–122, 124, 126, 129,
        133–134, 136, 140
Lightning pages
    layout, 128
    object, 117–118, 126
    sections, 131
    standard, 117, 126

M

Marketing Cloud, 325
Member access, 182
Members, 3–7, 9
Member types
    customers, 21–22, 24, 30, 34–35, 37, 39
    employees, 21–22, 27, 34–35, 37, 39
    group, 21–22, 24, 34–39
    partners, 21–22, 34–35, 37, 39
Messages, 308, 320
Moderation, 307–310
Modes, 105–109, 112

N

Napili, 43–44
Navigation, 77, 83, 90, 97, 115
Notifications, 321

O

Objects, 179–180, 182, 184–190,
    192–195, 199
Organizationwide sharing, 179, 185, 188

P

Packaging, 291, 300–301

Pages, 62–63, 65, 67–71, 73–86, 88, 90–98, 101–105, 107–109, 115

Page variations, 259, 272, 278–279, 284, 286, 288

Partner Central, 43–44

Permissions, 217–219, 222

Personalization, 259

Personas, 3–4

Pluralsight, 335

Prerequisites, 217–221, 229

Process builder
    new members, 236–237, 239, 251
    reputation point, 242–245

Processes, 3–7, 292, 294, 298, 301

Q

Quip, 326

R

Related records, 203–204

Release notes, 331

Requirement
    features, 12–13
    functions, 11, 15

S

Salesforce, 1–9

Salesforce app, 316–318

Search, 220, 222, 228–229, 319–320

Setup domain, 148

Share groups, 179, 196, 199

Sharing, 179

Sharing sets, 179, 188, 190–192, 196, 199

Solutions, 290–291, 301–304

T

Tabs, 41–52, 54–60

Targeting, 259

Templates, 289–291, 296, 298, 301, 303
    considerations, 52, 56
    selection, 41–42, 52–58
    template types, 41–58, 60

Theme
    branding, 69, 75, 77
    colors, 69–70
    fonts, 75–77
    images, 71–75
    settings, 69–70, 75, 77–78, 81, 84–86, 115

Topic assignment, 202, 204, 213

Topics, 54, 217, 222–224, 226, 227, 229

Trailhead, 329

TrailheaDX, 333–334

Training, 334–335

Twitter, 332–333

Types
    featured, 211, 215
    navigational, 201, 208, 215
    standard, 201, 206, 215

U

Unlisted groups, 213

User experience, 3, 5–7

Users
    creation, 28, 30
    login, 22, 30–33, 39
    named, 30–31, 33, 39

V

Vision
    approach, 12
    strategy, 12, 14
Visualforce, 41–52, 54–58, 60

W, X, Y, Z

Workflow
    cases, 233, 257
    email alerts, 235, 237, 244
    group membership, 233, 236
Workspaces, 61, 97–100
World Tours, 333–334

CPSIA information can be obtained
at www.ICGtesting.com
Printed in the USA
LVHW05s2012010818
585585LV00002B/2/P